JONATHAN MANTLE

COMPANIES THAT CHANGED THE WORLD

Quercus

Quercus Publishing Plc
21 Bloomsbury Square
London
WC1A 2NS

First published in 2008

A catalogue record of this book is available from the British Library

Cloth case edition:
ISBN 13: 978 1 84724 614 1

Printed case edition:
ISBN 13: 978 1 84724 241 9

Printed and bound in China

10 9 8 7 6 5 4 3 2 1

PICTURE CREDITS

Private Collection/Bridgeman Art Library 8, Mary Evans Picture Library 12, G Robertson/Lowry/Mary Evans
Picture Library 16, TopFoto 19, Hulton Archive/Getty Images 24, Bettmann/Corbis UK Ltd. 27, American
Stock/Hulton Archive/Getty Images 32, Hulton Archive/Getty Images 35, Hackett/Archive Photos/Hulton
Archive/Getty Images 41, Associated Press/PA Photos 43, Bettmann/Corbis UK Ltd. 49, Mary Evans Picture
Library 52, Mary Evans Picture Library/Alamy 56, Bettmann/Corbis UK Ltd. 60, The Coca-Cola Company/
The Advertising Archives 65, The Advertising Archives 69, John Loengard/Time Life Pictures/Getty Images
72, Mary Evans Picture Library 77, The Advertising Archives 81, Reproduced from the BP Archive 85,
Central Press/Agence France Presse/Hulton Archive/Getty Images 89, Hulton Archive/Getty Images 94,
Associated Press/PA Photos 99, Mary Evans Picture Library, R. Gates/Hulton Archive /Getty Images 106,
Bettmann/Corbis UK Ltd. 111, Hulton-Deutsch Collection/Corbis UK Ltd. 114, Margaret Bourke-White/Time
Life Pictures/Getty Images 118, akg-images 121, Pictorial Press Ltd/Alamy 126, David Magnus/Rex Features
129, The Advertising Archives 133, Three Lions/Hulton Archive/Getty Images 138, The Advertising Archives
142, Robert S. Crandall/Time Inc./Time Life Pictures/Getty Images 144, Alain Nogues Sygma/Corbis UK
Ltd. 148, Greg Baker/Associated Press/PA Photos 153, Don Ryan/AP Photo/PA Photos 157, Court Mast/
Getty Images 161, Rex Features 164, Sipa Press/Rex Features 169, DB Apple/Photoshot 172, Ian Cook/Time
Life Pictures/Getty Images 177, Rex Features 182, Manuel Zambrana/Corbis UK Ltd. 185, Reuters/Corbis UK
Ltd. 187, Rex Features 191, David Duprey/PA Photos 197, Corbis UK Ltd. 199, Sipa Press/Rex Features 203

Edited by Ian Crofton
Editorial and project management: JMS Books LLP
Design: cbdesign
Picture research: Zooid Pictures Ltd

CONTENTS

INTRODUCTION

Few companies literally and unilaterally 'change' the world. Those that did include the Coalbrookdale Company, Western Union, Union and Central Pacific, Bell, Ford, DuPont, Searle and Microsoft – yet only some with a product of their own invention. Many more companies, such as Eastman Kodak, IKEA, Apple or Google, have taken and improved an invention, product or service and created new markets, changing human behaviour and building 'communities'.

Companies that changed the world, had they been companies, would have included The Wheel Tribe (transport, Mesopotamia, 4000 BC), Pharaoh Corporation (infrastructure, Egypt, 3000 BC), Delphic Oracles Ltd. (misinformation systems, Greece, 500 BC), Johan Gutenberg AG (printing, Germany, 1455), Lombard Spa (banking, Italy, 1100), the Manhattan Project Inc. (nuclear energy, USA, 1943), NASA Inc. (space travel and exploration, USA, 1958) and Der Mauer (Berlin Wall) AG (infrastructure, Germany, 1961–89).

Other companies that changed the world, yet are mentioned here tangentially or not at all, include the South Sea Company (the leveraged investment trust whose collapse triggered the first regulatory backlash), Remington (the typewriter), Consolidated Edison (the light bulb), Westinghouse (refrigeration), the British Broadcasting Corporation (BBC), Bell Laboratories (the transistor), Bayer (aspirin), Hewlett-Packard (the beginnings of Silicon Valley), McDonald's (fast food) and Amazon (online retailing). All these companies – and many more – fulfil the role of invention, marketing and technology in the transformational process. My rationale for inclusion is broad in its geographical spread, but also provocative – for example, in the case of King Kullen over Wal-Mart, where size is exceeded by influence.

The 'company', as originally conceived, was intended to serve the public good. The 'corporations' that then arose, from the 19th century, advanced as a result of the integration of mass production and mass distribution. Their management techniques took over and internalized transactions previously done by the market: they *made* the market. These corporations were transformed by invention. However, they did not invent the steamship, the railroad, the telegraph, the internal combustion engine or the aeroplane; they capitalized on them. In the process, their priority was no longer the public good, but the wealth of their private owners; they became increasingly independent of the governments that enabled their creation.

Many believe that the era of 'managerial capitalism' has now all but come to an end. The corporate, driven by executives, mergers and stockholders, is smothering the company, the vehicle of entrepreneurs. People rebel. Companies are becoming smaller and businesses disaggregated. Shifts are taking place between the centre and the margins. At the same time, the changes that companies reflect and engender are as great, if not greater, than ever. The company that changes the world is getting smaller in many ways; and yet has greater than ever power to make and break the planet. Moreover, the gravitational pull of success is always from the margins to the centre. Thus, what begins with the individualistic kick against the prevailing order always ends with the new orthodoxy.

In such a world, a husband leaves in his Toyota for work at Johnson & Johnson, while his wife programmes her iPod, laces her Nike trainers in order to jog to the Body Shop and wonders whether or not she remembered to take the Pill. Back home, she logs on via her Apple laptop to MSN, googles the World Wide Web and sells her own glass beads on eBay. Her brother, a soldier in Iraq, puts on his Kevlar vest and watches Al Jazeera. He takes out a Kodak photograph of his girlfriend and his Nokia mobile rings. Later, footage of the contact in which he is involved will be transmitted by satellite and shown on CNN. Whether he is alive or dead, this will probably be the first his sister – and the world – will know of it.

Behind all these companies are and will always be the entrepreneurs: the 'pilgrims' who, in the words of James Elroy Flecker, 'go a little further ... beyond that last blue mountain'. What makes an entrepreneur is subject enough for another book: genetics, fortunes and misfortunes of birth, nature, nurture, necessity, alienation, displacement, bigamy, war, asthma, dyslexia, pranksterism and serendipity, all can play a part. There are myriad and often unlikely inspirational threads, varying for Thomas Cook, Julius de Reuter, Bill Boeing, Walt Disney, Masaru Ibuka, Akio Morita, Anita Roddick, Bill Gates, Larry Page or Sergey Brin. Keeping the vision of the founder can be as dangerous as losing it, as Allen Lane found. Lew Platt of Boeing observed that, unlike his former company, Hewlett-Packard, Boeing no longer had a value-based culture of ethics, but an ethics 'policy'. A company may have, lose and then rediscover a value-based culture. A company may face the loss of the founder, or lose the founder and yet keep the vision to its benefit, seemingly forever, as was the case with Johnson & Johnson. The worth, and self-worth, of companies is invariably linked to the worth, and lack of worth, of their product. There are icons of modest but determined beginnings that we can identify with: Levi Strauss's packhorse in the California gold fields, Bill Boeing's boathouse, Ingvar Kamprad's shed, Sony's abandoned department store, Anita Roddick's garage, or Larry Page's dorm.

If India and China succeed in changing the world in the 21st century, they will not do so by coupling with the American model established in the 19th and 20th centuries. India and China rely on technology transfer as suppliers of goods and services to the West, much of this underwritten by Western capital seeking short-term profit. The company that changes the world will need its equivalent of 'lean production', Windows or the iPod to do so on its own terms. In changing the world, invention and serendipity – and disruption – are the keys.

The joint-stock company model and its descendants, the American corporation, the British limited liability company, the German *Aktiengesellschaft* (AG), the French *société anonyme* (SA) and the Japanese *kabushiki gaisha*, are the boreholes of the sweet-tasting, yet troubled well that is capitalism. I have chosen these companies from a long list that has triggered many an argument between friends. This much is certain: each company has changed and reflected change in the world of its time, through success and failure, and all in far-reaching and often unexpected ways.

THE HONOURABLE EAST INDIA COMPANY

1600 | *England*

The company that controlled a continent

Imports
Exports
Infrastructure

In 1600, only a dozen years after the English defeat of the Spanish Armada, Queen Elizabeth I granted a 21-year charter to 'the Company of Merchants of London trading into the East Indies'. This was the Honourable East India Company, founded in the interests of the nation and one of the first ever joint-stock companies, with 125 shareholders and capital of £72,000. Initial voyages to compete with the Dutch in the Spice Islands in what is now Indonesia met with mixed fortunes, and it was more by luck than judgement that the third voyage of the company's ships arrived off the west coast of India in 1608.

At first the British in India were little more than rivals to the Portuguese, Dutch, Swedish, Danish and French in a country dominated by the Muslim Mughal Empire. As the Mughals rotted from within, the emperors granted further trade concessions and the company exploited the power vacuum with the help of disaffected local Hindu rulers. It acquired governmental rights in Madras (Chennai) on the eastern coast in 1639, and in 1669 control of Bombay (Mumbai), which had passed to King Charles II of England as part of his dowry from the Portuguese Catharine of Braganza; the king granted the territory to the company in return for £10 a year. In 1690 the company also assumed control of Calcutta (Kolkata), in Bengal, which was later to become the seat of power of British rule in India.

WEALTH FROM THE ORIENT

By the end of the 17th century, the company was employing its own armed forces, fleets, administrators, tax collectors and judiciary, and even issuing its own coinage. The Mughal emperors became puppets, and the company adopted a policy of divide and rule towards local rulers, while seeing off the Portuguese, Dutch, French, Swedes, Danish and even a rival

> **'A VERY OLD FRIEND OF MY FATHER'S** presented me with a beautiful cut-and-thrust steel sword, desiring me to cut off a dozen rich fellows' heads with it, and so return a nabob myself to England.**'**
>
> William Hickey, the diarist, who went to Calcutta as a company cadet in 1769.

English company. The first modest offices of the company in the City of London soon gave way to magnificent headquarters on Lime and Leadenhall Streets, containing a compendious library and treasures such as Tipu's Tiger, a working model of an Indian tiger eating an Englishman (later transferred to the Victoria and Albert Museum in London), and topped by a gigantic statue of Britannia. Nearby on the River Thames the East India Docks sprang up to handle the import of cotton, spices, indigo dye, tea, jewels, ivory, silks and saltpetre. The fortunes made funded magnificent London town houses as well as many new businesses and political influence in Parliament. Above all, the huge accumulation of capital helped to kick start the Industrial Revolution.

Ten years' service with 'John Company' could set a man up with an estate and country mansion packed with exotic mementoes of the East – some of these houses, like that of the nabob Sir Charles Cockerell, Sezincote in Gloucestershire, were designed in the Indian manner. Robert Clive, commander-in-chief and governor of Bengal, and the richest nabob of all, demonstrated how blurred the boundaries could become between the fortunes of the individual, the East India Company and the British Empire. The vast wealth he accrued overshadowed his military achievements in ending French influence in India, and he died in 1774 by his own hand, one of the richest and most vilified men in England. A later governor of Bengal, Warren Hastings, a great reformer and administrator, was also accused of corruption, although his long-running trial before the House of Lords ended with an acquittal in 1795.

GOING NATIVE

Company men invariably took Indian mistresses; few English women were prepared to risk the threat of disease and a hostile climate. James Achilles Kirkpatrick – nicknamed the 'White Mughal' – went so far in 1801 as to fall in love with and marry a Mughal princess, Khair-un-Nissa, convert to Islam and become a double agent, working for her father against his own employers.

The mission of the company never seems to have been imperial in the later 19th-century sense of imposing the values of British Christian civilization on the 'natives', who came to be regarded as morally, culturally and intellectually inferior. Many of the early company men were great admirers of Indian culture, some

Uniting the subcontinent

In the 19th century the East India Company oversaw an astonishing feat of mechanical and social engineering, as the subcontinent began to be joined up – and controlled – by highways. By the 1850s a metalled road linked Calcutta and Bombay; and the Grand Trunk Road, restored and enlarged, ran for 1500 miles from Calcutta to the North-West Frontier. The first railroad – 20 miles of track – was laid in 1853, and by 1869 some 4000 miles were operational. Most stops were at junctions or fortified cantonments at a strategic distance outside the volatile cities. The effect of this transport network was unparalleled until the opening up and colonization – again by the railroads – of the American West.

of them even becoming great scholars and collectors. The business of the company was, after all, business – not evangelizing. The aim was to provide an annual dividend of 10 per cent for shareholders. By 1801 sales had risen to £7,602,041 – a staggering sum by today's reckoning and an increase from £4,988,300 eight years earlier.

In the 19th century the company's administrators declared their aim was to hand over a prosperous, efficient India to the Indians. The company instructed its judges in matters of local law to consult 'Equity or Good Conscience'; and it was committed to non-intervention in local customs and religious practices.

RELATIONS WITH THE BRITISH GOVERNMENT

Nevertheless, the company was not entirely divorced from the interests of the British government, with whom it had a somewhat ambiguous relationship. In 1773 the Bengal famine, combined with recession in Europe, prompted the directors to appeal to Parliament for financial help. Parliament responded by passing the Tea Act, which allowed the company to flood the American market with cheap tea – causing resentment there among the colonists, and resulting in the Boston Tea Party, in which a group of citizens boarded the tea ships and threw the cargo overboard. The likelihood is that they were hired thugs in the pay of smugglers whose

The ultimate 'nabob' – Robert Clive and family with Indian maid, painted by Sir Joshua Reynolds in 1765. 'Clive of India's' military conquests and vast wealth epitomized the imperial reach of the joint-stock company.

The origin of the Stars and Stripes

The design of the East India Company flag is commonly believed to have inspired the Stars and Stripes. Elihu Yale (1649–1721), co-founder of Yale University, had made his fortune as the company's governor of Madras (now Chennai) until he was relieved of his post for illegal profiteering.

business was undercut by the cheap company tea, but the 'official' version is that the incident helped trigger the American Revolution.

In 1773 the cash-strapped company took control of the opium trade in Bengal and circumvented the Chinese ban on imports of the drug by selling it in Calcutta on condition that it was exported on to China. The profits paid into the company's factory in Canton (Guangzhou) meant that the opium trade financed most of the company's imports of tea and silks from China. Renewed Chinese opposition resulted in the British government's seizure of Hong Kong in 1840, during what became known as the First Opium War. Jardine and Matheson, the original 'Tai-Pans' of Hong Kong, were company employees in Calcutta who had moved to southern China to develop the opium trade. During the handover ceremony of Hong Kong from Britain to China in 1997, the Chinese President Jiang Zemin's speech referred to this as the 'final chapter of the Opium Wars'.

THE INDIAN MUTINY

By 1839, the armed forces of the East India Company were larger than the queen's own forces and any European army, except that of Russia. It was an army of mercenary volunteers – Punjabis, Sikhs, and Gurkhas from Nepal – under the command of British officers. The officers, who trained at the company's academy at Addiscombe, in Surrey, learnt not only soldiering, but also Hindustani, mechanics and mathematics. The army was a microcosm of

1600
Queen Elizabeth I grants a charter establishing the **East India Company**.

1608
A company fleet arrives off the west coast of **India**.

1639
Company acquires control of **Madras (Chennai)**.

1669
Acquires control of **Bombay (Mumbai)**.

1690
Acquires control of **Calcutta (Kolkata)**.

1757
Robert Clive's victory at Plassey gives the company control of **Bengal**.

1764–7
Clive carries out many **reforms** as governor-general of Bengal.

1773
The British government helps the company out of financial difficulties by passing the **Tea Act**, to the fury of the American colonists.

1774–85
As governor-general of Bengal, and responsible for all British territories in India, **Warren Hastings** consolidates British rule, establishing the basis of subsequent British administration.

1801
The **turnover of the company exceeds £7.5 million** – a staggering sum at the time.

1839–42
The British fight the Chinese in the **First Opium War**, enforcing the company's desire to export opium to China.

1853
The **first railroad** is built in India.

1857
The **Indian Mutiny** marks the beginning of the end of company rule in India.

1858
The **Government of India Act** transfers the company's powers to the Crown.

1874
Final **dissolution** of the East India Company.

Anglo-Indian relations in all their contradictions and complexity. Yet the liberal-minded cosmopolitan outlook of the likes of Hickey and Kirkpatrick had by the mid-19th century given way to the narrower evangelism of the Victorian era, whose exponents both mistrusted and misunderstood the native Indians.

The result of the insensitivity on the part of a new generation of British rulers was the Indian Mutiny of 1857, in which the company's native troops, backed by some local rulers, rose in revolt against the British. The mutiny was marked by atrocities and massacres on both sides, and marked the end of company rule in India. The British government decided to take the administration of India into its own hands. Even before the end, Queen Victoria herself had noted in her diary 'a universal feeling that India should belong to me'.

THE END OF THE EAST INDIA COMPANY

The India Bill of 1858 proposed to abolish the powers of the company, including its Board of Control, and transfer all authority to the Crown. The political philosopher John Stuart Mill, an employee of the company in London, drew up a petition presented to Parliament protesting against the dissolution. The petition failed, the bill was enacted, and Mill retired with a handsome annual pension of £1500. The company effectively ceased to exist, and its once formidable army, weakened by ageing senior officers and desertions, became the Indian Army. Many company treasures went to the India Office, and India itself came under the full control of the British government, its governor-generals becoming the queen's viceroys. India formally became a crown colony and the 'jewel in the crown' of Queen Victoria.

'IT ACCOMPLISHED A WORK such as in the whole history of the human race no other company ever attempted and as such is likely to attempt in the years to come.'

The Times (London), commenting on the final dissolution of the East India Company in 1874.

The company lingered on for a few years, managing the tea trade for the British government. On 1 January 1874, when the East India Stock Dividend Redemption Act came into effect, the company was finally dissolved. *The Times* of London reported: 'It accomplished a work such as in the whole history of the human race no other company ever attempted and as such is likely to attempt in the years to come.'

The company's undoubted contribution to trade, administration and infrastructure must be weighed against the lack of indigenous development in areas such as manufacturing and the consequent resentment of the colonial power by many Indians. After independence in 1948, India remained for over 40 years a centralized and largely agricultural economy, a country that attempted to industrialize while resisting foreign investment. This began to change in the 1990s, when the world's largest democracy began to emerge as a would-be superpower. With economic growth at 9 per cent a year in the early 21st century, India is showing a determination to even up the balance sheet and attract foreign investment – this time on its own terms.

THE AMSTERDAM EXCHANGE BANK

1609 | *Netherlands*

2

The creation of modern money

The Amsterdam Exchange Bank was the first bank clearing house established in the Netherlands in the 17th century. This was the time of the Dutch 'Golden Age', when the Netherlands witnessed a great cultural flowering and Amsterdam became the commercial centre of the world. 'Bank money' freed entrepreneurs and currency from the limitations of intrinsic value, and created cashless transfers of funds that underpinned the ventures of merchants and joint-stock companies.

The Dutch Golden Age dawned during the Eighty Years' War – the long struggle for independence from Catholic Spain. The willingness of the tolerant Dutch to provide a refuge to Protestants from Flanders, Huguenots from France and Sephardic Jews from Portugal and Spain enhanced the already well-established commercial vibrancy of Amsterdam. Other key factors included the development of energy from windmills and the invention of the sawmill, which enabled the construction of great numbers of ships for trade and defence.

Holland's commercial reach was embodied in the Dutch East India Company, incorporated in 1602. It was the first company in the world to issue stock, and is often referred to as the first multinational. The States General granted the company a 21-year monopoly on Asian trade, particularly in spices, and it became the world's most powerful trading enterprise. The wealth created brought about a flowering in the law, mathematics, architecture, sculpture, painting and the sciences. The Amsterdam Stock Exchange, with its daily trading in the shares of the new joint-stock companies, was the epicentre of this activity.

> **'FOR NEVER COUNTRY TRADED SO MUCH** and consumed so little: They buy infinitely, but 'tis to sell again, either upon improvement of the Commodity, or at a better Market.'
>
> Sir William Temple, the English diplomat, comments on Dutch commercial vibrancy in the 17th century.

The volume of transactions at the Amsterdam Exchange in the 17th century inspired the concept of 'bank money', freeing coinage from literal value and creating the forerunner of the cashless transactions we know today.

THE ESTABLISHMENT OF THE BANK

The Amsterdam Exchange Bank (*Wisselbank*) was established in 1609 under the ownership and protection of the city. Its purpose was to receive deposits of gold and silver bullion and coin.

The early operations of the bank followed the Venetian model, concentrating on deposits of uncut gold and silver. The receipts issued for these deposits were redeemable six months later, and were worth 95 per cent of the value. Unlike some lenders, the bank also undertook that it would neither melt down or debase the bullion in question, nor would it ever lend these deposits, even when they went unreclaimed. The poor relation at this time was the deposit of coinage, for which the bank charged the lowest management fee.

STABILIZING THE CURRENCY

Money in Holland, as elsewhere in the 17th century, was coin-backed: its value was defined by the origin of the coin in question and its precious-metal content. This led to dozens of different types of regional and national coinage, and the widespread 'clipping', melting and debasement with tin or copper of coin of all kinds. Such activities led the value of the Dutch florin to fall by 1 per cent every year, with negative effects on commerce, the economy and society. The booming and often sophisticated financial transactions of the import and export trade were tormented by these unstable variables. Heavy gold and silver coins were often replaced by 'light' coinage when settling debts, and this would further diminish the consistency of the coinage in circulation. Early banks – and their cashiers – were active participants in these corrupt practices.

The solution of the Amsterdam Exchange Bank was to accept foreign and local cash of all kinds and denominations, deduct a modest management fee, and register the value in Dutch gilders in the owner's account on its books. Withdrawal of funds from the bank was exclusively by receipt and in coins of guaranteed quality. The bank also attracted customers by banning cashiers (this would be relaxed in 1621) and ensuring that transactions between accounts were carried out quickly and without a fee. The mechanism laid the foundations of the cashless transfer of funds between account holders at the bank, and is the origin of 'bank money'.

SECURITY AND PROFIT

Customers were thus reassured that their deposits would maintain a stable value. They could also be sure that their money was secure from fire and theft, and from losing value via debasement. The bank in turn imposed a range of fees: a ten-gilder fee for each new account opened; a fee for each additional account; a small fee for each transaction; a higher fee for transactions below a certain threshold, to discourage excessive traffic. It also imposed penalties for failure to balance the account twice a year and for becoming overdrawn, and a threshold above which all bills had to be paid in bank money; this created stability between debtor and creditor and compelled all merchants to keep an account with the bank. These fees and penalties, and the fact that bank money itself commanded a premium because of its reliability, engendered more than enough funds to cover the costs of the bank's management and operations.

Debasement of coinage continued to be widespread beyond Amsterdam, chief among the culprits being the *patagon* coin of the Spanish Netherlands, which infiltrated the Dutch Republic as a subversive 'light' rival to the *rixdollar*. Between 1609 and 1648 deposits at the Amsterdam Exchange Bank grew by 10 per cent a year, and the bank became a monetary haven and Europe's largest bank clearing house. As the incentives for debasement fell, so did Dutch inflation: to 1 per cent, half its previous level. The disconnection by the authorities of the price of Amsterdam Exchange Bank money from the price of other money in circulation engendered new forms of market behaviour, and is a defining moment in the history of banking.

FORTUNES FROM TRADE

Holland's economic growth throughout the 17th century can be measured today in the architecture and artistic treasures of Amsterdam, and in the extent of land reclamation funded during those years. Much of this growth came from the fortunes made by fair means or foul by the Dutch East India Company, the greater part of whose start-up capital was raised by the merchants of the Amsterdam Exchange Bank. As was the case with the British East India Company, the Dutch prosecuted their colonial expansion with a single-minded ferocity. In the 1620s,

TIMELINE

———1602———
Incorporation of the **Dutch East India Company**.

———1609———
Establishment of the **Amsterdam Exchange Bank**.

———1648———
The Amsterdam Exchange Bank becomes Europe's **largest bank clearing house**.

———1672———
Run on the bank following the French invasion of the Netherlands.

———1773———
Opening of the **first bank clearing house in London**.

———1853———
Opening of the **first bank clearing house in New York**.

in the pursuit of nutmeg and mace, the company massacred most of the population of the Banda Islands (part of what is now Indonesia) and attempted to force the survivors into a slave workforce. Elsewhere, the company introduced Christian missionaries and European technology to Japan, and became that country's sole link for many years with the Western world. By 1669 the company had 150 merchant ships, 40 warships, 50,000 employees, a private army of 10,000 soldiers and a dividend payment of 40 per cent.

The Amsterdam Exchange Bank embraced the proceeds of these and many other ventures, both abroad and at home. In 1672 a run on the bank following the French invasion reduced the value of florin deposits by 47 per cent over the following two years. But the bank survived with its credibility not only intact, but strengthened.

The end of the Golden Age came with costly wars against England and France and the stagnation of the Dutch economy. By 1700 Britain had taken the lead as a maritime power and in the colonial and slave trade, and London became the economic centre of Europe – the city's first bank clearing house opened in 1773. The Industrial Revolution in Britain further shifted the balance. The Dutch East India Company went bankrupt, and was dissolved in 1800. In 1853 the first bank clearing house opened in the United States, in New York City – ironically once known as 'New Amsterdam'.

Tulip fever

The 1630s in the Netherlands witnessed an extraordinary speculation in rare tulip bulbs. By January 1637, for example, the price of a single bulb of Semper Augustus, which had previously traded at a few florins, rose to 2000 florins. By February, the price was 6390 florins, but shortly afterwards collapsed to one-tenth of a florin, at which price it traded for the next century.

THE LEGACY OF THE AMSTERDAM EXCHANGE BANK

The concept of bank money began life as an obscure local counter-debasement measure, but it went on to become the foundation of central banking, and also of modern monetary and payment systems. It freed coinage from its literal value, and enabled transactions of ever-greater sophistication on an ever-greater scale. However, it also paved the way for the phenomena of inflation and hyperinflation. Where coinage for all its flaws had been tied to the value of precious metals, in Germany in the early 1920s a wheelbarrow filled with paper bank notes could barely pay for a loaf of bread. Above all, the dour and pragmatic burghers of Amsterdam bequeathed us the seeds of a stimulating paradox: modern money is neither worth the metal from which it is minted, nor the paper on which it is printed – yet its stability of value is worth much, much more.

THE COALBROOKDALE COMPANY

1717 | *UK*

Birthplace of the Industrial Revolution

The Coalbrookdale Company was founded by the Darby family in the ironworking belt of Shropshire, England, in 1717. It was Abraham Darby (1677–1717) – whose descendants managed the company until the mid-19th century – who had perfected the use of coke to smelt iron ore, turning Coalbrookdale into the birthplace of the Industrial Revolution. The large-scale production of iron was necessary for the manufacture of such things as steam engines, railway wheels, bridges and ships, and was a key element in Britain leading the world in the process of industrialization.

Coal mining and small-scale ironworks and smithies had been active in the parish of Madeley and Coalbrookdale on the Severn Gorge since before the Dissolution of the Monasteries in 1538. One of the earliest forges to smelt iron was at Bringewood, near the Welsh border. Coal could not be used in iron smelting and the use of 'charcoaled' wood to do so resulted in the deforestation of large parts of Europe. The arrival of the Quaker Abraham Darby at Coalbrookdale from Bristol in 1709 brought the new technology of iron smelting by coke – a fuel made by heating coal in the absence of air. Using coke was more economic than using charcoal, and enabled larger blast furnaces to cast bigger pieces of iron.

THE THREE ABRAHAMS

Abraham Darby did not invent the smelting of iron using coke, but he was the first to patent and apply the process on an industrial scale. Having rebuilt the derelict furnace at Coalbrookdale, he was soon turning out cast-iron pots, pans, kettles and other household items. These were transported by barge down the River Severn to Bristol, thence distributed throughout Britain and exported to mainland Europe and beyond. By 1717 Darby had built a second furnace and expanded his iron foundry by re-melting pig iron in air furnaces. He died intestate at the

Coalbrookdale in 18th-century Shropshire, England, the birthplace of the Industrial Revolution. The process of iron smelting perfected here by the Darby family helped to make Britain the world's first great industrial power.

The dark satanic mills

Abraham Darby I (1677–1717) and his grandson Abraham III (1750–91) died young, even by the standards of the time. In spite of the outstanding natural beauty of Shropshire, the immediate working environment at Coalbrookdale can have done nothing to improve the health of those who laboured there. To some, it brought to mind the mouth of hell. Charles Dibdin, dramatist, songwriter and author, wrote in 1801:

'Coalbrookdale wants nothing but Cerberus to give you the idea of the heathen hell. The Severn may pass for the Styx, with this difference that Charon, turned turnpike man, ushers you over the bridge instead of rowing in his crazy boat ... really, if an atheist who had never heard of Coalbrookdale, could be transported there in a dream, and left to awake at the mouth of one of these furnaces, surrounded on all sides by such a number of infernal objects, though he had been all his life the most profligate unbeliever that ever added blasphemy to incredulity, he would infallibly tremble at the last judgement that in imagination would appear to him.'

age of 39, swiftly followed by his widow. The Coalbrookdale works, valued at £3200, were placed in the ownership of the Coalbrookdale Company, owned by one of Abraham's creditors, Thomas Goldney, a fellow Quaker, and his son, Darby's son-in-law Richard Ford; the other owners were trustees on behalf of Darby's sons Edmund and Abraham II.

Abraham II put into practice his belief that iron should be used for as many purposes as possible: pavements, coffins – even houses. The company built more furnaces and produced the first iron steam-engine cylinders (previously made of expensive brass) and the first iron wheels, and laid what was probably the world's first iron railway. In 1755 Abraham Darby II and Thomas Goldney 'blew in' a new and more efficient furnace near Coalbrookdale. The company continued to expand until Abraham II's death in 1763, when he was succeeded by his son-in-law, the philanthropist and Quaker anti-slavery campaigner, Richard Reynolds.

Abraham Darby III, son of Abraham II, had entered the works in 1768 at the age of 18, and took over the company in the 1770s.

In 1775 a group of subscribers agreed to construct a bridge across the Severn gorge near the Coalbrookdale works. Darby was the lead shareholder with 20 per cent, and the bridge was to be made of 'stone, brick or timber'. By 1778 Darby and the family held 50 per cent, and determined that the bridge should not be made of stone or brick or wood, but of cast iron, the first iron bridge in the world. It was a tremendous engineering feat – a single span almost 200 feet long. The components were manufactured in the Coalbrookdale works, overseen by Darby and the great ironmaster John Wilkinson. People flocked from all over the country to attend the opening on New Year's Day 1781, and the image of the bridge amid the rural landscape passed into popular iconography in engravings, embroidery and china. Locally manufactured glass and porcelain, a cast-iron rotunda affording views over the Severn valley, and 'sabbath walks' attracted tourism to the area, also drawn by the ministry of Mary Fletcher at Madeley church, a famous centre of Methodism. The town that grew up around the bridge became known as Ironbridge.

In 1785 Abraham Darby III converted the furnaces to be run by the new improved steam engines invented by his friend James Watt. Other technological advances meant that Buildwas Bridge, built in 1795 two miles upriver from the first iron bridge, used only half as much cast iron in spite of being 30 feet longer. Thomas Telford's Longdon Aqueduct, begun in 1796, carried the Shrewsbury Canal over the River Tern and was supported by iron columns cast at Coalbrookdale.

COALBROOKDALE IN THE 19TH AND 20TH CENTURIES

Abraham Derby III was dead by the time the company built the first steam locomotive for the Cornish railway pioneer, Richard Trevithick. That was in the early part of the first decade of the 19th century. The Napoleonic Wars brought demand for cast-iron cannon; conversely, peace in 1815 brought recession to the Shropshire iron industry. Only the Coalbrookdale works continued as a major foundry, and in 1837 Charles Hulbert, an evangelical Christian, cotton master and author of books on Shropshire, described the two-mile conurbation of stepped canals, ironworks, brickworks, boatyards, stores, inns, houses and teeming employees as 'the most extraordinary district in the world'.

By 1849 members of the Darby and Reynolds families had ceased to manage the company, by this time best known for its decorative ironwork: the gates of London's Hyde Park were cast at Coalbrookdale. Although the smelting furnaces closed, the foundries continued, in spite of competition from South Wales and the Black Country. The Coalbrookdale Company survived by becoming part of a consortium of ironfounders called Light Castings Limited; this was taken over in 1929 by Allied Ironfounders. In 1969 the Glynwed Company took over Allied Ironfounders; Glynwed itself was renamed in 2001 as Aga Foodservice.

TIMELINE

1677
Birth of **Abraham Darby I**.

1709
Abraham I builds the **first coke-powered blast furnace** at Coalbrookdale.

1711
Birth of **Abraham Darby II**.

1717
The Coalbrookdale Company is established following the death of Abraham I.

1750
Birth of **Abraham Darby III**.

1755
Abraham II builds a new and more efficient type of **blast furnace**.

1763
Death of **Abraham II**.

1781
Opening of Abraham III's **iron bridge** over the Severn, the first such bridge in the world.

1785
Furnaces at Coalbrookdale are converted to be run by **steam engine**.

1791
Death of **Abraham III**.

1849
By this time the **Darbys have ceased to manage** the company.

1968
Foundation of **Ironbridge Gorge Museum Trust**.

INDUSTRIAL HERITAGE

For many years Coalbrookdale slumbered by the Severn. In 1959, with the 250th anniversary of Darby's arrival, excavations began to uncover and preserve the original blast furnace. In the 1960s, the creation of the new town of Telford began to regenerate the population of the largely forgotten area, and in 1968 the Ironbridge Gorge Museum Trust was founded, with the aim of excavating and maintaining the remains of Coalbrookdale's blast furnaces and engine houses.

Today, Coalbrookdale – together with Ironbridge and Coalport – attract thousands of visitors annually, and the Ironbridge Gorge is now a UNESCO World Heritage Site. Archaeologists are still uncovering the history and secrets of Coalbrookdale – that small valley in Shropshire where the Industrial Revolution began and a family company changed the world.

DUPONT

1802 | USA

4

Something old, something new

Chemicals

E.I. du Pont de Nemours and Company was founded in 1802 by refugees from the French Revolution as a gunpowder mill. When the du Ponts sailed from France they were reduced on the voyage to eating soup made from boiled rats, but in the course of time they became one of the richest families in the world.

The fortunes of this remarkable business dynasty were closely connected over the following two centuries with explosives, stockings, the Manhattan Project, automobiles – and cannabis.

CORNERING THE GUNPOWDER MARKET

Pierre Samuel du Pont de Nemours (1739–1817) was an economist, author and associate of the French royal family. Forced to flee the guillotine – which claimed the life of his friend, the French chemist Antoine Lavoisier – du Pont and his family migrated to America. Here, at Brandywine Creek in Delaware, Pierre's son Éleuthère Irénée du Pont (1771–1834), who had worked in the French royal gunpowder and saltpetre factory, founded a gunpowder mill. His revolutionary techniques of factory construction enabled the company to supply 1 million pounds of gunpowder to the American government for the War of 1812. Pierre du Pont died aged 77 in 1817 after helping to fight a fire at the powder yard. E.I. du Pont died in 1834. His descendants, who included eminent members of the Union Army, went on to supply 2700 pounds of gunpowder a day to the Union side during the American Civil War. Innovations in dynamite and smokeless powder followed, with attendant hazards: the founder's grandson Lammot du Pont died in an explosion. In 1902, with the death of company president Eugene du Pont, the company was on the verge of being taken over by non-family members when it was sold to three of the founder's great-grandsons.

The brilliant organic chemist Wallace Hume Carothers discovered nylon, neoprene and polyester while working for DuPont. Although the company became a multi-billion-dollar global brand, Carothers died a self-styled 'failure' by his own hand.

The du Ponts dominated the Powder Trust, which behaved in a similar fashion to Standard Oil over kerosene and gasoline. The Sherman Antitrust Act of 1912 forced DuPont (as the company was now known) and the Trust to divest into the Hercules and Atlas companies; in reality, as would be the case with Rockefeller and Standard Oil, the discrete elements remained under the same control. During the First World War, DuPont supplied 40 per cent of all Allied explosives, and it was alleged that at least a dozen members of the family earned $1 million a year.

DIVERSIFICATION

In 1914 Lammot du Pont's son Pierre invested in the failing General Motors automobile company and won a seat on the board. By 1920 he was president of the company, to which DuPont would supply rubber for tyres, and paint and varnish for bodywork. Pierre du Pont handed the management of General Motors to Alfred P. Sloan, under whom it would become a definitive American corporation. The 1920 Tariff Act, which protected the American chemical industry from foreign competition, was promoted by Senator T. Coleman du Pont (the latter having sold his shares in the company in 1915).

DuPont's near-monopoly in chemicals enabled the company to capitalize on the 1908 Swiss invention of cellophane, which had been imported as a commodity from France. In 1923 DuPont opened the first cellophane manufacturing plant in the United States, revolutionizing the packaging of foodstuffs and enabling the creation of adhesive tape. From the late 1920s, DuPont led the revolution in the development of industrial polymers, including neoprene, synthetic rubber, polyester and, in 1935, nylon, the world's first true synthetic textile fibre.

> **"BETTER THINGS** for Better Living ... Through Chemistry**"**
> DuPont slogan, 1939

DuPont and the du Ponts meanwhile consolidated their position in industry and society, buying 56 per cent of the Remington Arms Company and marrying into the Roosevelts. In 1937 the company was alleged to have lobbied for the criminalization of cannabis, or hemp, in order to strengthen the position of its synthetic products in the fibre market, in which hemp had a significant share.

THE SECOND WORLD WAR

An ironic light was thrown on DuPont's 1939 slogan 'Better Things for Better Living ... Through Chemistry' in the early years of the Second World War when an investigation began into the contribution by DuPont, General Motors and Standard Oil to the German chemical conglomerate IG Farben's manufacture of synthetic tetraethyl fuel for Nazi Germany's military vehicles.

As General Motors' Alfred P. Sloan observed: 'We're too big to be inconvenienced by these pitiful international squabbles.' The investigation was shelved after the cooperation of the American companies became essential to the Allied war effort.

During the war, DuPont manufactured 70 per cent of the explosives used by the US armed forces, reputedly earning the company $4.5 billion. In 1943 construction began of the top-secret plutonium plants that built the first atomic bomb for the Manhattan Project. DuPont's ballistic nylon flak jackets also helped protect American and British bomber crews.

Wallace Carothers, the tragic DuPont boffin

The development at DuPont from the 1920s of a revolutionary new range of materials – including neoprene, polyester and nylon – was largely down to the brilliant organic chemist Wallace Carothers, group leader at the company's experimental laboratory. On 29 April 1937, Carothers, convinced he had achieved little, checked into a Philadelphia hotel room and died after drinking a cocktail of lemon juice laced with potassium cyanide. He was only 41.

THE POSTWAR DECADES

After the Second World War DuPont's profits soared as America entered the era of plastics, the hydrogen bomb and the space age. Synthetic materials such as Orlon and Lycra followed Mylar and Dacron, and the company's onward progress was barely dented when in 1957 the Clayton Antitrust Act forced DuPont to divest its stockholding in General Motors. The following year DuPont opened its first European plant in Londonderry, Northern Ireland.

The 1960s saw a further rush of synthetic materials, some of which were essential to the Apollo space programme. The bulletproof material Kevlar, the result of long-term trials, became standard-issue for police forces and armies around the world. DuPont's acquisition of Conoco in 1981 was the largest merger in corporate history and secured supplies of petroleum feedstocks for fibre and plastics. The company was also an early investor in manufacturing in China.

CFCS AND THE OZONE LAYER

DuPont and General Motors between them accounted for 25 per cent of the global market in chlorofluorocarbons (CFCs) used in aerosol sprays and refrigerants. Having resisted public concern and congressional pressure over the depleting effects of CFCs on the earth's ozone layer, the company conducted a U-turn after NASA confirmed in 1988 that CFCs were not only thinning the ozone layer above Antarctica but also around the world.

The company committed itself in a full-page advertisement in the *New York Times* to the cessation of CFC sales in the United States and other developed countries by 1995, sold its Conoco holding and focused on new sources of chemicals from living plants. Its new corporate strapline proclaimed 'The miracles of science'.

DUPONT TODAY

One of the longest-lived corporations in America, DuPont today is one of the 30 huge US public companies that comprise the Dow Jones index, with annual sales of $30 billion and 60,000 employees around the world. In 2005, in a remarkable turnaround by a company that epitomized the synthetic revolution with its toxic consequences for the environment and the individual, DuPont was nominated Number One among 'The Top Green Companies' by *BusinessWeek* magazine. Its top scientists (either during their time at DuPont or afterwards) have won numerous National Medals of Technology and the Nobel Prize for Chemistry. The executive board of DuPont in 2007 included family member There du Pont. Other du Pont family interests have included Boeing, a company whose fortunes have similarly been intertwined with government policy in peace and war.

The du Pont dynasty continues to occupy a colourful place in American society. Irénée du Pont (1876–1963) was, like his contemporary Henry Ford, a keen admirer of Adolf Hitler and advocated the chemically assisted creation of a race of supermen. Henry Francis du Pont (1880–1969), was a livestock breeder, horticulturalist and noted connoisseur of European furniture and the American decorative arts. In 1996 John Eleuthere du Pont, a multimillionaire ornithologist, philatelist, wrestling sponsor and paranoid schizophrenic, was convicted of shooting to death an Olympic wrestler on his Philadelphia estate. He had believed the unfortunate man was an agent of an international conspiracy. Virgil Roger du Pont III (b.1972), became lead singer of American Goth/electropop band the Cruxshadows, using the stage name 'Rogue'.

TIMELINE

1739
Birth of **Pierre Samuel du Pont de Nemours**.

1771
Birth of Pierre's son **Éleuthère Irénée du Pont**.

1802
Foundation of **E.I. du Pont de Nemours and Company**, a manufacturer of gunpowder.

1817
Death of **Pierre du Pont**, fighting a fire at the gunpowder mill.

1834
Death of **Éleuthère Irénée du Pont**.

1902
The company is **acquired by three of the founder's great-grandsons**.

1912
The Sherman Antitrust Act forces the **breakup** of DuPont, although the company effectively remains under the same control.

1914
Pierre du Pont invests in **General Motors**, becoming president by 1920.

1920
Senator T. Coleman du Pont promotes the **Tariff Act**, which protects the US chemical industry from foreign competition.

1923
DuPont begins to manufacture **cellophane** in the USA.

1935
DuPont scientists invent **nylon**.

1943
DuPont becomes involved in the **Manhattan Project**, developing the atomic bomb.

1957
Anti-trust legislation forces DuPont to sell its holdings in General Motors.

1981
DuPont acquires **Conoco**, the oil giant, which it later sells.

1988
The company commits to phase out sales of **CFCs**.

2005
BusinessWeek names DuPont **first among 'The Top Green Companies'**.

THOMAS COOK

1841 | UK

> "God's earth, with all its fullness and beauty, is for the people." THOMAS COOK

Thomas Cook, born in 1808, was a Baptist minister from Market Harborough in the Midlands of England who, while waiting for a stagecoach one day, conceived the idea that the educational benefits of travel could further the cause of helping to wean working people off the 'fiend alcohol'. 'What a glorious thing it would be,' he observed, 'if the newly developed power of railways and locomotion could be subservient to the cause of Temperance.'

On 5 July 1841 Cook arranged for a train to carry 570 temperance supporters 11 miles from Leicester to a rally in Loughborough and back in open carriages for a shilling. The price included tickets and food. Cook, who was paid a share of the fares charged to the passengers, recorded: 'Thus was struck the keynote of my excursions, and the social idea grew upon me.'

THE FIRST TRAVEL AGENT

During the following three summers, Cook conducted outings for temperance groups and Sunday-school children. The success of these prompted the Midlands Counties Railway Company to offer Cook an arrangement, on condition that he supplied the passengers. Cook started up in business under his own name organizing rail excursions for pleasure and taking a percentage of the revenue from ticket sales. In the summer of 1845 he organized a trip for hundreds of people by railway to Liverpool from Leicester, Nottingham and Derby. Tickets cost 15 shillings for first-class passengers and 10 shillings for second-class. Cook carefully examined the route in advance and produced a 60-page handbook of the journey – the first travel

> "WHAT A GLORIOUS THING it would be if the newly developed power of railways and locomotion could be subservient to the cause of Temperance." Thomas Cook

brochure. 'Advertising is to trade what steam is to machinery,' he declared, stating that his aim was to make travel 'easy, cheap and safe for others'. He also – pragmatically – turned a blind eye to intemperance on the part of certain passengers, on the grounds that this would serve as a lesson to the remainder.

Encouraged by this success, Cook began to include accommodation for his tour parties as part of the service. However, an 1846 scheme for 350 people from Leicester to tour Scotland led to bankruptcy. To a man as pious, sober and respectable as Cook this must have been traumatic, but his reputation and mettle were such that, five years later, 165,000 customers signed up for Cook's tour from the Midlands to London, where they viewed the Great Exhibition in the Crystal Palace in Hyde Park and were accommodated in dormitories for two shillings a night. In

> **'ADVERTISING IS TO TRADE** what steam is to machinery.**'**
> Thomas Cook

1855 Cook undertook his first continental tour, personally conducting two parties by paddle steamer from Harwich to Antwerp, then on to Brussels, Cologne, Frankfurt, Heidelberg, Strasbourg and finally Paris for the International Exhibition. The parties included a high proportion of unaccompanied single women, reassured by the company's reputation for sobriety and responsibility.

By 1865 Cook had stopped personally conducting his 'grand circular tours' of Europe, Palestine and Egypt – the River Nile had become known as 'Cook's Canal' – and gone into partnership with his commercially minded son John Mason Cook as Thomas Cook & Son, travel agents, from offices in Fleet Street, London. Cook and his wife ran a small temperance hotel above the office, which contained a shop selling guidebooks, luggage, telescopes, footwear and other essentials for the traveller. The latter could also purchase 'hotel coupons' valid either for a restaurant meal or an overnight stay in a hotel, providing the establishment in question was on Cook's 'approved' list.

AROUND THE WORLD

The imagination of an increasingly affluent and educated Victorian Britain was fired by the Great Exhibition, by improved communications in the form of the press and telegraph, and by news of Empire. The desire of the British to see the world for themselves extended to the former colonies in North America, and in 1866 John Mason Cook led the first $250 tour of the United States. The itinerary included a month-long voyage each way across the Atlantic, during which customers were served three 13-course meals a day. In New York City they took in the Hudson River, Madison Avenue and Central Park, while in Richmond, Virginia, they visited Civil War battlefields, where a year after hostilities had ceased, mass graves were still being dug and piles of bones, human and animal, lay bleaching in the sun. In Washington they admired the Capitol and the White House, and returned via Vermont. In 1871 a brief Anglo-American partnership under the name Cook, Son and Jenkins was unsuccessful, however, and the company swiftly reverted to its original name.

In 1872, at the age of 63, Cook himself conducted the company's first world tour, costing 210 guineas per head. The 222-day excursion included a steamship across the Atlantic, a stagecoach across America, a paddle steamer to Japan and an overland journey across India and China. For the benefit of subsequent tours, his son invented the predecessor of the traveller's cheque.

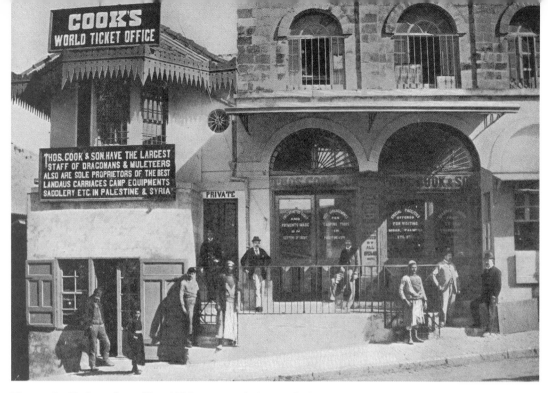

Thomas Cook's Jerusalem office, 1900 – one man's dream of a better world through temperance became the phenomenon of 'tourism' and transformed leisure travel from the privilege of a wealthy few to an activity open to all.

By this time there was something of a backlash from members of polite society, who had long considered travel in Europe to be their private preserve. British residents in Florence complained that Cook was swamping the Continent with 'everything that is low-bred, vulgar and ridiculous', while the critics John Ruskin and Leslie Stephen disdainfully referred to Cook's tourists as 'cockneys'. 'God's earth,' Cook retorted, 'with all its fullness and beauty, is for the people.'

FROM FAMILY FIRM TO PRIVATIZATION

Cook was persuaded to retire to Leicestershire in 1879. John Mason Cook, with whom Cook Senior had enjoyed a frosty relationship, expanded the company into military transport and postal services for Britain and Egypt, and led tours of the Middle East. In 1890 he and his sons set up the 'Princes' Department' to handle the European tours of Indian maharajahs: '200 servants, 50 family attendants, 20 chefs, 10 elephants, 33 tame tigers, 1000 packing cases and a small howitzer' read one early inventory. In 1898, six years after his father's death, John Mason Cook contracted dysentery while arranging a visit for the German Emperor Wilhelm II to Palestine and died the following year. His three sons took on the company, organizing the first air charter in 1919, from New York City to Chicago, to the world heavyweight fight between Jack Dempsey and Gene Tunney. They also expanded into winter sports and tours by motor car.

In 1928 the two surviving sons unexpectedly sold out to their only international rival, the Franco-Belgian Wagons-Lits company, operator of the Orient Express. The brand lived on – by 1937

> **'200 SERVANTS,** 50 family attendants, 20 chefs, 10 elephants, 33 tame tigers, 1000 packing cases and a small howitzer.'
>
> Items on the inventory for a tour of Europe organized by Thos. Cook & Son for an Indian maharajah, *c.* 1890.

Thomas Cook was advertising three-day flights by Zeppelin to Rio – but after the Fall of France in 1940 the Paris offices and business of Wagons-Lits fell into German hands, and the UK assets of Thomas Cook were requisitioned by the British government. In 1941, the year of its centenary, the British assets and name were sold to a consortium of four British railway companies, and nationalized in 1948 as part of the British Transport Commission.

RETURN TO THE PRIVATE SECTOR

In the 1950s air tourism ceased to be the preserve of the better off, and over 1 million Britons a year travelled abroad on holiday. By its 125th anniversary year in 1966 Thomas Cook was the world's largest travel organization, but its decision not to enter the growing market for cheap package holidays cost the company dear. In 1972 British Rail sold it to a consortium of Midland Bank, Trust House Forte and the Automobile Association, returning it to the private sector. This proved to be the salvation of the company, which was reorganized and rebranded and, unlike several major travel firms, survived the recession of the 1970s. During the same period, under US banking laws, Cook's American travel-agency operations were sold to Dun & Bradstreet. The division prospered, and in 1989 was sold on again to Crimson/Heritage for $1.3 billion.

The right – and wrong – kind of parent company has proved crucial to Thomas Cook, especially in Europe. In 1992 Midland Bank, now the sole owner distracted by bad lending in America and Third World debt, sold the company to the German LTU group and Westdeutsche Landesbank. Subsequent acquisitions included budget airlines and Club 18–30, the sex and 'booze cruise' operator for young adults whose advertising slogans included 'Beaver España'. In 1999 the JMC ('John Mason Cook') amalgamation took the company back into customized package holidays, including the lucrative gay-and-lesbian market. In 2007 the European Union approved a merger with MyTravel that made Thomas Cook the second largest travel company in Europe (after the German group TUI) and the third largest in the world. The company is now known as the Thomas Cook Group with its head office operating out of the UK, and is listed on the London Stock Exchange. It is owned 52 per cent by the German retail group Karstadtquelle and 48 per cent by the MyTravel shareholders.

Over a century and a half ago, a non-smoking, teetotal Baptist invented tourism and earned the title 'Grand Courier Extraordinary to the Human Race'. Today, his critics John Ruskin and Leslie Stephen would most likely be earning their living giving cultural lectures to the clients on a Cook's tour. By the early 21st century Cook had become a worldwide tourism and travel services conglomerate employing 16,000 staff in 1050 locations around the world.

SINGER

1850 | USA

As ye sew ...

The Singer Corporation was founded by Isaac Singer, actor, inventor and philandering bigamist. Singer saw the sewing machine 'invented' four times before his own version reached the market. The machine he perfected not only became a design classic, but also brought about social transformations, emancipating both the home-working seamstress and the housewife – although his own personal dealings with women were far from emancipated.

Isaac Merritt Singer was born in 1811 near Schaghiticoke, New York, the son of a destitute Saxon immigrant and his first wife (serial polygamy was to become a recurring feature of the Singer family). Singer's father, who would live to be 102, left home when Isaac was 12 years old. When young Isaac was 19 he was apprenticed as a machinist, and in the same year became a touring actor, married the 15-year-old Catherine Haley and fathered a son. He subsequently moved his young family to New York City, where he worked in a press shop.

A RACKETY LIFE

Before long, the ever-restless Singer took to the road again as an agent for a company of actors. In Baltimore he met Mary Ann Sponsler, to whom he bigamously proposed marriage before returning to New York, where he and his first wife had a daughter in 1837. In the same year, after Mary Ann arrived in the city and discovered Singer was married, he decided to leave with her for Baltimore, where they lived as a married couple and had a son, Isaac.

Singer's first patent, for a rock-drilling machine, was obtained in 1839. He had been inspired when he was working during a lean spell as a labourer clearing boulders on the Illinois–Michigan Canal. He sold his patent for $2000, a considerable sum, and with the proceeds went on tour again as 'Isaac Merritt', an actor in his own company, the 'Merritt Players', with Mary Ann as 'Mrs Merritt'. Five years down the road, in 1844, after touring the wilds of the West, they fetched up broke in Fredericksburg, Ohio. They were soon back in Singer's native

Pittstown, where he set up a shop making wood type and signage. In 1849, having patented a type-cutting machine, he moved back to New York hoping to market his latest invention. With barely enough funds to build a working prototype, Singer rented a shared workshop in Boston.

THE DEVELOPMENT OF THE SEWING MACHINE

Singer's landlord, Orson C. Phelps, was manufacturing Lerow & Blodgett sewing machines, which were difficult to produce and operate, and were often returned by disgruntled purchasers. With no orders for his type-cutting machine, Singer suggested improvements to the sewing machine in the form of the movement of the shuttle and the shape of the needle; he was also the first to see the advantage of a foot treadle over the hand-cranked mechanism standard to machines at the time. After laborious efforts, the machine began to stitch more effectively. Singer and Phelps secured backing and became partners in the 'Jenny Lind Sewing Machine Project', named after the famous soprano known as the 'Swedish nightingale'. By the time Singer was awarded a patent in 1851, the 'Jenny Lind' had become the 'Singer Sewing Machine'.

Litigation broke out between various developers until a 'patent pool' was established whereby the rivals agreed to share their intellectual properties and the profits. I.M. Singer & Company's machine, although

Mrs Singer and the Statue of Liberty

The Statue of Liberty, given by the French to the USA in 1884 and erected in New York Harbour as the gateway to America, has a face reputedly modelled by the sculptor Frederic Bartholdi on Isabella Singer, Isaac Singer's last wife.

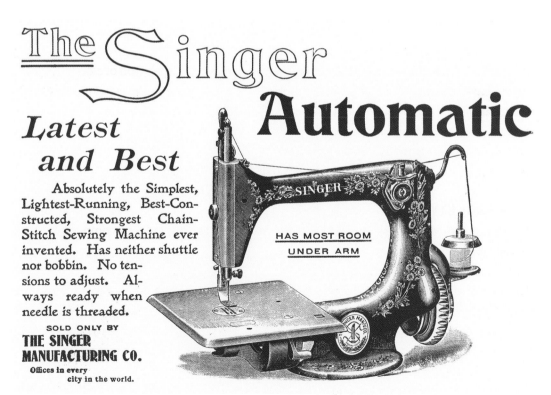

The Singer Automatic

Latest and Best

Absolutely the Simplest, Lightest-Running, Best-Constructed, Strongest Chain-Stitch Sewing Machine ever invented. Has neither shuttle nor bobbin. No tensions to adjust. Always ready when needle is threaded.

SOLD ONLY BY

THE SINGER MANUFACTURING CO.

Offices in every city in the world.

HAS MOST ROOM UNDER ARM

Behind the machine that revolutionized the garment industry and emancipated women the world over, was an extraordinary story of exile and invention spanning at least four 'wives' and two continents.

technically superior and comparatively portable, nonetheless initially failed to attract the garment trade, which was notorious for its aversion to investing in its own business and for its savage working practices. Instead, Singer resurrected his *alter ego* as a performer and used his Herculean personality to sell his machine to individual buyers through theatrical demonstrations at country fairs, carnivals and church suppers around the country. He dreamed up crude and effective slogans – 'It seams perfect' – and offered hire-purchase schemes. As word of the quality of

the machine spread, sales grew and more conventional advertising became feasible. In 1856 Singer produced 2564 machines; in 1860, 13,000. Singer's domination of the market for the home sewing machine enabled the company to expand abroad. It became one of the first American multinationals, with agencies in Paris, France and Rio de Janeiro.

SUCCESS AND SEXUALITY

Singer's success enabled him to buy a mansion on Fifth Avenue for his second 'wife' Mary Ann and their family. He divorced his legal wife Catherine on the somewhat surprising grounds that *she* was guilty of adultery, and went on to set up various mistresses in sumptuous apartments. Among his paramours was his employee Mary McGonigal, who had already borne him five children by the time Mary Ann spotted her driving with Singer down Fifth Avenue. She sued her 'husband' as a result, and Singer was arrested, fleeing to London on his release. A further Singer 'family' was shortly afterwards discovered in Lower Manhattan under the name of Merritt. Singer is thought to have fathered – and acknowledged – at least 18 children (16 surviving infancy) by four women. In 1863 he married Isabella Boyer, whom he had met in Paris. She was his last and, by all accounts, truest wife.

By this time the company had been renamed the Singer Manufacturing Company. Singer remained a major stockholder and on the board of trustees. Barred from New York society, however, he and Isabella emigrated to Paris, where they would have six children. The Franco-Prussian War forced them to London, and thence to the Devon coastal resort of Torquay. Here Singer built a large house, Oldway Mansion, where many of his children came to live. The house included its own theatre, in which the family performed and produced plays and comic operas. Singer also became widely respected for his generosity to the local poor, particularly on his birthday, on the Fourth of July, and at Christmas. He never returned to the United States, and the Singer family vault is in Torquay Cemetery.

Singer's children

The founder's penchant for a complex and exotic family life was inherited by some of his children. Isaac's 18th child, Winnaretta, married twice into the French aristocracy, became a patron of the composer Erik Satie and conducted a long affair with Violet Trefusis, also the lover of Vita Sackville-West. Her brother had a child by the dancer Isadora Duncan, while – somewhat more respectably – another brother became a donor to what would become Exeter University in southwest England, where a building is named after him.

INNOVATION AND EXPANSION

Singer died in 1875 leaving a fortune of around $14 million. Given the complexity of his 'families', a number of lawsuits followed before Isabella was declared his legal widow. The company he founded had already become synonymous with cutting-edge sewing-machine technology, building on his brilliant insights and unerring eye for detail. The red 'S' Girl logo was one of the best-known emblems in the world.

The company became known for its monumental buildings, to match its great success. In 1883, to meet demand in Europe, the company opened the largest sewing-machine factory in the world at Kilbowie – later Clydebank – in Scotland, employing up to 12,000 people and boasting the world's second-tallest clock tower, at 200 feet high, with the world's largest clock face. The factory would last for 99 years, closing in 1984. Singer's Russian headquarters, opened in St Petersburg in 1904, was the country's first steel-girder building. When the 47-storey Singer Building at 149 Broadway was completed in 1908, it was New York's first skyscraper, and at the time the tallest building in the world, at 612 feet.

FROM ELECTRIC MOTORS TO MICROCHIPS

Thomas Edison had supplied the motor for an early electrically powered sewing machine, but it was Singer who went on to introduce the electric model to the mass market. By the 1920s the company was producing a range of models of different shapes, weights and sizes, and in 1927 opened the first Singer Sewing Centre, in New York City. The pattern of product dominance, brand pre-eminence and education was established for the next half century. By the 1950s the Singer Sewing Centres were training 400,000 housewives in basic and advanced techniques.

Broadway remained the executive headquarters of the company until 1961, when it moved to Rockefeller Plaza (the original Singer Building was demolished in 1968). In 1973 the Singer Company – with over $2 billion in sales, 120,000 employees and 60,000 shareholders – was listed on the London Stock Exchange. When the world's first fully electronic sewing machine came onto the market two years later, it was Singer who made it. The company celebrated its 150th anniversary in 2001. Singer continued to invest in new materials and microprocessors, and to produce both simple and complex machines to suit a range of abilities and needs. In the early 21st century the home sewing machine as evolved by Singer became comparable in its different capabilities to the personal computer.

The Singer Corporation today is based near Nashville, Tennessee, and is part of SVP Worldwide, which is owned by Kohlberg & Company. Today, around the world, many of the earliest Singer treadle sewing machines are still hard at work – justifying the old Singer slogan 'At Home Worldwide'.

1811
Birth of **Isaac Singer**.

1839
Singer patents a **rock-drilling machine**.

1851
Singer is awarded a patent for his **sewing machine**.

1860
Production reaches **13,000 machines per year**.

1875
Death of **Isaac Singer**.

1883
The Singer company opens its **factory in Clydebank**, Scotland.

1908
The **Singer Building**, New York's first skyscraper, is completed.

1927
Opening of the **first Singer Sewing Centre**, in New York City.

1973
The Singer Company is **listed on the London Stock Exchange**.

WESTERN UNION

1851 | USA

From brand leader
to sub-prime

The Western Union Company transfers money around the world. It is based in Englewood, Colorado, with 1800 employees and 270,000 agent locations in 200 countries. Today's utilitarian black and yellow sign hides a history linking Thomas Edison, Samuel Morse, Alexander Graham Bell, the founder of Cornell University and one of the definitive corporate horror stories of the 1980s and 1990s.

By the 1850s telegraphy was the new new thing for entrepreneurs and governments in the United States and Europe. Verbal and numerical information encrypted in Samuel Morse's code could be electromagnetically transmitted by a telegraph operator down wire cable over long distances, at a fraction of the speed of the mail coach, railway, steamship, carrier pigeon or the Pony Express. Joining up America with the telegraph became the new obsession, and telegrams were used for both social and business communication, for the conveyance of good news and bad – the latter delivered in a black-edged envelope.

THE DREAM OF A TRANSCONTINENTAL TELEGRAPH

In 1851 a group of businessmen in Rochester, New York – including Hiram Sibley and Don Alonzo Watson – formed the New York and Mississippi Valley Printing Telegraph Company. Another of the founders was Ezra Cornell, a Quaker ejected from the Society of Friends for marrying a Methodist. Cornell had been a plough salesman and an associate of Samuel Morse, for whom he had dug underground telegraph cables before it became clear that telegraph poles and wire were cheaper. Cornell helped string the first significant telegraph line between Washington DC and Baltimore, Maryland, and would oversee many more lines for the company. In 1856, following Cornell's vision of a coast-to-coast telegraph, the company changed its name to Western Union.

The Pacific Telegraph Act of 1860 authorized the federal government to award the contract to build the first transcontinental telegraph. The contract went to Hiram Sibley, president of

Western Union, who formed a consortium that consolidated into the Overland Telegraph Company of California. Sibley himself incorporated the Pacific Telegraph Company of Nebraska. The route drove eastward from Carson City through Nevada and Utah, and westward from Omaha along the Oregon Trail. Building the line took nearly a year, but the company overcame the problems of provisioning the construction teams and a shortage of telegraph poles in the deserts of the Great Basin and the plains of the Midwest. On 18 October 1861 the line from Omaha reached Salt Lake City; six days later, the line from Carson City arrived and the final pole was driven into the ground.

By the time the coast-to-coast telegraph was completed, the Civil War had broken out between North and South, threatening to tear the country apart. Nevertheless, the first transcontinental telegraph was a milestone in the formation of the United States, and represented the greatest revolution in information technology since the invention of the printed word. Two days after the telegraphs joined up, the Pony Express announced its closure. Its assets were later sold to Wells Fargo and the name trademarked by the US Postal Service.

In 1865 Western Union embarked on the construction of the Russian–American Telegraph, an attempt to link Vancouver in British Columbia to Europe via Alaska, the Bering Sea, Siberia and Moscow. The epic two-year expedition succeeded in connecting British Columbia to Alaska, but was halted when the first submarine cable was successfully laid under the Atlantic between Europe and the United States. Ezra Cornell, having made his fortune from Western Union, retired and co-founded Cornell University.

TELEGRAMS, PHONES AND FAXES

In 1869 the single overland telegraph was replaced by a multi-line telegraph constructed along the route of the First Transcontinental Railroad. Half a century followed of capitalization on this and other inventions. In 1870 Western Union introduced standardized time at principal railroad stations and in major cities; the company's own clocks were synchronized with the US Naval Observatory. By this time its telegrams were delivered by uniformed messengers. In 1871 the company introduced the first money-transfer service by telegraph. In 1879 Western Union left the telephone business, allegedly over a patent dispute; other versions have it that the company saw no future for a 'toy' product that would require two users. Either way, this was one missed call. As the

Thomas Edison and Western Union

Among Western Union telegraph operators in the later 1860s was the young Thomas Edison, whose deafness helped him to concentrate while working alongside other operators. During his time with Western Union, Edison learned about electricity and applied this knowledge to his 1866 stock ticker, which enabled Western Union to supply New York City brokerage firms with stock-exchange quotations. The invention made Edison's first fortune. Western Union president William Orton also asked Edison if he could usurp Alexander Graham Bell's patent for the telephone. Edison, who in the words of a friend 'had a vacuum where his conscience ought to be', replied that he could. He could not.

'I WOULD FOUND an institution where any person can find instruction in any study.**'**
Ezra Cornell, 1865, one of the founders of Western Union, and co-founder of Cornell University.

Western Union Telegram Messengers *c.* 1940. Western Union operated at the leading edge of telegraphy and telephony for more than a century, but the 1980s brought a disastrous downturn in the company's fortunes.

telephone began to replace the telegraph for communications, the company concentrated on money transfer. In 1884 Western Union was among the first 11 companies selected for the Dow Jones Average on the New York Stock Exchange.

In 1914 the company introduced the first consumer charge card. This was followed by singing telegrams, roller-skating messenger girls and, in 1935, the intercity facsimile transmission (fax) service. During the Second World War, Western Union introduced the first commercial intercity microwave network to replace land lines, and its teletype operators worked in the secure bunker beneath the White House. At the end of the war, many Western Union employees who had served in the armed forces obtained places at Cornell, the university founded by their predecessor, before returning to work for the company.

CORPORATE MELTDOWN

In 1958 the advent of the telex saw the end of the uniformed messenger. In 1964 the company invested in transcontinental microwave, and by 1974 was operating its own satellites for communication within the USA. During the 1980s more and more financial transactions were being carried out by credit card over the phone and this, combined with the breakup of ATT and Bell, brought falling revenues and spiralling costs to Western Union from local operators. Meanwhile, the personal fax spelled the end of the telex.

The ensuing corporate meltdown featured ousted CEOs, failed satellite launches, cancelled dividends, slashed wages,

60 Hudson Street

Western Union's headquarters between 1930 and 1973 were in a splendid art deco building located at 60 Hudson Street in SoHo, Lower Manhattan. The building has been officially designated a New York City landmark.

redundancies, union lockouts, strikes, lines of credit withdrawn, major stockholders unloading, asset write-downs, real estate sell-offs, junk-bond issues, frozen pensions, stockholder-mounted executive purges, junk-bond default and three near brushes with bankruptcy. The Western Union Alumni website would call this the 'pathway to oblivion'. In 1994 Western Union's New Valley parent company filed for Chapter 11 bankruptcy. For the first time in 143 years, Western Union ceased to send telegrams.

A CHANGING WORLD

The financial markets identified value in the money-transfer business of the company. Western Union was sold at auction and became part of First Financial Management Corporation, subsequently First Data Corporation. The telegram service was resumed, and with only 20,000 agent locations there was a drive to build up agents and business in Mexico, Russia, Uzbekistan, South Africa and Eritrea. Much of this was and is business to customers without credit cards or bank accounts. Western Union is trusted by many migrants for safe transmission of remittances. However, after it came to light that the company was cooperating with government surveillance following the revelation that one of the last acts of the 9/11 hijackers was to wire money via Western Union to their families, it has been feared by people wanting to move money illegally. Another ploy by migrant users who manage to obtain a bank account is to order two ATM cards and mail one to their families, cutting out the cost of Western Union-style money transfer. Some online purchasers on auction sites are reluctant to use Western Union as there have been cases of users becoming the victims of fraud, especially from Nigeria, with which there is no extradition treaty; issues have also arisen of money laundering by criminal users and the exploitation of the service by financiers of terrorist groups. The company regularly advises its clients on payment security and endeavours to block suspicious transactions.

In 2006 Western Union, one of the first 11 components of the Dow Jones, once again became an independent, publicly traded corporation. The telegram service was again discontinued, this time for good. The communications revolution that had superseded the Pony Express was now itself superseded by the internet. Telegram services are still offered by other suppliers.

Today, Western Union Financial Services processes 250 million money orders a year. Its main competitors are banks, credit unions, CheckFree, MoneyGram and the US Postal Service. The company also sponsors community events around the world in aid of the diaspora communities that use its global money-transfer service.

TIMELINE

1851
Foundation of the **New York and Mississippi Valley Printing Telegraph Company**.

1856
The company changes its name to **Western Union**.

1860
The Pacific Telegraph Act authorizes the federal government to offer a contract to build a **transcontinental telegraph**.

1861
Completion of the transcontinental telegraph.

1871
Western Union begins its **money-transfer service** by telegraph.

1879
The company **withdraws from investment** in developing the telephone, dismissing it as a 'toy'.

1884
Western Union is listed with ten other companies in the **first Dow Jones Average**.

1914
The company introduces the **first consumer charge card**.

1935
Western Union offers the **first fax service**.

1958
Introduction of the **telex**.

1994
Western Union files for **Chapter 11 bankruptcy**, and is subsequently taken over.

2006
Western Union is **relaunched** as an independent, publicly traded corporation.

REUTERS

1851 | UK

Knowledge is power

Reuters is a global news service whose income derives principally from the supply of information to newspapers and to worldwide financial markets. For many years synonymous with breaking the news of events that changed the world, Reuters today is an £8.7 billion conglomerate merged with Thomson Financial of Canada. All this began with a pigeon in Aachen, Germany, 158 years ago.

Julius de Reuter was born Israel Beer Josaphat in Cassel, Germany, in 1816, the son of a rabbi. His father died when he was 13, and young Josaphat was sent to join his Uncle Benfy's bank in Göttingen. Josaphat went through a number of jobs in various German cities, and also spent time in London. Although he retained a lifelong affinity with the Jewish faith, like many in Germany he found Jewishness an obstacle to advancement, and in 1845 – having married Ida, the daughter of a Prussian bureaucrat – he converted to Christianity. He also changed his name to Paul Julius Reuter, Reuter being a common German surname.

BERLIN, PARIS, AACHEN

In 1847 Reuter bought into a Berlin bookshop and expanded into publishing under the name Reuter and Stargardt. The radical tone of the company's publications antagonized the Prussian authorities, and possibly for this reason the Reuters fled Berlin for Paris. Here in 1849 they set up a tiny agency supplying news articles and information about prices on the Paris Bourse – translated from French by Ida, printed by Julius, and conveyed by mail coach to German provincial newspapers. After eight months the venture failed through insufficient revenues from subscribers, not least because the Prussian authorities disliked uncontrolled information about other countries.

'**IF ST PAUL RETURNED** to the world today he would head Reuters.' Pope John Paul I, 1978

Undaunted, the Reuters returned to Germany. Julius opened an office in Aachen, on the border of Germany, Belgium and the Netherlands, and at the end of the Prussian state telegraph line. Reuter supplied market and stock-exchange prices to bankers and merchants and received information by mail from Paris and other centres. The telegraph line between Paris and Brussels was not yet complete, and Reuter spotted a gap in the market: he could beat the 76-mile seven-hour mail-train journey between Aachen and Brussels if he used pigeons. For seven months Reuter's pigeons were transported each day by train from Aachen to Brussels from where they flew back the next day bearing messages, beating the railway by five hours. Reuter's main subscribers were the *Kölnische Zeitung* of Cologne, which he supplied with news from France and Belgium, and *L'Independence Belge* of Brussels, which wanted news from Germany and Austria. When the gap in the telegraph narrowed to 5 miles, Reuter used horses. When it closed with the completion of the telegraph, so did his window of opportunity. In 1851, with the completion of the new submarine cable between Calais and Dover, the Reuters moved once more to London.

SETTLING IN ENGLAND

This time Reuter's persistence was rewarded. London was the centre for free trade and home to a large Jewish business community. He opened the 'Submarine Telegraph' office in the City and agreed a contract with the London Stock Exchange to provide brokers with opening and closing prices from Continental European exchanges in return for access to the London prices, which he telegraphed to brokers in Paris. Reuter also began supplying merchants with information about grain markets and prospects in Russia – Britain's chief supplier – and the Danube

The editorial staff at Reuters Press Agency, *c.* 1900. From humble beginnings – in its heyday the agency proved the power of news to influence world opinion and move markets.

basin. This was technology harnessed as a switchboard or clearing centre where the latest news of a commodity was a valuable commodity in itself. The cost of a telegram – 60 words to Trieste could cost as much as £4.17s.6d in 1852 – was well worth the price to the wholesale traders and market makers of their day.

The telegraph helped Reuter to sell the idea of a faster and more accurate general news service to *The Times* and other British newspapers. Reuter's terms were 2s.6d for 20 words if his name was used; if not, 5s. for the same despatch. He offered a 24-hour service, often going down to his office by hansom cab in the middle of the night in his nightshirt and dressing gown, copying out messages by hand and sending them round by cab to the newspaper offices. He built up an unrivalled network of contacts in the highest circles of commerce and even royalty, and his choices of agent and correspondent were as shrewd as his commercial judgement. In 1857 Reuter was naturalized as a British citizen.

THE VICTORIAN INTERNET

Reuter's first major news scoop came in 1865 with the assassination of President Lincoln. With the transatlantic telegraph out of action, in order to get the news to London, Reuter's US correspondent chartered a tug and chased a departing mail boat across New York Harbour, writing his story as he did so. Catching up with the mail boat, he threw it aboard with instructions that it was to be taken ashore to Reuter's telegraph station on the coast of Ireland and cabled to London. While the rest of the New York press pack waited for the next mail boat, Reuter in London received the story so far ahead of the competition that many believed it to be a hoax perpetrated by Stock Exchange speculators. The truth established, Reuter's Telegram Company Limited – with its by-line 'Reuter's Telegrams' – was confirmed as the leader in breaking news.

By the time of his death as Baron Julius de Reuter in 1899, the former Israel Beer Josaphat had invested in his own cable to link England and Germany and co-invested in the cable between France and North America. Through the reach of the British Empire, Reuters had agents in Asia, Africa and Australia; yet the original two-room offices in the Royal Exchange lasted until 1866.

> ## Our man in the USSR
>
> During the 1930s, Reuters' Moscow correspondent was Ian Fleming, who went on to become a senior officer in naval intelligence during the Second World War, and subsequently gained fame as the creator of James Bond.

Even after a move to Lothbury and then Old Jewry there were still only a dozen senior men in the London headquarters. In 1879 Reuter had been succeeded by his son Herbert, who saw the company through the newspaper frenzy of the Boer War in South Africa, where Rudyard Kipling, author of *The Jungle Book* and later winner of the Nobel Prize for Literature, was among its correspondents. Herbert de Reuter – a 'sociable recluse' – unsuccessfully diversified the company into banking and was estranged from his only son Hubert, who declined to work for Reuters and died a hero's death in the First World War. When his wife Edith died in 1915, Herbert committed suicide.

FIRST AND BEST WITH THE NEWS

Reuters was on the brink of insolvency by the time the company was restructured in 1916 by Roderick Jones, who saw off a hostile takeover, disposed of the bank established by Herbert Reuter and greatly enriched himself in the process. The Reuters aim – to be first and best with the news – remained unchanged throughout the 20th century, although during the Second World War it received secret subsidies from the British government in return for departing from 'objective truth'. Subsequently, Reuters created, jointly invested in and in some cases handed back to local control numerous news agencies around the world. Some of these – no longer branded Reuters – have since proved to be less than impartial reporters of truth.

By the late 1960s and early 1970s, Reuters itself was reporting losses, with falling subscriptions and competition from television news. Ironically, the company was rescued by the screen: floating currencies meant that commodities traders and bankers' dealing rooms required constantly updated electronic financial information. Reuters invested in new information technology and ramped up operations in the United States, particularly in Washington, the political news capital of the Western world.

GOING PUBLIC

The 1980s saw business booming, with Reuters operating one of the largest private communications networks in the world through computer data centres in London, Hong Kong, New York, Frankfurt and Geneva. Inevitably the costs and opportunities involved in this expansion raised the issue of flotation. Reuters uniquely had a 'Founder's Share', which protected its integrity from unwelcome ownership and editorial interference, and this was much discussed in the context of possible flotation. But going public was inevitable, and went ahead in 1984. The share issue was undersubscribed on the Nasdaq in New York, but 2.7 times oversubscribed in London, and the valuation of £770 million raised £53 million for Reuters to spend. It also made multimillionaires of the senior executives.

The 1990s bull market saw Reuters riding high until 1997, when pressure came in the United States from Bloomberg, founded by ex-Salomon Brothers trader Michael Bloomberg, who had spotted a niche that Reuters had ignored in the bonds and derivatives markets. Finding the 'Bloomberg Killer' product became an obsession within Reuters. But in the meantime, management ignored more fundamental issues of overmanning and lost competitiveness, and even the *Sunday Times* dropped its subscription. By 2001, Reuters' 150th anniversary, the dotcom bubble had burst, and in 2002 Reuters was the worst-performing company on the FTSE 100. Thousands of jobs and hundreds of product lines were shed, followed by a move to Canary Wharf in London's Docklands. In 2007 Reuters and Canadian-based Thomson Financial, part of the group that had sold the *Sunday Times* and *The Times* to Rupert Murdoch, announced an £8.7 billion merger to create the world's largest provider of financial data, with only Bloomberg left as a significant competitor.

TIMELINE

1816
Birth of **Israel Beer Josaphat**, later Baron Julius de Reuter.

1845
Josaphat converts to Christianity and changes his surname to **Reuter**.

1847
Starts a **publishing business** in Berlin.

1849
Sets up a **news agency** in Paris.

1857
Reuter is naturalized as a **British citizen**.

1879
Reuter's **son Herbert** takes over the company.

1899
Death of **Julius de Reuter**.

1915
Herbert de Reuter commits suicide.

1916
Roderick Jones restructures the company.

1984
Reuters is **floated** in New York and London.

2007
Reuters **merges** with Thomson Financial.

LEVI STRAUSS

1853 | USA

From working clothes
to fashion classic

Levi Strauss & Co. is best known for its eponymous blue jeans, now sold in more than 110 countries around the world. The largest and most successful brand-name clothing company in the world began with two men and a horse in the California gold fields. The company is a leader in corporate citizenship, and is privately owned by descendants of the founder, Lob Strauss, a Jewish immigrant who first came to the United States in 1843.

Lob Strauss was born in Buttenheim, Germany, in 1829. In 1843 he set sail with his mother and two sisters from Bremerhaven for New York, where his half-brothers had established a whole-sale textile and tailoring business. Lob Strauss and his family soon moved on to the ranch of his uncle Daniel Goldman in Louisville, Kentucky, where they spent the next four years. At first Strauss was expected to take over, but he had other ideas and took to walking the roads of Kentucky selling cloth and other items from his backpack. In 1847 Lob Strauss, together with his mother and sisters, returned to New York City, where he joined his half-brothers. By 1850 he had adopted the name 'Levi' and in 1853 became an American citizen. In the same year, aged 23, he left New York City for San Francisco.

MEETING THE NEEDS OF THE FORTY-NINERS

California was in the grip of the Gold Rush. By 1855 some 300,000 'Forty-Niners' had arrived in search of the ore first discovered at Sutter's Mill in the Sierra Nevada. Few of these would leave rich, but by 1857 alone $43 million a year in gold was being taken out of the California mines, most of this transported by Wells Fargo. Strauss and his brother-in-law David Stern saw in the thousands of miners and prospectors and tented camps and covered wagons a market for fabric, scissors, buttons, threads and blankets, as well as canvas sailcloth. They opened a wholesale dry-goods business to supply stores across the American West. The business quickly prospered, and in 1854, the year after Levi had gone West, he donated $5 to a San Francisco orphanage – $110 in today's values.

Levi also sold direct around the mining camps, leading a packhorse laden with merchandize. On these trips Levi noted the complaint of miners and prospectors that their cotton britches tore easily and the gold ore split and spilled from their pockets. This was the inspiration for his move into manufacturing. Initially he made overall trousers of brown canvas sailcloth with storage pockets that were virtually impossible to split, and thus ideal for holding gold ore. Sales boomed, and with his supply of canvas exhausted Levi switched to a sturdy fabric made in France. The material was called *serge de Nîmes*, after the city in the south of France. The name was soon shortened to 'denim'.

THE BIRTH OF BLUE JEANS

For the next 20 years Levi Strauss & Co. flourished, and during this time moved headquarters to Battery Street, San Francisco. In 1872 Levi received a letter from a customer, Jacob Davis, who was a tailor in Reno, Nevada. Davis had invented a process of placing metal rivets at the points of strain on men's work pants. Lacking funds, he suggested Levi pay for the paperwork and they take out the patent together. On 20 May 1873 Strauss and Davis received US patent 139,121 for using copper rivets on men's pants. With denim supplied by the Amoskeag Manufacturing Company in Manchester, New Hampshire, they began manufacturing blue copper-riveted 'XX' top industry quality 'waist overalls' – the first blue jeans.

Features that followed over the decades included the trademark 'LS&CO' embossed buttons, the two-horse leather patch above the right back pocket, the 'arcuate' (bow-shaped) decorative stitching on both back pockets (the oldest American trademark in constant use), the '501' lot number introduced in 1890 and the tiny but distinctive red tab introduced in 1936, originally designed to help salesmen identify and count Levi's jeans at rodeos.

A BENEFICENT EMPLOYER

Shortly before his death in 1902, Levi Strauss endowed 28 scholarships at the University of California in Berkeley. These are still in place today. He also left bequests to Bay Area charities helping children and the poor. His four nephews inherited the thriving company with its headquarters and two factories. When these were destroyed in the 1906 San Francisco earthquake and fire, employees continued to receive their salaries and worked from a temporary headquarters and showroom until new permanent premises were built. The company also extended credit to its wholesale customers to give them time to recover. The following year Jacob Davis sold back his share of the company, but his son Simon continued as superintendent of the factory on Valencia Street and invented 'Koveralls', a one-piece children's playsuit, which became the company's first nationally distributed product.

Throughout the 1920s and 1930s, in spite of falling revenues, the company adopted assembly-line production, maintained its investment in advertising and adopted the cowboy as its image-building icon. Levi's paid bonuses – rare at the best of times in the garment industry – and during the worst of the Depression put employees on a short week to avoid lay-offs and gave them non-manufacturing

> **'I WISH I HAD INVENTED BLUE JEANS:** the most spectacular, the most practical, the most relaxed and nonchalant. They have expression, modesty, sex appeal, simplicity – all I hope for in my clothes.' Yves Saint Laurent

tasks such as laying the hardwood floors that are still in use at Valencia Street today. During the Second World War, while US soldiers wore Levi's jeans and jackets overseas, African-American employees at the company's California plants worked in integrated facilities. Twenty years before the Civil Rights Act, this was a ground-breaking policy. When tried elsewhere it sometimes met with (unsuccessful) local opposition – as in 1960 when the company purchased and desegregated what had been a racially segregated factory in Blackstone, Virginia.

YOUTH APPEAL

During the 1950s, while a US army colonel in Frankfurt, Germany, was banning army wives from wearing Levi's on the grounds that this reflected poorly on America, teenagers back home had started buying the overalls and calling them 'blue jeans'. By 1964 Levi's had become part of the permanent collection of the Smithsonian Institution in Washington DC, and the genderless yet sexy uniform of the generation of Vietnam, Woodstock and *Easy Rider*. This was the latest, softest and most iconic incarnation yet of the dogged sweat and toil of the gold miner, the rugged individualism of the cowboy and the darker nonconformity of the biker. But the company, which went public in 1971, seemed unaware of the treasure in its possession, and instead diversified into baby clothes and polyester suits.

> '**THE DESIGN IS SO RIGHT IT NEED NEVER ALTER,** a timeless classic of clothes. Adaptable, like any well-designed object you can wear them with almost anything.'
>
> The designer Margaret Howell gives her view on Levi jeans.

By the 1980s the brand and company were haemorrhaging money for the simplest reason: they had lost touch with the 15-to-19-year-old core market that had made them what they were. The situation that Levi's found itself in has become a classic corporate case study: the company could either have broken itself without even the excuses of competition or distribution problems; or it could have remade itself. It chose the latter. Non-core product lines were discarded, while advertising campaigns all over the world gradually recaptured the market perception: Levi's were the original, the authentic American blue jeans. Throughout the 1980s and 1990s Original Levi's Stores were established in Europe, North America and Asia – over 1000 company-owned or franchised stores have opened to date. In Moscow, the entire stock sold out in one day. In 1985, in the largest leveraged buy-out the clothing industry had ever seen, the company was taken into private hands again by descendants of the founder, and has remained privately owned ever since. It is difficult to separate the significance of this move from the company's return to profitability and the recovery of its soul.

SUCCESS AND ENLIGHTENMENT

Today, Levi's customers pay the premium price and earn the company twice the profit made by other manufacturers. Carefully cultivating its image, Levi Strauss & Co. has sponsored concert tours by the Rolling Stones and Christina Aguilera. The company has been named by *Fortune* magazine and others as one of America's most-admired corporations for dismantling stereotypes about women, and for the opportunities it offers to Hispanic, gay and transgender employees. It has also been praised for providing medical benefits for employees' partners and financial assistance for retired employees, and for its transparency in naming designers and suppliers.

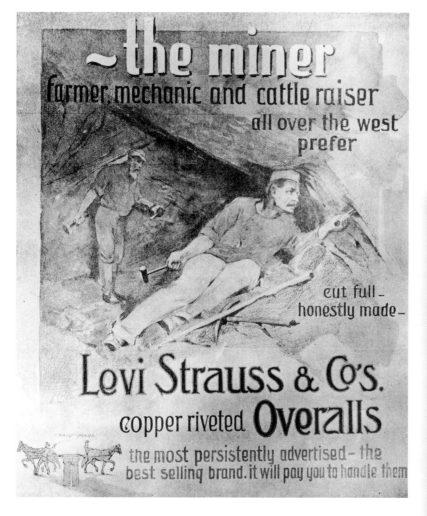

Levi's have been worn by a wider range of people than any other fashion item, from James Dean, Paul Newman and Andy Warhol to Julia Roberts and George W. Bush. As the designer Margaret Howell has said: 'They are the original ... The design is so right it need never alter, a timeless classic of clothes. Adaptable, like any well-designed object you can wear them with almost anything. They are good-looking, well-made, functional and unobtrusive. What is more, they improve with age and increase in value with every wash.' Blue jeans not only provide acceptable and ubiquitous conformity; they give presidents, prime ministers, movie stars and billionaires credibility and self-expression – and in doing so they uniquely represent the contradictions in American culture. They embody an economic superpower's need to recall its origins in the American belief that opportunities are available to everybody, provided they work hard enough. The Levi's brand is as hard-wearing as the core product, as mythical and yet virtually as tough to break.

The California Gold Rush and the rodeo tested 'Levi's' to the limit, giving generations of wearers a piece of American mythology as credible and durable as any brand in the world.

TIMELINE

1829
Birth of Lob (later Levi) **Strauss**.

1843
Strauss **emigrates to the USA** from Germany.

1853
Strauss becomes a US citizen, and leaves New York City for California, where he creates the **first blue jeans**.

1873
Strauss and Jacob Davis are awarded a patent for using **copper rivets** on men's pants.

1890
Introduction of the **'501'** lot number, later a key part of the Levi's brand.

1902
Death of **Levi Strauss**.

1964
Levi's become part of the permanent collection of the **Smithsonian Institution**.

1971
The company goes **public**.

1985
Levi Strauss & Co. is taken back into **private hands** by descendants of the founder.

CENTRAL PACIFIC AND UNION PACIFIC

1869 | *USA*

10

The first transcontinental railroad

The first transcontinental railroad was built across the United States in the 1860s, linking the railways of the east with California in the west. The most challenging and ambitious engineering enterprise of the 19th century, it united the country in the aftermath of the Civil War, joined up the domestic economy, and unleashed the export potential of the world's greatest industrial power. The railroad brought an end to the era of the covered wagon and the Wells Fargo stagecoach, enabling millions of white homesteaders and immigrants to populate the West. In the process it helped to destroy the culture of the Native Americans of the Great Plains.

Talk of a transcontinental railroad began in 1830, a year after the first (British-manufactured) locomotive made its appearance in the United States. Given the fearsome barriers presented by the Rocky Mountains, the Sierra Nevada and the Coast Ranges the debate was not over *if* but *where*. A northern route through Montana and Idaho to Oregon was ruled out because of the likelihood of heavy snow. The central route followed the pioneer trails that opened up the West and avoided the worst of the Rocky Mountains by passing through Nebraska and Wyoming, but was also vulnerable to snow. The southern route avoided the Rockies by going through Texas to Los Angeles.

THE CENTRAL ROUTE

In 1845 Asa Whitney led a team along the central route. Along the way he canvassed support, and went on to submit proposals to Congress at his own expense. His proposals were turned down. Eight years later the government purchased land to enable the southern route to be built, but this was thwarted by the build-up to the Civil War. The railway engineer Theodore Judah also championed the central route, and in 1860, in Sacramento, California, a consortium of businessmen known as 'The Big Four' raised the investment to found the Central Pacific Railroad Company. Judah was appointed chief engineer, only to die from yellow fever before major construction began.

California, booming after the Gold Rush and safely distant from the Civil War, was physically isolated from the Union. Secessionist elements were gaining ground, and this added a political imperative to the commercial need for the railroad as far as Washington was concerned. The Pony Express had been superseded as a carrier of light mail by the first transcontinental telegraph, but the transport of goods and people from New York City to California still took up to six months. The journey – by train to the Mississippi River and thence by covered wagon or stagecoach across plains and through mountains – was fraught with hazards such as bad weather, wild animals, outlaws and hostile Native Americans. Items such as railway locomotives and Wells Fargo's Concord stagecoaches had to be transported from east to west by ship. The voyage took several weeks, as in the days before the Panama Canal ships had to sail all the way down the Atlantic seaboard, round Cape Horn, and then sail back north again up the Pacific coast of South and Central America to California.

'MY FOLKS CAME TO THE UNITED STATES** from Sweden in 1866… when they got to Omaha they had $5, no job and couldn't speak a word of English. Then they got work on the new Union Pacific Railroad … Father worked on the road and mother cooked and washed for twenty-two men … when they got back to Omaha they had $900 saved up.' Mrs Will H. Berger, 1938

Railroad officials celebrate the joining of track laid from coast to coast, 10 May 1869, at Promontory Summit, Utah. The transcontinental railroad unlocked the vast domestic and export potential of the United States.

CONGRESSIONAL APPROVAL

The 1862 Pacific Railway Act passed by Congress and signed by President Lincoln authorized the building of the first transcontinental railroad by the Central Pacific Railroad Company working eastward from California and the Union Pacific Railroad Company working westward from the Missouri River. Each company was required to build only 50 miles of track per year; each was subsidized to the tune of $16,000 per mile over easy ground, $32,000 in the high plains and $48,000 in the mountains.

Theoretically, a healthy competition was under way to see which company could build the longest section of track. However, unlike Central Pacific's 'Big Four' (a grocer, a hardware merchant, a jeweller and a dry goods merchant, all of relative probity), Union Pacific's major investor, Thomas Clark Durant, was an unscrupulous manipulator who had made his money smuggling Confederate cotton.

WORK BEGINS ON THE RAILROAD

In January 1863 the Central Pacific Railroad broke the first ground at Sacramento. Progress was good until they reached the foothills of the Sierra Nevada, where worsening weather saw many of the white workforce strike or quit amid rumours of the latest gold-mining boom. The company began to hire Chinese immigrant labourers, thought at first to be insufficiently robust for the work, but who soon proved otherwise. Thousands more were recruited from the gold mines, laundries and kitchens of California, and from China. Underpaid compared to the whites – eventually they went on strike and won a small increase – the Chinese were the heroes of the Central Pacific Railroad. Hundreds were injured or died during the blasting of tunnels, to the point where the company switched to less volatile explosives and devised a method of suspending the Chinese blasters in baskets, which were then pulled to safety after the fuses were lit.

Later the same year, Union Pacific broke its first ground at the Missouri River bluffs near Omaha. The workforce consisted of Irish labourers and Union and Confederate veterans. Durant see-sawed the eastern track through land he owned, making the most of the federal subsidy. He circumvented Congress's stipulation that no one hold more than 10 per cent of stock in Union Pacific by part-funding friends to buy in their own names and then sell on to him. Railroad stocks became the 19th-century equivalent of Dutch tulips in the 1630s or shares in the South Sea Company in 1720. Durant also ensured Union Pacific was overcharged by the contracting company Crédit Mobilier, also controlled by Durant. By the end of the Civil War in 1865, Durant had made fortunes for himself and his cronies – but the Union Pacific track had barely reached 40 miles west of Omaha. However, with the return of peace, the government began to scrutinize Union Pacific's operations more closely.

> '**MAY GOD CONTINUE** the unity of our Country, as this Railroad unites the two great Oceans of the world.'
>
> Inscription on the ceremonial golden spike driven in during the completion ceremony, 10 May 1869.

DRIVING THE GOLDEN SPIKE

As the railroad began to enter the lands of the Plains Indians, Sioux and Cheyenne war parties attacked Union Pacific labour camps in response to the threat posed by the 'Iron Horse' to their territorial sovereignty. The railroad reacted by building forts along the line and shooting the

COMPANIES THAT CHANGED THE WORLD

bison on which the Plains Indians depended for food. In 1867 a party of Cheyenne uprooted the track at Plum Creek, Nebraska, derailing and looting a freight train, but such incidents were never going to halt the railroad. As Central Pacific closed from the west, the two companies vied to see who could build furthest and fastest – even sabotaging each other's tracks and at one point altering paths to run parallel in order for both to claim government subsidies over the same plot of land. An equally fierce battle took place between the 'New York Crowd' and the 'Boston Crowd' of investors over control of Crédit Mobilier. Congress eventually stepped in to determine where and when the railroads should meet. Central Pacific meanwhile set the record by laying 10 miles of track in a single day; while for all its shoddy workmanship and overcapitalization, Union Pacific would succeed in building two-thirds of the total 1777 miles of track.

Six years after Leland Stanford – one of the 'Big Four' – had driven the first spike, the two railroads met at Promontory Summit, Utah. On 10 May 1869 Stanford drove the symbolic 'golden spike' to mark the completion. This was then removed and replaced by a permanent iron spike. In the event both Stanford and Durant – whose own carriage had been chained to the track by workers until he settled their back pay – missed when trying to drive in the iron spike. Nevertheless, the on-site telegraph operator transmitted the single word 'DONE' to east and west coasts, and the nation erupted in celebration. Travel across the United States – at least from Omaha to Sacramento (the actual coasts were linked shortly afterwards) – was reduced to a single week.

FULFILLING AMERICA'S 'MANIFEST DESTINY'

Less than three years later the Crédit Mobilier overcharging scandal broke and Union Pacific faced bankruptcy. Durant himself had been forced out, but he had bought himself political protection: a number of Congressmen including future President James Garfield were stock-holders. Within ten years of the 'golden spike', borrowings fell due and a debt crisis ensued. However, even this made no difference to the economic consequences of linking up the continent.

America's 'Manifest Destiny' was fulfilled in the link between the coasts and points in between. The fortunes of towns and cities were made by their proximity to the railroad, while the stagecoaches and wagon-based freight service of Wells Fargo only survived in increasingly remote areas. The consequences for the Plains Indians, with the loss of tribal lands and cultural identity, were entirely negative. By 1890 the population of the United States had grown, largely through immigration, to 76 million – from 31 million only 30 years earlier. Over the same period the length of railroad track grew from 30,000 to 270,000 miles. The transportation revolution shortened the vast distances of the continent, enabling the export of American agricultural produce overseas and giving American industry a global reach.

TIMELINE

1830
A **transcontinental railway** is first proposed.

1845
Asa Whitney reconnoitres a route, via Nebraska and Wyoming, known as the 'central route'.

1860
Foundation of the **Central Pacific Railroad Company** in Sacramento, California.

1862
The **Pacific Railway Act** authorizes the construction of a transcontinental railroad. The work is to be undertaken by the Central Pacific and the Union Pacific, the latter being incorporated following passage of the act.

1863
Work on the railroad **begins**.

1869
The **railroad is completed** when lines from the east and west meet at Promontory Summit, Utah.

1885
Central Pacific is **absorbed** by Southern Pacific.

1901
Union Pacific **takes over** Southern Pacific.

1913
The US Supreme Court orders Union Pacific to **surrender control** of Southern Pacific.

1996
Union Pacific finally **acquires** Southern Pacific.

For many Americans the railroad remained the definitive transcontinental link well into the 20th century – this only began to change when American Airlines offered the first non-stop internal flights by Boeing 707 jet airliner in 1959. Today, hundreds of miles of the original route are still in service in the Sierra Nevada, Utah and Wyoming. Interstate 80, the east–west automobile highway, closely follows the path surveyed by the engineers of the first transcontinental railroad nearly a century and a half ago. Thousands of tracklayers, blacksmiths, teamsters, carpenters, surveyors, masons, telegraphers and cooks lived and sometimes died by the railroad.

As for Leland Stanford, the grocer turned railway entrepreneur, he became governor of California, and today the golden spike resides in the Cantor Arts Center of the university that bears Stanford's name. Theodore Judah, the chief engineer of Central Pacific, is commemorated in Judah Street in San Francisco. Thomas Clark Durant died in affluent obscurity in the Adirondacks. Central Pacific Railroad was taken over by Southern Pacific in 1885, which in turn was absorbed by Union Pacific in 1901; thereafter Union Pacific was forced by the US Supreme Court to divest on grounds of monopoly. Almost a century later, in 1996, Union Pacific eventually managed to complete the takeover.

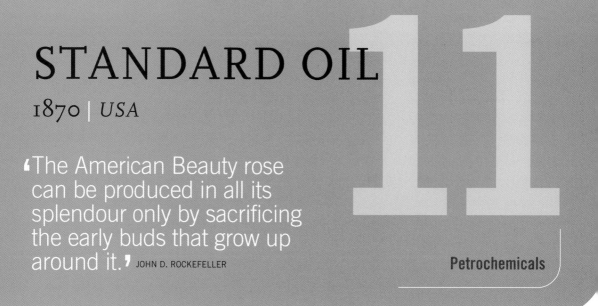

STANDARD OIL 11

1870 | USA

'The American Beauty rose can be produced in all its splendour only by sacrificing the early buds that grow up around it.' JOHN D. ROCKEFELLER

Petrochemicals

Standard Oil, founded in 1870, went on to become one of the first and biggest multinational corporations. It resulted from the subjugation of unruly interests and above all the drive of one man, John D. Rockefeller, who became the world's richest man. It also came to symbolize the anti-competitive practices that are the natural outcome of unregulated free-market economics, becoming the subject of the first and biggest anti-trust lawsuit in American industrial history.

John D. Rockefeller, born in Richford, New York, in 1839, was the son of a devout Baptist mother who would tie him up and beat him when he was disobedient. His father was a bigamous lumber trader and snake-oil salesman whose habit was to trade with his sons and cheat them to 'make 'em sharp'. As a child Rockefeller excelled at mathematics, and rejoiced that in mental calculations he could 'beat a Jew'. His own first business venture was selling turkeys at the age of 7. At the age of 20 he left his job with a Cleveland shipping-produce company and went into business with Maurice Clark. The Civil War and the opening up of the West were good times for entrepreneurs, and the two men dealt in Ohio wheat, Michigan salt and Illinois pork. Within two years they were also dealing in, and refining, oil from the newly discovered fields in Pennsylvania. Clark later recalled that Rockefeller was 'methodical to an extreme'.

THE PENNSYLVANIA OIL BOOM

Clark's comment belies the fact that the Pennsylvania oil fields during the boom of the 1860s presented a squalid vision of ramshackle oil derricks, wildcat drillers, reneged deals, prostitution, pollution and unmanaged pricing – a barrel of oil at times became cheaper than drinking water, and it was here that the phrase 'the bottom fell out of the market' was coined. This was the kind of environment in which Rockefeller's father might have prospered. But the young Rockefeller was made of sterner stuff.

In 1865, at the age of 26, Rockefeller bought out the easy-going Clark and set about combining all aspects of the oil business, from prospecting to marketing, and standardizing the supply of refined oil. His great weapons were his systematic approach to

> **'A FRIENDSHIP BASED ON BUSINESS** is better than a business based on friendship.'
>
> Harry Flagler, business partner of John D. Rockefeller

every aspect of business, and his proximity to the newly extended Atlantic and Great Western Railroad. He was greatly assisted by a new partner, Harry Flagler, whose ebullient and piratical personality complemented that of Rockefeller. It was Flagler who coined the adage: 'A friendship based on business is better than a business based on friendship.'

ELIMINATING THE COMPETITION

Rockefeller and Flagler devoted every waking hour to the business, buying warehouses in New York, boats on the Hudson River, tank cars for transporting oil by railroad, and land on which to grow white oak to make barrels. The expansion of the business enabled them to extract rebates secretly from the railroad companies, lowering their transportation costs and giving what many later held to be an unfair advantage over their competitors. Rockefeller was pathological in competition: he won further concessions from the railroads, and even when he bought up his smaller rivals in Cleveland he tried to keep the fact secret, so that they continued to appear to compete, effectively acting as spies among other genuine competitors. He also built up large cash reserves, which would see him through times of recession and overcapacity. For all these reasons, he soon became the most envied and hated man in the oil industry.

In 1870 – with a million dollars in capital, of which he owned 27 per cent – Rockefeller and five partners established the Standard Oil Company. They already controlled one-tenth of the oil industry in America. The company's name was chosen to project the 'standard quality of product' on which the customer could depend at a time when badly refined kerosene in a household lamp could and often did accidentally ignite, with sometimes fatal results. The highly liquid and expertly run company rapidly expanded its market share through the next downturn, and responded to uncontrolled overproduction by covertly buying up more and more struggling refiners by whatever means necessary. Many never knew that their nearest competitor slashing prices was actually part of Standard Oil, or that the latest 'barrel famine' was orchestrated by the same. Criticism grew vocal, but Rockefeller was unperturbed. Even Harry Flagler was moved to exclaim on one occasion, 'John, you must have a hide like a rhinoceros!'

> '**JOHN, YOU MUST HAVE** a hide like a rhinoceros!'
> Harry Flagler to John D. Rockefeller

AN ALL-POWERFUL MONOLITH

By 1879 Standard Oil controlled over 90 per cent of America's refining capacity, including pipelines and transportation. Kerosene – and other refined oil products such as gasoline and Vaseline – transformed the American way of life, paving the way for the likes of Henry Ford to drive the 'American Century'. Edison's invention of the electric light bulb would supersede the kerosene lamp and threaten Standard Oil with the loss of its market – but Ford's invention of the gasoline-powered mass-produced automobile saved the company.

This efficient, all-powerful monolith sat uncomfortably with a young democracy. As early as 1871 Charles Francis Adams had written that corporations such as Standard Oil 'have declared war, negotiated peace, reduced courts, legislatures and sovereign states to an unequalled obedience to their will'. Such broadsides had no immediate effect, but Rockefeller would later acknowledge the downside of Standard's secretiveness: 'I shall never cease to regret that at that time we never called in the reporters.' In 1881 excoriating press challenges by Henry Demarest Lloyd in the *Chicago Tribune* and an article entitled 'The Story of a Great Monopoly' in *Atlantic Monthly* again appeared to have little effect, but Rockefeller and his partners were taking no chances. In 1882, partly in response to these attacks and partly to ensure the stability of the company after their deaths, they established the Standard Oil Trust Agreement – the first of its kind. Thereafter, Standard Oil could no longer be accused of owning or controlling the vast empire of 14 wholly owned and 26 partly owned

Miss Tar Barrel and the pirate of Wall Street

Rockefeller's image was defined for posterity by the campaigning journalist Ida Tarbell (1857–1944), herself the daughter of an oil driller whom Rockefeller had put out of business, and with whom he maintained an indulgent relationship, calling her 'Miss Tar Barrel'. Tarbell's 1904 book, *The History of the Standard Oil Company*, an exposé of the company's anti-competitive practices, was listed in 1999 by the *New York Times* as among the five most important pieces of American journalism in the 20th century. But when Tarbell heard in 1937 that Rockefeller was dying, she rushed to visit him, calling him 'as fine a pirate as ever flew his flag in Wall Street'.

John D. Rockefeller created the Standard Oil Trust out of an industry in chaos. In the process he made himself the richest man in the world and the most hated man in America.

companies – from which it nonetheless drew colossal profits and over which Rockefeller, Flagler and a handful of dominant stockholders still held sway. Rockefeller remained for many the most hated man in America, while Theodore ('Teddy') Roosevelt, the chief trust-buster, became a national hero.

By 1885, 70 per cent of Standard Oil's business was overseas, and its agents around the world – and its own espionage service – enforced Rockefeller's dictum: 'It is not the business of the public to change our private contracts.' The company's headquarters at 26 Broadway in New York City were synonymous with impregnable secrecy, yet within the boardroom a management style evolved that was far from autocratic and in many ways anticipated the flatter and more creative consultative approach espoused by corporations a century later.

Rockefeller's charitable donations (over his lifetime he gave away some $550 million, including the endowment of the University of Chicago), together with his determination that his children should learn the values of thrift and hard work, distinguished him and his wife Laura from the flashier *nouveaux riches* of the day. But the pressures, although self-imposed, were inexorable. In 1897, in poor health, he stepped aside from executive responsibility in favour of John D. Archbold. Harry Flagler, having made one fortune in partnership with Rockefeller, went on to make another by building a railroad down the coast of Florida and founding both Miami and West Palm Beach.

BUSTING THE TRUST

The Standard Oil Trust – itself the first such trust in America – provoked the first anti-trust laws, and in 1909 a US Department of Justice suit demanded the breakup of the monolith, citing: 'Rebates, preferences and other discriminatory practices in favour of the combination by railroad companies; restraint and monopolization by control of pipelines, and unfair practices against competing pipe lines; contracts with competitors in restraint of trade; unfair methods of competition, such as local price cutting at the points where necessary to suppress competition; espionage of the business of competitors, the operation of bogus independent companies, and payment of rebates on oil, with the like intent.'

> **'IT IS NOT THE BUSINESS** of the public to change our private contracts.' John D. Rockefeller

In 1911 the empire was broken up into 38 parts. The largest of these were Standard Oil of New Jersey (later Exxon) and Standard Oil of New York (later Mobil and Socal, which became Chevron). Not only did these progeny go on to outstrip their parents, but the price of oil went up. Rockefeller, who retained holdings in all these companies, became the world's richest man. The legacy of Socal and Exxon would include Aramco's Saudi Arabian Tapline.

Rockefeller turned down at least one biographer, a certain Winston Churchill, who had accepted a fee of $50,000. Rockefeller observed without bitterness to a neighbour: 'I tell you things have changed since you and I were boys. The world is full of socialists and anarchists. Whenever a man succeeds remarkably in any particular line of business, they jump on him and cry him down.' The Rockefeller Foundation, under his son John D. Rockefeller II and grandson Nelson Rockefeller, has given away billions of dollars to charitable causes (and paid hundreds of millions in taxes). Rockefeller's ruthless commercial logic, personal rigour and vast philanthropy cast both light and shadow over America and its troubled capitalist identity to this day.

12

BELL TELEPHONE COMPANY

1877 | USA

It's good to talk

Alexander Bell was born in Scotland to a family of speech therapists. At the age of 11 he adopted the middle name 'Graham' out of admiration for a family friend. The device he invented, bridging the worlds of the telegraph and the internet, made him rich and famous. A century and a quarter later, an Italian was acknowledged as the first true inventor of the telephone.

The Bell family of Edinburgh was closely associated with the teaching of elocution and working with the deaf. Alexander's mother was herself deaf, and the teenage 'Alec' made it his mission to find a 'cure'. This was an age of authoritarian scientific rationalism that regarded disabilities as treatable 'defects' to be 'bred out' of future generations. In the early 20th century this would engender the eugenics movement, of which Bell would be a prominent member in later life. By the age of 16, in 1863, he was teaching elocution and music; the following year he attended Edinburgh University, and later held a teaching post in Bath. In 1870, when he was 23, the Bell family emigrated to Canada, where they settled in Brantford, Ontario. Here Bell's father, Professor Alexander Melville Bell, promulgated his 'System of Visible Speech' for mutes.

ALL FOR LOVE

When Professor Bell was invited to take up a position at a large school for mutes in Boston, Massachusetts, his son was already experimenting with a device whereby the sound of a piano could be transmitted over a distance by electricity. Bell Senior declined the Boston position in favour of his son, and thus Alexander Graham Bell became professor of vocal physiology and elocution at the Boston University School of Oratory. Here he encountered, and became attracted to, one of his deaf students, the 20-year-old Mabel Hubbard.

> '**MR WATSON** – Come here – I want to see you.'
>
> The first words heard via telephone, spoken by Alexander Graham Bell to his assistant, 10 March 1876.

1892: Alexander Graham Bell inaugurates the Chicago–New York telephone line. Western Union first rejected the invention as 'a toy' and then tried to usurp the patent with the help of Thomas Edison.

Mabel Hubbard was the daughter of a family who owned much of downtown Boston. Bell routinely taught his deaf students to touch their own throats lightly, then to feel his, in order to feel the changing vibrations and different sounds that were being produced. He complimented her on her voice – 'Nobody had told me that before,' she wrote – and the attraction, although platonically conducted, was mutual and powerful. Mabel's mother, however, sent the Scottish immigrant packing into the rain when he called one night at their Nantucket summer house to ask for her hand in marriage, falsely adding that her daughter had no desire to requite his affections.

Bell by all accounts channelled his determination to marry Mabel into the great invention that would make him rich, famous and accepted across the Hubbard family threshold in Nantucket. He was to find an unexpected ally in the form of his future father-in-law, the lawyer Gardiner Hubbard. As was the case with the light bulb and the telegraph, electricity was the key.

THE QUEST FOR THE 'TALKING TELEGRAPH'

The quest for the 'talking telegraph' had become something of an obsession for many inventors. Antonio Meucci, who had migrated from Italy to America, had already developed a 'telettrofono' (an electric telephone'), testing long-distance voice transmission in Cuba and demonstrating his invention in New York. In 1872 he had supplied Edward B. Grant of the American District Telegraph Company with a working prototype, documentary evidence and a patent caveat. By 1874, unable to raise the $250 required for a full patent, Meucci had renewed the caveat and asked Grant about the status of his invention; there was no reply. In the same year, Western Union President William B. Orton had instructed Thomas Edison and Elisha Gray to research means whereby multiple messages might be sent down telegraph lines.

In the meantime, Bell, after much labour, had been making progress with an electronic multi-reed apparatus that responded to the sound of his voice. When he communicated this to Joseph Henry, director of the Smithsonian Institution, the latter declared that he had 'the germ of a great invention'. To Bell's concern that he lacked the necessary knowledge, Henry simply replied: 'Get it!' Mabel Hubbard's father, Gardiner Hubbard, and Thomas Sanders, father of another of Bell's students, gave Bell the funds to employ the electrical designer and mechanic Thomas A. Watson. On 2 June 1875 Watson accidentally plucked one of the reeds, and Bell, at the other end of the wire, heard the overtones that would be necessary for transmitting speech.

PATENTS AND PRIORITIES

Elisha Gray, meanwhile, had devised a prototype water transmitter for which he filed a patent caveat on 14 February 1876. The same morning, Gardiner Hubbard's patent lawyer Anthony Pollok filed Bell's application with the Patent Office. Three weeks later, on 7 March, Bell's patent number 174,465 was issued for 'the method of, and apparatus for, transmitting vocal or other sounds telegraphically ... by causing electrical undulations, similar in form to the vibrations of the air accompanying the said vocal or other sound'. Three days after this, Bell shouted into a mouthpiece and the vibration of a diaphragm caused a needle to vibrate in an acid-water mixture, varying the electrical resistance in the circuit. His words, 'Mr Watson – Come here – I want to see you,' were clearly heard by Thomas Watson at the receiving end of the wire.

Antonio Meucci had waited two years for an answer from Edward Grant concerning the status of his prototype telephone and accompanying papers, only to be told that both had been 'lost'. Meucci was unable to raise the relatively minor sum needed to renew his patent caveat. With only his memory to fall back on, Meucci brought a lawsuit against Bell to prove his priority, but he lost the case due to lack of material evidence.

———1847———
Birth of **Alexander Graham Bell**.

———1870———
Bell **emigrates** with his family from Scotland to Canada.

———1871———
Bell **moves to the USA**.

———1872———
The Italian inventor **Antonio Meucci** supplies a working prototype of an electric telephone, but this is subsequently 'lost'.

———1875———
Bell, working independently on his own device, manages to **transmit sound**.

———1876———
Bell is **awarded a patent**, and three days later **transmits speech** on his device.

———1877———
The Bell Telephone Company is incorporated.

———1878———
Western Union declines to buy the patent, dismissing the telephone as a 'toy'. The **first telephone exchange** opens the same year.

———1887———
Meucci fails in his bid to have the Bell patent annulled.

———1889———
Meucci dies in obscurity.

———1915———
Bell makes the **first transcontinental telephone call**, from New York to San Francisco.

———1922———
Death of **Alexander Graham Bell**.

———2002———
The US House of Representatives **recognizes Antonio Meucci** as the true inventor of the telephone.

The case scared the newly founded Bell Telephone Company. A few days after the company was incorporated, Bell married Mabel Hubbard. The following year, in 1878, Bell, Gardiner Hubbard and Thomas Sanders offered the Bell patent to Western Union for $100,000. The latter company turned them down; the telephone, they said, was a 'toy' that would never catch on. Two years later, in 1880, after Western Union had encouraged Thomas Edison to try to usurp Bell's patent, and the Bell Telephone Company had acquired Edison's patent for the carbon microphone, the same president of Western Union apparently declared he would have paid $25 million for the Bell patent and still considered it a bargain.

PHONES ACROSS AMERICA

The first telephone exchange, operating under licence from the Bell Telephone Company, opened in New Haven, Connecticut, in 1878. Within three years, telephone exchanges licensed by what was by this time the American Bell Telephone Company existed in most towns and major cities across America. By 1886, 150,000 Americans possessed a telephone, and Bell and his fellow investors were millionaires. A further lawsuit brought in 1887 by Antonio Meucci again failed to annul the Bell patent. Meucci died in obscurity two years later.

'MOST EXTRAORDINARY'
Queen Victoria's verdict on the telephone

By the time Bell's patent expired in 1894, the telephone, through the Bell subsidiary American Telephone and Telegraph Company, had reached outwards from New York to Chicago. In 1915 Bell himself made the first transcontinental telephone call, speaking from New York to Thomas Watson in San Francisco. The American Telephone and Telegraph Company, AT&T or 'Ma Bell', became at one point the world's largest telephone company, and one of the biggest and most efficient natural monopolies in America, until it was divested and restructured in 1984.

Bell, loaded with honours from many countries, died in 1922, having propagated numerous far-sighted ideas, ranging from aircraft and the metal detector to air conditioning and solar energy. He had also been a founder member of the National Geographic Society. Across America, telephones were silent for one minute in tribute.

THE TRUE INVENTOR OF THE TELEPHONE

More than one hundred years after Antonio Meucci's last lawsuit, papers surfaced proving collusion between the Bell Telephone Company and the American District Telegraph Company of New York, whereby the former paid the latter 20 per cent of the profits from Bell's invention for 17 years, in return for the permanent 'loss' of Meucci's invention.

In 2002, due primarily to the efforts of the Italian-American Congressman Vito Fossella, Meucci's 'extraordinary and tragic' career was posthumously recognized by the US House of Representatives. While Bell had independently reached his own solution, 'if Meucci had been able to pay the $10 fee to maintain the caveat after 1874, no patent could have been issued to Bell'. Thus Meucci was formally acknowledged as the true inventor of the telephone.

MANCHESTER UNITED FC

13

1878 | UK

The theatre of dreams

Football / soccer

Manchester United Football Club began life as Newton Heath LYR FC in 1878, the works team of the Newton Heath depot of the Lancashire and Yorkshire Railway. Today, based at the Old Trafford stadium in Greater Manchester, the club is one of the most successful in English football, and probably the most celebrated in the history of the sport. 'Man U' is a £1 billion business whose core product is football and the merchandizing and television revenues garnered thereby. Most Manchester United fans do not even live in England, let alone Manchester.

Newton Heath FC separated themselves from the railway depot after 1890, but did not join the newly established Football League until 1892. They were near bankruptcy when rescued in 1902 by the managing director of Manchester Breweries, J.H. Davies. Davies decided a change of name might bring a change of fortunes, and after considering 'Manchester Central' and 'Manchester Celtic', at the suggestion of an Italian immigrant called Louis Rocca he chose 'Manchester United'. Davies also changed the strip from green and gold to red and white.

A ROLLERCOASTER OF SUCCESS AND FAILURE

Having been relegated and fought their way back into the First Division, Manchester United won the Football League Championship at the end of the 1907/08 season, and in 1909 the FA Cup. Old Trafford, purchased for £60,000, became the club's home in 1910. Further relegation and rescues from near-bankruptcy followed in the 1930s.

During the Second World War the ground and stadium were bombed and the club was forced to rely

> '**MATT BUSBY IS A SYMBOL** of everything that is best in our national game.'
>
> Harold Wilson, the former Labour prime minister, in 1978

on the goodwill of its more successful neighbour, Manchester City, which allowed the use of its ground at Maine Road. This situation lasted until Old Trafford was rebuilt in 1949, by which time management of the team had been taken over by former Manchester City and Liverpool player Matt Busby.

THE BUSBY BABES AND AFTER

Busby was the first of the modern managers, picking his own players, joining his squad for training and, with assistant coach Jimmy Murphy, developing the youth team as an academy for the first team. The average age of the 'Busby Babes' who won the League in 1956 was only 22. The following season they repeated this success, reached the final of the FA Cup, and became the first English team to compete in the European Cup. In 1958, after a European Cup match against Red Star Belgrade, the aircraft carrying the team crashed in snow on take-off at Munich, killing or fatally injuring 8 of the players – including Duncan Edwards, regarded by Busby as the best player in the world – and 15 other passengers. With such youthful promise cut short, the whole nation felt the tragedy as a blow not only to the club, but to the prospects of the English national side, which in the years after the Second World War had been making something of a recovery. All this drove up attendances at Old Trafford, and as Busby struggled to recover from his own injuries, a makeshift team under Jimmy Murphy managed to reach the final of that season's FA Cup. A legend was born.

'The Reds' in 1905–6, shortly after they had changed their strip to red and white and before they moved to Old Trafford. One hundred years on, the world's most famous club would come into American ownership.

The Munich tragedy

The news of the deaths of eight young Manchester United players in a plane crash at Munich in 1958 shocked the whole of Britain. The following account by the novelist H.E. Bates was published in the *FA Yearbook 1958–59*: 'At six o'clock, out of pure curiosity, I turned on my television set. As the news came on, the screen seemed to go black. I sat listening with a frozen brain to that cruel and shocking list of casualties that was now to give the word Munich an even sadder meaning than it had acquired on a day before the war, after a British prime minister had come home to London waving a pitiful piece of paper and most of us knew that new calamities of war were inevitable.'

TIMELINE

1878
Manchester United founded as **Newton Heath LYR FC**.

1892
The club joins the **Football League.**

1902
J.H. Davies rescues the club from near bankruptcy, and renames it **Manchester United FC**.

1907/08
The team wins the **Football League Championship**.

1909
Manchester United win the **FA Cup**.

1910
Old Trafford becomes the team's home.

1945
Matt Busby becomes manager of Manchester United. During his tenure (1945–69, 1970–1), the team wins the League five times, the FA Cup twice and, in 1968, the European Cup.

1958
Eight Manchester United players are killed in an **air crash** at Munich.

1986
Alex Ferguson becomes manager. To the end of the 2006/07 season, the club wins the Premier League nine times, the FA Cup five times and the League Cup twice. Other wins included the UEFA Champions League and the UEFA Cup Winners' Cup.

1991
Manchester United is **floated** on the London Stock Exchange.

1998
The British government blocks a **takeover bid** by Rupert Murdoch.

2005
The American tycoon **Malcolm Glazer** acquires the club.

Busby rebuilt the team in the 1960s, and in 1968 United became the first English club to triumph in Europe. Bobby Charlton, Denis Law and the doomed genius George Best, rated by many as the most gifted player ever, were all nominated European Footballers of the Year. The glamour of the 60s and success in Europe was turning English footballers into celebrities; but after Busby resigned in 1969 a messy period followed on and off the pitch. Wilf McGuinness and Frank O'Farrell were succeeded at the top by Tommy Docherty, Dave Sexton and Ron Atkinson, under whom the club began to recover some kind of form. In 1986 the appointment of former Glasgow pub landlord and Aberdeen manager Alex Ferguson marked the beginning of the modern era.

THE FERGUSON ERA

Ferguson had something of a shaky start – at one point he was rumoured to be on the brink of being fired – but the former publican persisted, selling two of the team's top players (and hardest drinkers) within months of taking over. He also introduced the feared and famous 'hair dryer' treatment – standing so close and shouting so hard that the victim's hair was blown backwards – for players whose performance he deemed unsatisfactory. The 1990s under his stewardship saw the resurgence of the team, and turned into the most successful decade in the club's history. Success brought multimillion-pound TV and licensing deals, and in 1991 the club was floated on the London Stock Exchange at a value of £47 million. Two years later, bolstered by the charismatic Frenchman Eric Cantona, the team won the League Championship for the first time since 1967, and in 1994 the double (the League and the FA Cup) for the first time. This unprecedented run of success, and Man U's status as a publicly quoted company, made the club theoretically open to takeover. This turned it into a political football when, in 1998, the British government blocked a bid by the Australian media tycoon Rupert Murdoch. In 1998/99 Manchester United became the first and only English club to win the treble – the Premiership, the FA Cup and the UEFA Champions League – in one season.

Gate takings, TV revenues and worldwide merchandizing deals pushed the value of the club towards £1 billion, and with a new generation of players –notably the sublimely skilful David Beckham – rumours of who was acquiring large numbers of shares became national news. One such speculator was Talpa (from the Latin meaning 'mole') – the investment vehicle of the creator of *Big Brother*, John de Mol – which bought a 5 per cent stake and sold it at a substantial profit. In reality, however, the club was thought to be too big to be bought.

THE GLAZER TAKEOVER

Malcolm Glazer was a Beverly Hills businessman who had made his fortune in food processing, failed to take over the Harley-Davidson motorcycle company, but succeeded in buying out Zapata, the oil and gas company founded by George Bush Snr. Glazer also owned an American football club, the Tampa Bay Buccaneers. His son Joel had never attended a match but was reputedly a Manchester United fan. Glazer had held a 3 per cent shareholding in Manchester United since at least 2003. Throughout the next two years he increased this holding through his vehicle Red Football Ltd., buying out three big shareholders: the Irishman J.P. McManus, the Scot John Magnier, and the mining entrepreneur Harry Dobson. With a 75 per cent controlling interest, Glazer delisted the club from the London Stock Exchange, valuing it at nearly £1 billion and saddling it with £256 million of debt.

Vociferous and violent protests ensued at this 'foreign' takeover, in spite of the fact that there was a long tradition of United players going on to North American Soccer League teams such as LA Galaxy and the San Jose Earthquakes. Few blamed the three major shareholders who had allowed the bid to succeed. Glazer himself suffered two strokes, while his sons reaffirmed their commitment to the club. The Glazer business plan – boosted when in the 2006/07 season United won the Premier League title and reached both the semi-final of the UEFA Champions League and the final of the FA Cup – appeared to be to take the brand further into America and Asia, where the club has a strong following and the issue of ownership is immaterial. The club also expanded the capacity of Old Trafford and signed a new shirt sponsorship deal with the American International Group. Meanwhile, disgruntled supporters at home formed FC United of Manchester, which was accepted into the second division of the North-West Counties League, six promotions below the Football League.

'Man U' is the world's biggest football brand. From the corporate boxes of the 'theatre of dreams' at Old Trafford to kids kicking a ball against a wall in the slums of Mumbai or Rio de Janeiro, the red shirt with the player name and number in its latest version is *the* coveted football merchandize, whether legitimate or pirated. Decades before the idea of 'communities of consumers', and largely through the medium of the camera, the 'Reds' had already established their own community among their fans. Cantona, Van Nistelrooy, Beckham, Rooney, Ronaldo – the overpaid, pampered, petulant players come and go. But the club remains.

EASTMAN KODAK

1881 | *USA*

14

You get the picture

George Eastman became a breadwinner at the age of 14 after the death of his father and the failure of the family business. The images his photographic film and camera captured brought millions a record of the family he never had.

Eastman was born in 1854 in Waterville, Oneida County, in upstate New York. His father, George Washington Eastman, ran a nursery, and when George Junior was five years old the family moved to Rochester, where George Senior established the Eastman Commercial College. The sudden death of his father brought about the closure of the college and left Eastman, his mother and two sisters in financial difficulties. Judged to be 'not especially gifted', Eastman dropped out of high school at 14 in order to support the family and took a job as an insurance-company messenger boy. His first pay cheque was $3 a week.

The plight of his mother and sisters, one of whom was severely handicapped, was worsening, and Eastman found a new job as office boy for another insurance company. He impressed his employers to the point where they let him write policies, but the money was still insufficient and Eastman took up the study of accounting in the evenings. In 1874, at the age of 20, he became a junior clerk with the Rochester Savings Bank. His salary tripled, to more than $15 a week; many might have settled at this point for a secure job with the prospect of becoming manager. But something – probably in Eastman's all-female domestic life – would combine this bursarial ability with an inexorable pull in a different direction.

> **'PHILOLOGICALLY, THE WORD KODAK** is as meaningless as a child's first "goo" – terse, abrupt to the point of rudeness, literally bitten off by firm and unyielding consonants at both ends, it snaps like a camera shutter in your face. What more would one ask?'
>
> George Eastman, who devised the name Kodak with his mother.

A PASSION FOR PHOTOGRAPHY

In 1878, with his mother and sisters secure and himself in need of a holiday, Eastman resolved to visit Santo Domingo in the Dominican Republic. At the suggestion of a colleague, he purchased a wet-plate camera, together with tripod, plates and tent – 'a pack-horse load' – to record the trip. In the event, the vacation did not materialize, but Eastman's fascination was fired by the complicated, cumbersome and compelling activity of photography. He became obsessed with improving on photographic technology – possibly sensing an escape from the bank.

British journals of the time revealed how photographers were making their own gelatine emulsions to create more manageable dry-film plates. Eastman took one of these formulas and after a day's work at the bank began experimenting at night with his own emulsion in his mother's kitchen; she would sometimes discover him asleep on the floor in the morning. By 1879 Eastman had invented not only an effective dry-plate formula but also the machine that would coat the plates in large numbers. In the same year he obtained a patent in London, and the following year one in New York. In April 1880 he leased small offices on the third floor of a building on State Street, Rochester, and began to manufacture dry plates. Henry A. Strong, a local businessman, came aboard as an investor. In 1881 Eastman resigned from the bank, and he and Strong founded the Eastman Dry Plate Company.

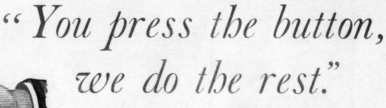

The Kodak Camera

"You press the button, we do the rest."

OR YOU CAN DO IT YOURSELF.

The only camera that anybody can use without instructions. As convenient to carry as an ordinary field glass World-wide success.

The Kodak is for sale by all Photo stock dealers.

Send for the Primer, free.

The Eastman Dry Plate & Film Co.

Price, $25.00 — Loaded for 100 Pictures.   ROCHESTER, N. Y.
Re-loading, $2.00.

Picture this: George Eastman's brilliant refinement of photographic film, allied to his marketing genius, defined a new visual age for millions around the world.

THE INVENTION OF FILM

Eastman's plan was to exploit the market for his dry plates principally among professional photographers. On at least one occasion he was forced to replace a defective batch for a customer at no cost: 'Making good on those plates took our last dollar,' he recalled, 'but what we had left was more important – reputation.' Having invented and patented a plate, he began looking for an alternative to glass, experimenting with photographic emulsion on paper mounted in a holder that was loaded into the camera. In 1885 Eastman wrote and circulated advertisements to the effect that 'shortly there will be introduced a new sensitive film which it is believed will prove an economical and convenient substitute for dry glass plates both for outdoor and studio work'. With further refinements Eastman created the modern transparent roll of film. The market consequences, however, were surprising: 'When we started,' Eastman recalled, 'we expected that everybody who used glass plates would take up films. But we found that the number which did so was relatively small. In order to make a large business we would have to reach the general public.'

In 1884 the Eastman Dry Plate and Film Company was formed with 14 shareholders. Its aim was to create a mass market for a camera 'as convenient as the pencil'. Four years later, in 1888, Eastman's Kodak hand-held camera, pre-loaded with enough film for 100 exposures, was released into the market at a price of $25 with the slogan, coined by Eastman, 'You press the button, we do the rest.' The customer took the pictures and returned the entire camera to Rochester where the film was developed, prints were made and a new film was inserted – all for $10.

KODAK – CAMERAS FOR ALL

Eastman and his mother had come up with the name Kodak with the help of an anagram set. The letter 'K' was a favourite of his, and mother and son tried out a number of combinations before they came up with the word that began and ended with the letter. As Eastman would recall: 'Philologically, the word Kodak is as meaningless as a child's first "goo" – terse, abrupt to the point of rudeness, literally bitten off by firm and unyielding consonants at both ends, it snaps like a camera shutter in your face. What more would one ask?'

The 'Kodak Girl', with her winning smile and yearly change of clothing style and camera, became an advertising icon, and 'Kodak' would be one of the first words to feature on an electric sign in London's Trafalgar Square. By 1889 the Eastman Company (as it was renamed) had opened an office in London to handle trade beyond the United States, and the first factory outside Rochester was opened in Harrow in 1891. In 1892 the company changed its name to Eastman Kodak, after its most successful product. The 100,000th Kodak camera was produced four years later, and in 1900 the introduction of the $1 Kodak 'Brownie' – designed by Frank Brownell and named after the popular Brownie cartoon characters – made everyone a photographer. A fatherless high school drop-out and former bank clerk had defined the visual age.

A GENEROUS EMPLOYER

From early in his management career Eastman made substantial gifts to each member of staff, and was among the first American company leaders to distribute employee bonuses in proportion to the value of Eastman Kodak stock. In 1919 he distributed one-third of his personal holdings – worth $10 million – among his employees. Retirement annuities, life insurance and disability benefits followed.

> **'A STUPENDOUS FACTOR** in the education of the modern world.'
> The *New York Times* pays tribute to George Eastman after his death in 1932.

In 1925 Eastman himself retired, taking up the position of chairman. In retirement he indulged in yearly visits to European art galleries, often bicycling from one to another, and building up one of the finest private art collections in America. His mother's final illness confined her to a wheelchair, and when he realized he had inherited a similarly debilitating condition, he committed suicide at the age of 78 in 1932. 'My work is done,' read his suicide note, 'Why wait?' He was buried in the grounds of Kodak Park, Rochester. The *New York Times* editorial paid tribute to him as 'a stupendous factor in the education of the modern world'.

Eastman's immense philanthropic and cultural legacy includes music, the theatre, dentistry clinics, the education of African-Americans and an anonymous donation as 'Mr Smith' of $20 million to Massachusetts Institute of Technology, where the rubbing of the plaque in his honour is regarded by students as a way of ensuring good luck.

TECHNICAL INNOVATION AND STULTIFICATION

The Eastman Kodak company since Eastman's death has been synonymous with the technology of Hollywood movies, space exploration, the 8 and Super 8 home movie formats, medical imaging, office technology, the Instamatic cameras and many others. However, by the 1990s, in common with many of the great companies that began life in the 1880s and triggered the 'American century', a company that had once been an American treasure had become a bureaucratic, sluggish and complacent corporation, constantly and unfavourably compared with Japan's Fuji. The company also had losses to match.

Towards the end of the first decade of the 21st century, Kodak was still a company in turnaround. The billion dollar-plus loss of 2005 was halved in 2006, but the fight was on to reinvent the company for the age of consumer digital imaging and graphic communications. Nearly half the 200 buildings in Kodak Park, Rochester, have been demolished since the late 1990s. The house on the old Eastman homestead where his father was born and George spent his early years has since been moved to the Genesee Country Museum in Mumford, New York.

Eastman himself has long been claimed as a pre-'coming out' gay American. The Gay Alliance of the Genesee Valley meets for its training runs and walks in the parking lot at George Eastman House International Museum of Photography and Film at 900 East Avenue, Rochester. To the end of his life, Eastman could, and probably preferred to, walk unrecognized down the main street of Rochester, where today's paparazzi would have pursued him relentlessly with his own invention.

COCA-COLA

1885 | USA

15

From soda fountain
to global brand

Coca-Cola began life in 1885 as a pharmacist's patent medicine during an era of prohibition in Covington, Georgia. Today, the sweet yet acidic liquid in the 'contour' bottle is the biggest-selling soft drink in history, and Coca-Cola is the most successful brand in the world. A copy of the original secret formula is held in the main vault of the Sun Trust Bank in Atlanta, Georgia.

This unlikely story starts in the American South in the late 19th century. Pharmacist John Stith Pemberton's 'French Wine Coca' was inspired by 'Vin Mariani', a powerfully alcoholic drink invented by the French chemist Angelo Mariani. Vin Mariani allegedly cured a variety of ailments, from dyspepsia

> **'COCA-COLA IS NOW DRUNK** in every state and territory in the United States.'
>
> Asa Griggs Candler, in 1895

to headaches and impotence – but more probably it induced all three. When in 1885 Atlanta and Fulton County passed prohibition legislation, Pemberton developed a carbonated, non-alcoholic version of his French Wine Coca and called it Coca-Cola. The name was chosen for its alliterative qualities by Pemberton's bookkeeper Frank Mason Robinson: 'Coca' refers to the South American coca leaves that provided the drink's stimulant, and 'Cola' refers to the kola nut flavouring, which also supplied caffeine. Even without alcohol, this was a powerful cocktail. Robinson also devised the forward-slanting red-on-white Coca-Cola logo in the 'Spencerian' script used for formal handwriting in the United States at the time.

CANDLER TAKES OVER COCA-COLA

Coca-Cola first went on sale – at five cents – in 1886 at Jacob's Pharmacy in Atlanta. For the first eight months, sales were no more than an average of nine drinks a day, in spite of Pemberton taking out advertising for the 'new and popular soda fountain drink' in the *Atlanta Journal*. Pemberton himself became a morphine addict and his son Charley an alcoholic. The Pembertons increasingly ceded the rights in Coca-Cola to others, including another pharmacist,

Asa Griggs Candler. Forced to sell his version of the drink under the names 'Yum Yum' and 'Koke', Candler was determined to wrest legal control of the business. In 1888, claiming to have secured exclusive rights, Candler set about placing the business on an organized footing. In 1892 he incorporated the Coca-Cola Company.

Candler now revealed the genius for marketing and advertising that would make Coca-Cola the nation's best-known product. He introduced coupons for complimentary glasses of the drink, and merchandizing such as clocks, souvenir fans, calendars and dozens of other novelty items, all bearing the logo. He also created and exploited the association between the 'delicious' and 'refreshing' drink with healthy and discerning customers, both male and female. The public responded, and sales of the drink, still served through soda fountains, took off. Candler arranged for bottling of the drink at the Biedenharn Candy Company in Vicksburg, Mississippi, and in 1894 the first cases of the drink were sold to farms and lumber camps. He also set up his own syrup factories, the first one in the small town of Dallas, outside Atlanta.

In 1895 Candler was able to announce to shareholders that 'Coca-Cola is now drunk in every state and territory in the United States.' By the end of the 19th century, most of the country was supplied by a large-scale mechanized bottling plant in Chattanooga, and over the next two decades the number of plants would grow to over 1000, 95 per cent of them locally owned and operated, establishing what was to become the worldwide franchising and distribution model. In 1900 Candler's son Charles took a jug of syrup with him on vacation to England and mailed back the company's first export order – for five gallons – to Atlanta.

COCAINE, CAFFEINE AND CONTOUR BOTTLES

Asa Candler claimed his formula contained only one-tenth of the amount of coca leaf of Pemberton's original, and by 1904 the company was using 'spent' leaves with a far lower residual cocaine content. The high caffeine content of the drink led to a lawsuit alleging that the product was harmful to children. In 1910 Candler had the earliest records of the company burned; in 1914 Margaret Dozier, one of the original partners he claimed to have bought out, declared her signature on the bill of sale had been forged. Years later, analysis of the signature of John Pemberton, who had died in 1888, would suggest this too was a fake.

Candler meanwhile turned competition from rival drinks into a means of strengthening his own brand, and the slogans 'Demand the genuine' and 'Accept no substitute' became widely recognized. In 1915 the company invited bottlers to design the container that would distinguish it from lesser rivals. The brief was to create 'a bottle which a person could recognize even if they felt it in the dark, and so shaped that, even if broken, a person could tell at a glance what it was'. Earl Dean's 'contour' or 'hobble skirt' bottle – inspired by a picture of a gourd-shaped cocoa pod in *Encyclopaedia Britannica* – was patented in 1915 and marketed in 1916. By the mid-1920s the standard Coca-Cola bottle was on the way to becoming one of the most recognized packaging items on the planet.

> **'A BOTTLE WHICH A PERSON COULD RECOGNIZE** even if they felt it in the dark, and so shaped that, even if broken, a person could tell at a glance what it was.'
>
> The original brief to designers that resulted in the world-famous 'contour' bottle, first marketed in 1916.

The 1897 Coca-Cola calendar – the story behind 'The Real Thing' is one of corporate transformation, global domination and perhaps the greatest triumph of branding in history.

TIMELINE

———1885———
John Stith Pemberton develops his recipe for Coca-Cola.

———1886———
Coca-Cola **first goes on sale**, in Atlanta, Georgia.

———1888———
Asa Griggs Candler claims to have acquired the rights in Coca-Cola.

———1892———
Candler incorporates the **Coca-Cola Company**.

———1915———
The **trademark 'contour' bottle** is patented.

———1919———
The company is bought by a group of investors headed by **Ernest Woodruff and W.C. Bradley**.

———1923———
Ernest Woodruff's son Robert becomes president.

———1928———
Coca-Cola starts its long-term sponsorship of the **Olympic Games**.

———1954———
Woodruff retires as president, but stays on the board of directors until 1984.

———1960———
Coke begins to be **sold in cans**.

———1981———
Roberto Goizueta becomes chairman and CEO.

———1985———
The **'New Coke'** debacle.

———1997———
Death of **Roberto Goizueta**.

———2007———
Coca-Cola acquires **Glaceau** for $4 billion.

THE WOODRUFF ERA

In 1919 a group of investors headed by Ernest Woodruff and W.C. Bradley bought the company for $25 million. In 1923 Woodruff's son Robert became president. Robert Woodruff's influence would span six decades, and he became one of the most successful American corporate leaders of the 20th century. In 1926 he created the 'Foreign Department', which evolved into the Coca-Cola Export Sales Corporation. He also invested heavily in training for sales and marketing, with the stress on quality, and pushed the bottled drink beyond the soda fountain. A string of his innovations are commonplace today: the six-pack portable carton; the cooler in the workplace; the operator-less automatic fountain dispenser.

In 1928 Coca-Cola became the first ever sponsor of the Olympic Games, held in Amsterdam that year, and has been a sponsor of every Olympic Games since. By the 1930s even Santa Claus was advertising Coca-Cola, although the legend that Coca-Cola 'created' the modern image of Father Christmas is erroneous. But during the winter – normally a period of lower sales – the company used the image of Father Christmas in his red-and-white livery to echo and promote their own (by now white-on-red) brand logo to such effect that many thought Coca-Cola and Santa Claus were synonymous. After minor sourcing changes, the drink was also pronounced kosher by Rabbi Tobias Geffen.

> **'A BILLION HOURS AGO,** human life appeared on earth. A billion Coca-Colas ago was yesterday morning.'
>
> Roberto Goizueta, CEO of Coca-Cola, 1981–97

During the Second World War 'Coke', by now an American icon, was deemed essential to the war effort, and 64 bottling plants were established close to areas of combat in Europe and the Pacific between 1941 and 1945. In 1953, after six decades at the same 5 cent price (originally set in an era of low inflation and low bottling costs), Woodruff realized it was time for a price rise, but given the high cost of replacing vending machines, he felt it reasonable to write to his friend President Eisenhower suggesting the introduction of a nickel-sized 7.5 cent coin.

In 1960 the first Coke cans (originally designed for the armed forces) appeared. Through the following decade TV ads featuring movie stars, sports men and women and popular singers endorsed Woodruff's alleged desire that everyone on earth should not only drink Coke, but that Coke should be their favourite drink. 'It's the real thing', a slogan first used in 1942, was revived in 1969 to tap in to the youth-culture explosion. The 1970s saw the more anodyne 'I'd like to buy the world a Coke' ads, the song being sung by young people from around the world on a hilltop in Italy. 'Rum and coke' also became a youthful gateway to the other real thing – as an entry-level alcoholic drink.

DEBACLES AND DIVERSIFICATION

Coca-Cola was nearly a century old when Cuban immigrant Roberto Goizueta was appointed chairman and CEO in 1981, at a time when competition from Pepsi-Cola was heating up. Some of Goizueta's initiatives, such as the purchase of Columbia Pictures in the cause of product placement, backfired. He was also responsible for the 1985 'New Coke' debacle, where the original recipe was changed, for the better according to the company but not in the eyes of the public. But when Goizueta died aged 65 in 1997, he was one of the most admired managers of his time – and the first corporate manager to have become a billionaire. The value of Coca-Cola stock under his leadership had increased by 7200 per cent; he had neither cashed in any of his 16 million Coke shares in two decades, nor sipped a rival Pepsi for a decade.

In the aftermath of Goizueta's death, the company was slow in capitalizing on the boom in 'sports' and 'enhanced water' drinks. Coca-Cola's $4 billion acquisition of Glaceau in 2007 made it a major player in the lifestyle drinks market, and furthered its image to some as a company that 'owns much and produces little'.

Today, with Irish-born CEO Neville Isdell and a board including a former chairman of Paramount Pictures, the president of Hearst Magazines and former US Senator Sam Nunn, Coca-Cola is a $124 billion company operating in 200 countries with 400 brands, including

Coke, Diet Coke, Fanta, Sprite, Tab, Enviga and Full Throttle. The original contour bottle is to be found in the most remote parts of the world, from the slopes of Everest to the deserts of the Sahara and the Amazon jungle. In addition to Pepsi, local competition in such places as Iran and the Middle East (Zam Zam Cola and Parsi Cola), Peru (Inca Cola), China (Future Cola) and Madagascar (Classiko Cola) is finely tuned to variations in local taste. Some may surpass Coke sales locally, but all depend upon the original as a reference point. If 'America' is the first English word uttered by many an indigenous person, 'Coca-Cola' is often the second: the brand is therefore a prime target for opponents of US 'cultural globalization'.

Love or hate it, Coke transcends its constituent parts in the manner of no other brand and no other range of products. Even the legendary investor Warren Buffett has said: 'If you gave me $100 billion and said take away the soft-drink leadership of Coca-Cola in the world, I'd give it back to you and say it can't be done.'

JOHNSON & JOHNSON

1887 | USA

'Workers need appreciation and recognition.' GENERAL ROBERT WOOD JOHNSON II

Healthcare

16

Johnson & Johnson was founded by Robert Wood Johnson and his brothers in New Brunswick, New Jersey, after Johnson had heard a speech by the British antisepsis pioneer Sir Joseph Lister. Lister was appalled at the practice of surgeons operating in bloodstained frockcoats without gloves or sterile instruments, using dressings made from cotton collected from the floors of textile mills. He in turn had been inspired in his campaign against the 'invisible assassins' of airborne bacterial infection by the great French chemist Louis Pasteur.

More than ten years after Lister's speech, on the fourth floor of a former wallpaper factory, Robert Wood Johnson, his brothers and 14 employees manufactured the first antiseptic surgical dressings, creating a new defence for masses of people against the tyranny of sepsis and post-operative mortality. The founder's son, General Robert Wood Johnson, engendered an ethos between employer, employee, customer and stockholder that encapsulates modern corporate thinking and makes Johnson & Johnson one of the most successful and admired companies and brands in history.

PLASTERS AND TALCUM POWDER

Lister's carbolic-spray method had proved effective but required cumbersome equipment that was only practical in the larger hospitals. The first Johnson & Johnson products were adhesive plasters containing medicinal compounds; these were followed by absorbent cotton and gauze dressings shipped to hospitals, physicians and pharmacists. The company produced a book entitled *Modern Methods of Antiseptic Wound Treatment*, which would remain for many years the standard text on antiseptic practices and set an example of knowledge transfer between the developer of commercial healthcare products and medical and surgical providers. Johnson & Johnson magazines such as *Red Cross Notes* and *The Red Cross Messenger* maintained and expanded this relationship under the direction of the company's scientific director, Fred B. Kilmer.

In 1890 Kilmer received a complaint from a doctor that the company's plasters caused irritation on the skin of some patients. He suggested a can of Italian talcum powder be sent to the patient. The results were successful and the company began packaging the talc with its plasters. The 'Wonderful Mother' advertising campaign followed (see box).

Johnson's Baby Powder opened up the vast market for nursery items, and remains one of the most recognized and trusted products in the world. It has also provided the company with perhaps the most positive corporate image of all time. In 1892 the company began manufacturing sterile dressings, using dry heat, then steam and pressure, which gave rise to the slogan 'The Most Trusted Name in Surgical Dressings'. A stream of products followed, including procedures for sterilizing catgut sutures, and a stronger, less irritant zinc-oxide surgical adhesive plaster.

OVERSEAS EXPANSION

Robert Wood Johnson served until his death in 1910, when he was succeeded by his brother James W. Johnson. Where the carnage of the American Civil War had demonstrated the need for antisepsis by its absence, the First World War and the horror of the trenches began to illustrate the benefits. In the immediate aftermath, the founder's two sons undertook a world tour and returned home convinced that this was the time to capitalize on the company's position in the domestic market and expand overseas. The company had been represented in the United

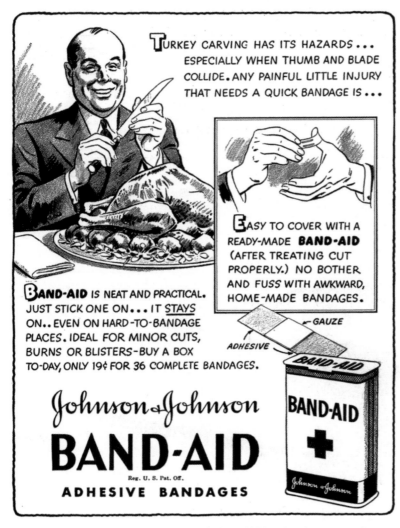

TURKEY CARVING HAS ITS HAZARDS . . . ESPECIALLY WHEN THUMB AND BLADE COLLIDE. ANY PAINFUL LITTLE INJURY THAT NEEDS A QUICK BANDAGE IS . . .

EASY TO COVER WITH A READY-MADE **BAND-AID** (AFTER TREATING CUT PROPERLY.) NO BOTHER AND FUSS WITH AWKWARD, HOME-MADE BANDAGES.

GAUZE

ADHESIVE

BAND-AID IS NEAT AND PRACTICAL. JUST STICK ONE ON . . . IT STAYS ON . . EVEN ON HARD-TO-BANDAGE PLACES. IDEAL FOR MINOR CUTS, BURNS OR BLISTERS—BUY A BOX TO-DAY, ONLY 19¢ FOR 36 COMPLETE BANDAGES.

Johnson & Johnson

BAND-AID

Reg. U. S. Pat. Off.

ADHESIVE BANDAGES

The imagery of Baby Powder and the likes of this 1930s advertisement made Johnson & Johnson one of the most trusted companies and respected corporate citizens on earth.

Kingdom through agents such as Thomas Gilmour and John Timpson since 1888, making the association with Britain only one year younger than the American parent. In 1924 the first overseas affiliate, Johnson & Johnson Ltd., was established in Slough, and the new British company, with the backing of New Jersey, soon set about exploiting the trade routes of the British Empire. By this time an employee of the parent company, Earle Dickson, had devised an adhesive bandage for his wife to treat a succession of household cuts and burns: they called it Band-Aid.

The stock market crash of 1929 and the Great Depression coincided with the appointment of Robert Wood Johnson II as vice-president and general manager; he became chairman in 1932. Johnson had inherited the entrepreneurial and managerial skills of his father, and while other manufacturing companies went under or laid off workers by the thousand, few jobs were lost at Johnson & Johnson. Johnson pushed ahead with overseas expansion, again leveraging the company's financial soundness and strength in the American domestic market to open up operations in South Africa, Mexico, Australia, Brazil and Argentina.

A NEW APPROACH TO MANAGEMENT

Johnson was a keen advocate of President Roosevelt's New Deal. He increased wages while promoting the concept of 'decentralization' – new market opportunities would become products and then autonomous divisions and subsidiaries, staffed and managed by motivated and incentivized individuals in a good working environment: 'Workers need appreciation and recognition,' he declared. In 1943, during the war in which he himself would be elevated to the rank of brigadier-general for his services to war procurement, he formulated these and other thoughts in two key documents, *Our Credo* and *Our Management Philosophy*.

The *Credo* laid out the company's four responsibilities: to customer, employee, community and stockholder. If the first three were met, the fourth would be served. General Johnson's second document still reads as freshly over half a century on as when it was first published: 'Our concept of modern management may be summarized in the expression "to serve". It is the duty of the leader to be a servant to those responsible to him ... High position does not imply the wielding of authority but rather to inspire others by effort within the framework of corporation policy.'

DIVERSIFYING INTO PHARMACEUTICALS

The company went public on the New York Stock Exchange in 1944, and thereafter expanded from healthcare products into pharmaceuticals, acquiring companies such as McNeil Labs in the USA and Janssen in Belgium and developing the markets for pain relief and antipsychotic drugs. Throughout these decades of prosperity, Johnson & Johnson came to rule the world.

> **'THE GREATEST RESPONSIBILITY** of modern management is to develop the human intellect in order that it may express its talent.'
>
> General Robert Wood Johnson II,
> *Our Credo* (1943)

Yet General Johnson was in a different mindset: 'Now is the time to try some of these things,' he wrote in 1962, 'We have rid ourselves of the traditional management and it might be well to experiment a little before the new management develops its own frozen traditions.'

General Johnson retired as chairman and CEO in 1963, and was briefly succeeded by his son Robert III, the last of the Johnsons to hold the position. Since 1965 the company has only had five men in the role, including Ralph S. Larsen, who worked his way up from third shift operator. It was under his predecessor, James E. Burke, that the Chicago Tylenol cases of 1982 and 1986 occurred, when persons unknown contaminated the Johnson & Johnson painkiller – the company's most profitable product – with cyanide, killing eight people. The company won respect for its handling of the crises from the industry, the media and its customers, and eventually regained its market position.

Today the 'Johnson & Johnson Family of Companies' is a $53 billion global network of 250 operations with 121,000 employees in 57 countries. Its products range from Band-Aid and Baby Powder to pharmaceuticals, skin and beauty products, contact lenses, surgical technologies and internet publishing. The global company that has consistently ranked Number One in the National Corporate Reputation Survey paradoxically combines a strong centre in New Jersey and a large number of decentralized initiatives. In 2005 the US Department of Labor posthumously inducted General Robert Wood Johnson II into the Labor Hall of Fame in recognition of his contributions to improving the life of the American worker.

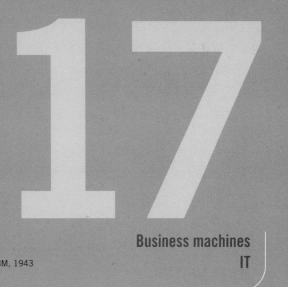

IBM

1889 | *USA*

❝I think there is a world market for maybe five computers.❞ THOMAS J. WATSON, CHAIRMAN OF IBM, 1943

International Business Machines Corporation – nicknamed 'Big Blue' – is a $100 billion company, and the largest IT employer in the world. IBM employees have won three Nobel Prizes, four Turing Awards, five National Medals of Technology and five National Medals of Science. The company also holds more patents than any other US-based technology company. Nobody is certain where the nickname derives, but one thing is certain: Big Blue was there first.

The origins of IBM are generally dated back to 1889 and the patent established by the pioneering German-American statistician Herman Hollerith. Hollerith had developed an electrical mechanism whereby personal data could be numerically encoded and stored in columns on punch cards, which could be sorted mechanically. In 1890 his machines were used by the US Census Bureau and reduced the time taken to record the census from seven to two and a half years. In 1896 Hollerith founded the Tabulating Machine Company, which leased machines and supplied punch cards to census bureaux and insurance companies around the world. In 1911 the Tabulating Machine Company merged with the International Time Recording Company and the Computing Scale Corporation to form the Computing Tabulating Recording Corporation. In 1916 the company was floated on the New York Stock Exchange. The name was changed in 1924 to International Business Machines, and IBM became a *Fortune* Global 500 company.

> ### THINK
> Under Thomas Watson Snr, 'THINK' became the motto of IBM. The word was displayed conspicuously in every room in every IBM building, on company stationery, on company matches, on company scratchpads. Every employee carried a notebook with 'THINK' on the cover, in which to jot down any brilliant thoughts they might have.

IBM UNDER THOMAS J. WATSON SNR

Hollerith died in 1929, a fan of good cigars, fine wines and his cat Bismarck, and a passionate opponent of the hard sales techniques practised under IBM president Thomas J. Watson Snr. Watson had joined the company as general manager in 1914. He was an asthmatic loner, who had already been convicted under anti-trust legislation for his activities in the cash-register industry. Under Watson the Computing Tabulating Recording Corporation grew and acquired its corporate culture; he was also responsible for the change of name to International Business Machines. Throughout the 1920s IBM secured market dominance at home and abroad in tabulating machines and time-keeping systems – and even in weighing scales and automatic meat slicers – before concentrating on punch-card equipment. The 1935 US Social Security Act gave IBM the contract to maintain employment data for 26 million people, in what the company later described as 'the biggest accounting operation of all time'.

Watson was a complex character. Like Henry Ford, he was something of an autocrat, yet he was a lifelong Democrat who would remain loyal to President Franklin D. Roosevelt and become a trustee of Columbia University. A sincere, even simplistic, believer in 'World Peace Through World Trade', his election to the Chamber of Foreign Commerce in the 1930s brought him and IBM close to Mussolini's Fascist Italy and Hitler's resurgent military-industrial Germany. Awarded the Order of Merit of the German Eagle with Star, Watson accepted Hitler's assurance that there would be no war, and expanded IBM's operations inside Nazi Germany and France.

PROFITING FROM THE HOLOCAUST?

Watson, in common with Henry Ford, Alfred P. Sloan of General Motors and other leading industrialists, regarded war as a passing phenomenon in the greater scheme of capitalism. There are some who argue that, when hostilities did break out, Watson transferred IBM's European interests to a Swiss holding company, which received supposedly 'frozen' profits from its German and French operations throughout the war. They claim that these profits derived from the commission-driven sale of IBM machines used to track and tattoo millions of European Jews, gypsies, homosexuals, prisoners of war and slave labourers in order that they could be more efficiently processed through the gas chambers. Anne Frank would have been tracked and

New York 1957: 'The most successful capitalist who ever lived.' Thomas J. Watson Jr transformed the culture of IBM and turned 'Big Blue' into one of the largest industrial corporations in the world.

tattooed with the help of an IBM machine. IBM insist that IBM Germany was a separate company taken over by the Nazis over which it had no control.

After the Japanese bombing of Pearl Harbor and America's entry into the conflict, IBM manufactured engine parts, bombsights, the Browning automatic rifle and the M1 carbine for Allied forces. Watson also posted a 1 per cent profit ceiling on transactions with the Allied military, and even this was to be donated to widows and orphans from the conflict and the United Negro College. In the immediate postwar period, despite the onset of the Cold War, IBM courted the leaders of the Soviet Union.

THE FIRST COMPUTERS

Watson has been much mocked for his 1943 remark, 'I think there is a world market for maybe five computers.' However, his assessment was accurate for its time, given the intellectual challenge faced by the British pioneer Alan Turing and others, and the sheer physical scale of Colossus, the first mainframe computer, which was built at Bletchley Park in wartime England for the purpose of decrypting German military radio traffic, most crucially that between U-boats.

Despite Watson's doubts about the market potential, IBM did get involved in computer development. In addition to contributing its punch-card technology to the Manhattan Project, IBM sponsored the research that led Grace Hopper and Howard Aiken to construct the 5-ton Harvard Mark 1 computer: 55 feet long, 8 feet high and containing nearly 760,000 separate parts, including 3000 decimal storage wheels, 1400 rotary dial switches and 500 miles of wire. The Harvard Mark 1 was used between 1944 and 1959 for gunnery and ballistic calculations by the US Navy.

THE SON ALSO RISES

Thomas J. Watson Jr, who took over from his father as CEO in 1956, was a brilliant modernizer whom *Fortune* would call 'the most successful capitalist who ever lived' and *Computerworld* would describe as 'One of the 25 people who changed the world.' IBM's mainframe computers for the United States Air Force defence system earned the company $1.7 billion through the 1950s and 1960s, and gave IBM access to research sponsored by the military and conducted at the Massachusetts Institute of Technology. IBM was different things to different people: a maker of mainframes

TIMELINE

— *1889* —
Herman Hollerith patents a machine for storing personal data on punch cards.

— *1890* —
The **US Census Bureau** uses Hollerith's machines.

— *1896* —
Hollerith founds the **Tabulating Machine Company**.

— *1911* —
The company merges with two others to form the **Computing Tabulating Recording Corporation**.

— *1914* —
Thomas J. Watson Snr joins the company as general manager.

— *1916* —
The company is **floated** on the New York Stock Exchange.

— *1924* —
Watson changes the company's name to **International Business Machines**.

— *1935* —
IBM acquires a **US government contract** to maintain employment data for 26 million people.

— *1944* —
The **Harvard Mark 1** computer, sponsored by IBM, enters service with the US military.

— *1956* —
Thomas J. Watson Jr takes over as chief executive officer

— *1967* —
IBM moves its headquarters to **Austin, Texas**.

— *1973* —
IBM's patent on the digital computer expires, **ending its monopoly** of the hardware market.

— *1981* —
IBM launches the **PC**.

— *1993* —
IBM suffers a **record loss** of nearly $5 billion.

— *2005* —
IBM **sells its PC business**, concentrating instead on supercomputers and business solutions.

to governments and corporations, while for smaller businesses it was a maker of copiers and electric typewriters. It also produced the world's first commercial hard disk drive system.

IBM was one of the few companies that could put a town on the map. In 1967 IBM came to Austin, Texas, to make electric typewriters; over the next 20 years, thousands of high-tech companies and entrepreneurs set up in Austin, including Michael Dell. Yet IBM – in spite of Thomas Watson Jr's leadership and clarity of vision – failed to provide the culture in which innovators could flourish. This was the company whose decision – partly forced by anti-trust suits – to separate the pricing of software and hardware effectively created the software industry and the market for Microsoft and Apple. In 1973 the expiry (after a landmark court case) of the patent on ENIAC, the world's first general-purpose digital computer, placed the production of digital computers in the public domain, and also ended IBM's long monopoly in the hardware market.

IBM's first PC cost $1500 in 1981 and was bought by business managers who saw the value of the 'killer app', VisiCalc spreadsheet. 'Big Blue' was otherwise outsold, outclassed and made to look outdated by Apple and Microsoft in the high-technology consumer markets throughout the 1980s. The long shadow of the big mainframes, the blue suits and ties, the past-sell-by-date CEO John Akers and 110 lesser CEOs, was unappealing to the 'PIBs' ('People in Black') who were the target consumer market. IBM's 1991 and 1992 losses were only a prelude to the record corporate loss of nearly $5 billion in 1993, when Akers was replaced by Lou Gerstner. Even when the mainframe brand versus the workstation user became the key issue, IBM seemed unable to shake off its mainframe heritage and address the needs of the new workstation generation, to the point where many of its most loyal customers were forced to move on to technologies from other manufacturers. This began to change with the IBM ThinkPad range, initially expensive and uncompromisingly engineered, but like a car you had to work to drive it. This proved a powerful and rugged utilitarian tool for the user – a selling point when compared with the plastic, sensationless Apple laptops.

BUSINESS SOLUTIONS

The growth in the business market for departmental and desktop computing saw IBM expand its hardware and operating systems. In the process it bought Lotus to build up its software 'family', and the consulting arm of PriceWaterhouseCoopers to grow its share of the market for business solutions. It also increased the number of its patents to the point where revenues from licensing intellectual property alone reached $1 billion. A $10 billion programme to provide access to 'supercomputers on demand' was put in place in 2002, and reportedly active by 2004.

In 2005 IBM sold off its loss-making PC business to the Chinese Lenovo Group. As part of the deal, IBM acquired 19 per cent of Lenovo stock, and the Chinese company moved its headquarters to New York State under an IBM chief executive. Lenovo retained the right to use certain IBM brand names for five years, and inherited the ThinkPad range that had put the company into the laptop market. Part of Big Blue became Big Red: an American icon was humbled, and the Chinese increased their reach into the United States and Europe.

BEYOND THE BIG BLUE HORIZON

With the divestment of the PC business, the mainframe ruled. IBM's Mare Nostrum is Europe's most powerful supercomputer, while its Blue Gene is the most powerful supercomputer in the world: it is capable of operating speeds of 360 teraFLOPS (360,000,000,000,000 operations per second). The Square Kilometre Array project uses IBM technology as part of the world's largest radio telescope to pick up radio signals from deep space. Big Green, a $1 billion energy-saving initiative across the IBM businesses, aims to consolidate 4000 IBM computer servers in six locations worldwide into 30 refrigerator-sized mainframes.

Ultimately, IBM's longevity and capacity for self-reinvention depend upon the calibre of the people who work for the company. In a competitive job market it is not always easy to recruit the best, but IBM in the early 21st century shows signs of having moved on from the monopolistic monolith of its first hundred years. But whatever the flaws of its past management style, IBM's role in leading the way has made it more synonymous with the computer industry than any other company.

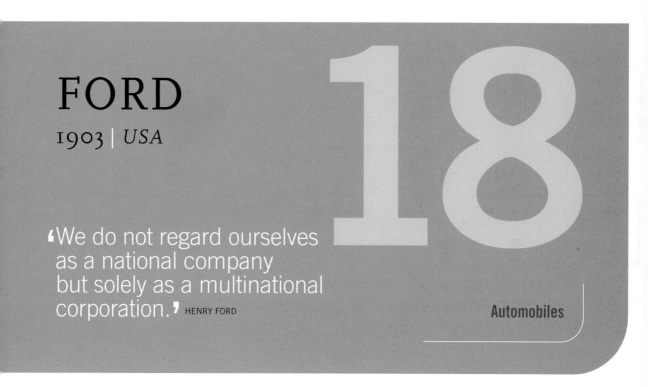

FORD

1903 | USA

'We do not regard ourselves as a national company but solely as a multinational corporation.' HENRY FORD

18

Automobiles

The Ford Motor Company is an American icon. In a paradigm of the American Dream, Henry Ford came out of the Michigan farming belt, and applied his great engineering and organizational talents to the mass production of the world's first affordable motor car, the Model T. The company he founded became the largest family-controlled corporation in the world, mobilized the American economy and, by providing motoring for all, brought about a transformation in American society.

Henry Ford was born to a part-Irish, part-Belgian immigrant family in 1863 on a farm near Greenfield Village, Michigan. Two events shaped his ambition and character. The first occurred when he was 12, when he first saw a steam traction engine; the second, the following year, was the death of his mother. His father expected Henry to take over the farm, but as Ford said: 'I never had any particular love for the farm – it was my mother on the farm I loved.' He had also gained a reputation as a watch repairman and expert dismantler and reassembler of friends' and neighbours' timepieces. In 1879, at the age of 16, he found work as an apprentice machinist in Detroit. He subsequently returned to the farm, where he maintained a Westinghouse portable steam engine; this led the company to hire him as an engineer. Ford married Clara Bryant in 1888, and supported her by farming and running a sawmill. In 1891 he moved to the Edison Illuminating Company, becoming chief engineer. Two years later he and Clara had their only child, Edsel.

A PASSION FOR ENGINES

Ford's obsession was the internal combustion gasoline engine invented by Karl Benz. As early as 1885 he was working on an Otto four-cycle engine, and in 1896 he completed a two-cylinder, air-cooled engine powerful enough to drive the horseless carriage he was assembling in a brick shed behind his home in Detroit. He was 36 years old when, in 1899, he found backers to form the Detroit Automobile Company and quit his job with Edison. Only 25 vehicles had been manufactured when the company went out of business in 1900. A further attempt failed, but in 1903 Ford – with 11 other investors, $28,000 in start-up capital – incorporated the Ford Motor Company.

'**WELL, THIS CHARIOT MAY KILL ME,** but they'll say afterwards that I was going like hell when she took me over the bank.'

Frequent remark by the racing driver Barney Oldfield on his publicity tours around the USA in the early 1900s with Ford's record-breaking 999 racing car.

Manufacture of the first 'Fordmobile' started on Mack Avenue, Detroit, but business was slow until Ford himself drove a powerful Ford racing car to a world land speed record of 91.3 mph over a mile on the ice of Lake St Clair. This prompted the famous racing driver Barney Oldfield to name the car the '999' in honour of a racing locomotive of the day and take it around the country, spreading the Ford brand across the United States. But Ford and his handful of men on Mack Avenue were more interested in developing not flashy racing cars but rather the affordable, four-cylinder utility car with enclosed engine and transmission they called the 'Model T' or 'Tin Lizzie'.

THE MODEL T

The Model T was introduced on 1 October 1908 with a massive publicity campaign. The price fell from $825 in 1908 to $600 in 1913, when Ford introduced moving assembly belts, an innovation created by four employees inspired by the overhead trolley used by Chicago meat packers. These assembly belts reduced the time taken to finish a car to 98 minutes, and Ford's mass-production techniques became known as 'Fordism'. By 1918 half of all the automobiles in America would be Model Ts. Ford's famous dictum 'Any customer can have a car painted any colour that he wants so long as it is black' was rooted in the fact that black was the paint that took least time to dry; until the introduction of the assembly line, the cars had been available in other colours, including red.

Henry Ford with his son Edsel – the man who invented mass-production and democratized motoring was a despotic father and controversial figure who inspired the admiration of Hitler and Stalin.

By 1914 Ford's independent dealers and franchisees had made themselves rich and the company synonymous with private motoring. Above all, the Model T converted rural America from its antipathy to the automobile, hitherto seen as a flashy fad for city slickers. Farmers adapted the car to carry hay and livestock and to supply power to grind grain and saw wood. Even more significantly, people in remote areas could now travel to town on a regular basis, for shopping and socializing. The Model T starred – pejoratively – in Charlie Chaplin's *Modern Times*, and in numerous Keystone Cops movies. Ford himself astonished the world in January 1914 by announcing he intended to share $10 million in profits with his workforce and double their wages to $5 a day. Turnover of staff fell, the number of skilled mechanics rose, and training costs plummeted. A week after the announcement, 12,000 unemployed men gathered outside the factory gates. The Detroit police drove them away with fire hoses.

BIGOT, DESPOT, PACIFIST

Although ill-educated and dyslexic (at the age of 50 he was still spelling 'coal' as 'cole', even though his company owned several coal mines in Kentucky and West Virginia), Ford was the best-known and most respected private citizen in America. His bigotry and distrust of intellectuals, foreigners (ignoring his own immigrant origins) and organized labour played well with devotees of cracker-barrel philosophy, yet sat uncomfortably with his democratic free-market liberalism. It was the latter that led him to campaign on the pacifist ticket during the First World War and to accept Woodrow Wilson's invitation to run for the Senate in 1918. The 'welfare capitalist' and lateral thinker who invented mass production and the $5-day resisted the introduction of the Model 'A' in spite of growing competition from General Motors and Chrysler, and condoned a dehumanizing regime in the Ford plants after the Depression. He was also a despotic father who both encouraged and undermined his only son, Edsel.

Ford's early associates had been the likes of marketing genius James Couzens, who became a Democratic senator. But by the 1930s they were hatchetmen such as Charles Sorensen and Harry Bennett. Ford's heroes were Hitler and Stalin, and the two despots returned the compliment: Hitler publicly admired *Der Fordismus* and kept a photograph of Ford on his wall, while Stalin declared Ford to be 'One of the great industrialists ... may God preserve him.' Ford himself observed, 'I have no patience with professional charity. The moment human help is systematized, it becomes a cold and clammy thing.' In 1932, when Ford was manufacturing one-third of all the world's automobiles, a column of hunger marchers converged on the Ford factory. The Dearborn police opened fire, killing four.

WAR PROFITEERING

The Second World War brought these ambiguities and contradictions to a head. Henry Ford refused to manufacture Rolls-Royce aero engines for Britain, urged Britain to surrender and bitterly opposed President Roosevelt's decision to take America into the war. The company's subsidiaries in Nazi Germany, like those of General Motors, manufactured half-track troop transports and trucks for Hitler's Wehrmacht and the SS, with the increasing use of slave labour.

A series of lawsuits in 1998 on behalf of survivors of Ford Werke in Cologne would fail to secure convictions against the company in the United States. However, documentary evidence in Ford's archives shows that wartime managers in Dearborn wanted the profits repatriated to the USA, and an authorized Ford historian, Dr Mira Wilkins, has written that the proceeds from Ford's operations inside and on behalf of the Third Reich did find their way 'to Ford-US, and the Ford family, who had a share ... after the war'. In 1967 Ford received $1 million in tax exemption on profits for damage done by Allied bombing to its military truck lines in Cologne.

CONTROL PASSES TO HENRY FORD II

The death of Edsel Ford in 1943 led to a power struggle that was resolved only when Mrs Edsel Ford, supported by her mother-in-law Clara, threatened to sell her Ford stock unless Henry Ford passed control of the company to her son, Henry Ford II. The Mrs Fords prevailed, and in 1945, with the company losing $9 million a month, Henry Ford II fired his grandfather Henry's candidate, Harry Bennett, reformed negotiating practices and began the turnaround that saw Ford overtake Chrysler in the 1950s.

The Ford Motor Company remained bigger than nearly all the European car manufacturers put together. In the 1960s, under Henry Ford II and Lee Iacocca, the Ford Falcon and Ford Mustang distanced the brand from the 'Tin Lizzie' and brought glamour by

> **'ONE OF THE GREAT** industrialists ... may God preserve him.**'**
>
> Joseph Stalin on Henry Ford

association with the high-performance sports car. Throughout the 1970s and 1980s, Ford, in common with General Motors and Chrysler, suffered from periodic national recessions and OPEC oil shocks, but less from Japanese competition in the domestic market. The global recession of the early 1990s, however, saw the third-largest industrial corporation in the world begin to cede market share at home and in Europe, losing $1.5 million a day in its British operations alone. In 2001 the company would end more than 80 years of car production in the United Kingdom.

A STRUGGLING GIANT

In the late 1990s, as the American economy boomed with low fuel costs and a soaring stock market, William Clay Ford Jr and British-born chief executive Alex Trotman introduced 'Ford 2000', an ambitious plan to transform the company into a global corporation, cut costs, shorten lines of communication and increase profits. The company also greatly increased its commitment to hybrid alternative-fuel vehicles. Others however have seen the vast size and global reach of Ford as a potential disadvantage in the event of the next downturn: 'Why?' asked Chrysler president Bob Lutz simply, 'What's the value of being big?'

By 2005 Ford owned Lincoln and Mercury in the United States, Jaguar and Land Rover in the United Kingdom, the car division of Volvo in Sweden, and one-third of Mazda in Japan. The company was bedevilled by soaring healthcare costs for ageing employees, dependence on declining sales of fuel-inefficient sports utility vehicles at a time of rising gasoline prices, and loss of market share to superior Japanese cars. Ford bonds were downgraded to junk status, and in 2006 Ford posted an all-time record loss of $12.7 billion. The company declared its intention to close factories, drop unprofitable models, shed 30,000 of its 280,000 employees and raise its borrowing capacity to $25 billion, effectively putting up all corporate assets as collateral. 'Bankruptcy is not an option,' stated William Clay Ford Jr, but he stepped down as president and CEO. Ford sold Aston Martin in 2007 and Jaguar and Land Rover in 2008, and even Volvo was on the block. Negotiations with the United Auto Workers Union were crucial if the company was to survive. The company that put the world on wheels was cornering dangerously, on the brink of becoming the biggest company casualty of the 21st century.

TIMELINE

1863
Birth of **Henry Ford**.

1879
Begins work as an **apprentice machinist** in Detroit.

1891
Joins the **Edison Illuminating Company**.

1899
Leaves Edison to form the **Detroit Automobile Company**, which goes out of business.

1903
Forms the **Ford Motor Company**.

1908
Introduction of the **Model T**.

1913
Ford introduces **moving assembly belts** in his production lines.

1914
Doubles the wages of his workers.

1918
Half of the automobiles in America are Model Ts.

1932
Ford accounts for **one-third of the world production** of automobiles.

1943
Death of Ford's son Edsel leads to **power struggle** that results in Ford's grandson, Henry Ford II, taking over the company.

1947
Death of **Henry Ford**.

1960s
The company changes its image with the introduction of sports cars such as the **Mustang**.

1987
Death of **Henry Ford II**.

1990s
Ford begins to **lose market share**.

2001
Ford **ends production in the UK**.

2006
Ford posts an all-time **record loss** of $12.7 billion.

HOOVER

1908 | USA

Cleaning up

Vacuum cleaners

Today, the Hoover Company's American operations are owned by the Hong Kong corporation, Techtronic Industries, while in Europe, Hoover is one brand among many in the portfolio of the Italian-based Candy Group. In the United Kingdom, the word 'hoover' has become a generic term for 'vacuum cleaner' (often shortened to 'vacuum'), and is used regardless of the manufacturer.

The origins of the device lie in a bout of coughing, and its consequences for hygiene, the home and the homemaker have been immense. The vacuum cleaner has replaced the domestic servant – a species made scarce by the First World War and practically rendered extinct by the Second – and in place of the servant has helped to create a new job in families all over the industrialized world, that of unpaid housewife.

THE EARLY BEHEMOTHS

Attempts to clean floors mechanically date back to 16th-century England, but it was not until 1869 that Ives McGaffey of Chicago patented the first 'sweeping machine' to clean rugs. He called the hand-pumped, wood-and-canvas contraption the 'Whirlwind.' Later in the same century, John Thurman started a horse-drawn door-to-door cleaning service in St Louis, and in 1899 patented the first gasoline-powered pump cleaner. It was a massive contraption. In 1901 the British inventor Hubert Cecil Booth, known for designing fairground rides and mechanical installations for exhibitions, independently developed an equally enormous machine – 'Booth's vacuum cleaning pump'. This was parked outside the building to be cleaned, and long hoses were fed through the windows.

Booth's device inspired two Americans, who had witnessed one of his demonstrations in a restaurant. Corinne Dufour, a woman from Savannah Georgia, produced a machine that sucked dust into a wet sponge. She was awarded the first ever patent for an electrically driven 'carpet sweeper and dust gatherer'. David E. Kenney came up with a system in which the vacuum device was installed by a squad of men in the cellar of the house to be cleaned, and connected to pipes leading to each room.

THE FIRST PORTABLE VACCUUM CLEANER

James Murray Spangler was an asthmatic janitor working in a department store in Canton, Ohio. In 1907, suspecting that the dust from the carpet sweeper he used was the trigger for his cough, he improvised a solution. The components were an electric fan motor, a soap box stapled to a broom handle, and a pillow case. The suction generated by the modified fan motor gathered the dust into the pillow case, so reducing his coughing fits. Spangler had invented the portable electric vacuum cleaner.

Spangler improved the device with a cloth filter bag and cleaning attachments, successfully applying for a patent and forming the Electric Suction Sweeper Company. One of his first customers was his cousin, Susan Hoover, who enthused about Spangler's patent electric suction sweeper to her husband, W.H. 'Boss' Hoover, a leather-goods manufacturer in New Berlin (later North Canton). When in 1908 Spangler ran out of funds to market his invention Hoover bought the patent and took on Spangler as superintendent and partner in the business. The Hoover Company was born.

THE EARLY DAYS

At first, sales were slow, but improved after Hoover placed an advertisement in the *Saturday Evening Post* offering a ten-day free trial. In time, aided by his advertising campaign, Hoover built a network of local retailers across the country. He also pioneered payment by instalment and door-to-door sales techniques, with his salesmen often carrying the demonstration model by bicycle.

The first Hoover Model 'O' machine cost $60 ($75 with cleaning tools) and weighed 40 pounds – over half of the weight was down to the 'whisper-quiet' 1750 rpm Westinghouse motor. These machines were hand built at a rate of only six to eight a day by a team of no more than 20 in a room at Hoover's leather-goods factory. The first few machines were painted black with a bright red sateen bag, but the colour

Hoover's 1952 'Constellation' floated on its own exhaust, epitomizing an era of unparalleled affluence and unchallenged technological reach, for an America that knew no limits at home and abroad.

scheme was soon changed to grey with ornate red detail and grey bag to match. Within a year Hoover had established a research-and-development department at the factory. James Spangler died in 1915 having contributed to further Hoover models and shared in the success of his invention.

'LIGHTER, HANDSOMER, CLEANER'

Only the well-off were as yet able to afford the machines, and the Hoover vacuum cleaner displayed in the hallway became a status symbol to show off to visitors. By 1919, the machines were being mass-produced using the latest sand-casting techniques, and the company was making its own electric motors. In the same year the first machines were shipped from Hamilton, Canada, to Britain, where a shortage of domestic servants lost to war work in factories had led to the emergence of the 'housewife', eager for any new device to make her life easier. 'Lighter, handsomer, cleaner', proclaimed the advertising

> **'IT BEATS** as it sweeps as it cleans'
>
> Long-running slogan for Hoover, coined by Gerald Page-Wood in 1919. It became one of the most famous advertising slogans ever.

for the die-cast Model 541 in 1923, promoting the machine as a labour-saving accessory that emancipated the fashionable housewife from domestic drudgery. Hoover sold 648,896 models in America in the three years from 1923 to 1926 – nearly 250,000 more than the previous design.

The de luxe Model 700 with its silver, orange and black livery, polished aluminium body, handle-integrated on/off switch and agitator brushroll brought the most famous slogan of all, 'It beats as it sweeps as it cleans', coined by Harold Evans Schiltz. The progressive and stylish nature of Hoover design and advertising began to be reflected in the company's architecture. In 1933 construction began at Perivale in west London of the first British Hoover factory, an Art Deco masterpiece decorated with glazed ceramic tiles inspired by ancient Egypt, and floodlit at night in green neon.

The Hoover Company remained in the ownership of the Hoover family until it was floated in the USA in 1943. During the Second World War, many children of Hoover employees in London were evacuated to stay with the families of Hoover staff in Hamilton, Canada. In 1947 the *Illustrated London News* reported that among the wedding presents to Princess Elizabeth and Prince Philip were a Hoover 160 and a Hoover 402: 'Gifts of sumptuous utility: Electric cleaning machines presented to the Princess by the Directors and Employees of Messrs. Hoover Ltd.' It is not recorded whether or not the princess, subsequently Queen Elizabeth II, personally tested the appliances.

The Hoover with the headlamp, and other innovations

Henry Dreyfuss's 1938 Model 825 included a headlamp: many houses were still only wired for electric lighting, meaning that all electrical appliances had to be plugged in via an overhead light socket. In poor visibility, without the overhead light, vacuuming could be a tricky procedure – hence the headlamp.

Another innovation was Hoover's 1952 Constellation model, which was remarkable for its wheel-less hovercraft technology: the spherical machine floated on its own exhaust. The Constellation was later relaunched under various names including the Maytag Satellite.

The Hoover heritage

Hoover today still uses Henry Dreyfuss's red and white 'Generation Future' logo, but faces strong competition from other brands, including the bagless Dyson. James Dyson himself has paid tribute to the strength of the Hoover patents. The 'Hoover', with its few concessions to aesthetics, has become a cult object that connects the consumer with industrial design and engineering, often with deep childhood associations. Many early Hoover cleaners still work perfectly after nearly one hundred years, and models such as the Junior are coveted by collectors and celebrated on websites such as Hooverland and Vacuumland.

The Art Deco Hoover factory in London – once threatened with demolition, but now a Grade 2 listed building – is a landmark to all drivers heading into London from the west, and has been celebrated by Elvis Costello in his song 'Hoover Factory'.

THE YEARS OF DECLINE

Hoover dominated the vacuum-cleaner market in the first half of the 20th century, and in the 1960s and 1970s diversified into washing machines and tumble driers, but increasingly suffered falling profits from price competition and its own high operating costs. Chicago Pacific bought the company in 1985, but was in turn bought by Maytag in 1989. With Hoover UK/Europe split from the American parent in 1993, the brand was weakening with the company.

Maytag's decision in 2004 to 'consolidate' its corporate and back office in Newton, Iowa, saw the loss of many Hoover jobs in North Canton, Ohio. When Maytag was in turn bought by Whirlpool in 2006, Hoover was deemed to be an 'underperforming brand' and was sold to Techtronic Industries of Hong Kong.

In 2007 Techtronic Industries announced the closure of the Hoover plant in North Canton, Ohio – one hundred years after James Spangler plugged in his first machine. In the same year, the centenary of Spangler's invention was celebrated in an exhibition dedicated to him at the Gallery Aferro in Newark, New Jersey. The exhibition, entitled *The Vacuum Cleaner in Art*, featured avant-garde 'dust art' and paintings by robotic vacuum cleaners.

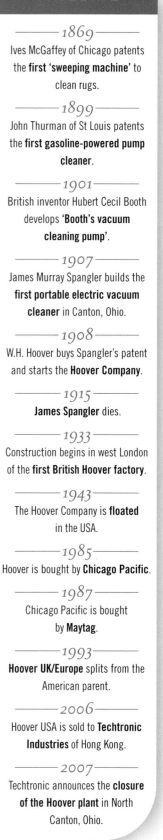

TIMELINE

1869
Ives McGaffey of Chicago patents the **first 'sweeping machine'** to clean rugs.

1899
John Thurman of St Louis patents the **first gasoline-powered pump cleaner**.

1901
British inventor Hubert Cecil Booth develops **'Booth's vacuum cleaning pump'**.

1907
James Murray Spangler builds the **first portable electric vacuum cleaner** in Canton, Ohio.

1908
W.H. Hoover buys Spangler's patent and starts the **Hoover Company**.

1915
James Spangler dies.

1933
Construction begins in west London of the **first British Hoover factory**.

1943
The Hoover Company is **floated** in the USA.

1985
Hoover is bought by **Chicago Pacific**.

1987
Chicago Pacific is bought by **Maytag**.

1993
Hoover UK/Europe splits from the American parent.

2006
Hoover USA is sold to **Techtronic Industries** of Hong Kong.

2007
Techtronic announces the **closure of the Hoover plant** in North Canton, Ohio.

BRITISH PETROLEUM

1909 | *UK*

Hydrocarbons, war,
peace, the environment
and practically everything

20

Oil
Gas

British Petroleum (BP) is synonymous with the fortunes of a
nation, but its true country of origin is Persia. Founded as the
Anglo-Persian Oil Company, BP became one of the most powerful
players in the greatest business enterprise of the 20th century.
From the Persian Gulf to the North Sea and Alaska, the story of
BP has involved need, greed, geology, high politics, *kismet* –
and the caribou.

William Knox D'Arcy was rich from gold mining and a 'capitalist of the highest order' when,
in 1901, he responded to an emissary of the shah of Persia offering 'a source of riches incalcu-
lable as to extension'. Antoine Kitabgi was peddling an oil concession in southern Persia, and
his reasons were simple: the shah 'wanted some ready money'. D'Arcy knew that no less a
person than Baron Julius de Reuter had in 1889 obtained concessions in Persia that had
foundered on opposition and failure. D'Arcy had always wanted to outdo John D. Rockefeller,
the US oil magnate. After negotiations facilitated by Kitabgi and backed by a British government
determined to pin back Russian influence in Persia, D'Arcy's man in Tehran handed over
£20,000 in cash, with another £20,000 in shares and a share of the profits, in return for a
60-year concession covering three-quarters of the country. D'Arcy appointed George Reynolds,
a graduate of the Royal Indian Engineering College and a man of 'solid English oak' to run the
operation. In 1902, after enormous difficulties, they began drilling on a remote and desolate
plateau near what would become the Iran–Iraq border.

D'ARCY AND THE ADMIRAL

By 1903, when D'Arcy met Admiral John ('Jacky') Fisher at the Bohemian health spa of Marien-
bad, his Persian venture was on the verge of collapse. D'Arcy was nearly £200,000 overdrawn
at the bank, having been told it would cost £10,000 to drill two wells. Fisher was recovering from

dysentery, and as second sea lord of the Royal Navy was already branded an 'oil maniac' for his unshakable belief in oil, rather than coal, as the best fuel for British warships. He was also downcast: a test of oil versus coal had recently resulted in the warship in question becoming engulfed in a cloud of thick black smoke. Fisher returned to London to become first sea lord, having promised D'Arcy help.

Fisher had another ally in Marcus Samuel, the head of Shell, who had broken Standard Oil's kerosene monopoly and was ambitious to supply the Royal Navy. Fisher, who would be dubbed by Samuel the 'godfather of oil', lobbied on D'Arcy's behalf; the latter was approaching bankruptcy before being rescued by the Scottish Burmah Oil Company, which had close links to the British Admiralty. In 1905 D'Arcy was refinanced by Burmah, and within three years Reynolds and his team had struck significant reserves of oil in southern Persia. The dispatch from Persia cited Psalm 104, verse 15: 'That he may bring out of the earth oil to make a cheerful countenance.' In 1909 the Anglo-Persian Oil Company was incorporated and went public, triggering wild scenes among would-be stockholders outside the Glasgow branch of the Bank of Scotland.

Reynolds was nonetheless fired by an impatient Burmah, and by 1912 the company was in fresh crisis. This time Fisher's promise to help came good: 'This liquid fuel problem has got to be solved,' Winston Churchill, then first sea lord, wrote to Samuel. In 1914 the British government invested £2.2 million in a 51 per cent stake in Anglo-Persian, a right of veto (which it never exercised) and two seats on the board. Details of the 20-year contract with the Royal Navy were only revealed decades later. The deal turned out to be good for the navy and even better for the British taxpayer. George Reynolds, meanwhile, had been paid off with £1000. William Knox D'Arcy died in 1917, a rich man, but written out of the Anglo-Persian story. British sea power, fuelled by oil, triumphed over Germany in the First World War.

The postwar years saw Anglo-Persian capitalize on Britain's imperial position while remaining at arm's length from the British government. In 1929 the company became a partner in the Iraq Petroleum Company – but as for the other side of the Persian Gulf, Anglo-Persian's new head declared, 'There is no oil in Arabia.' When Shah Reza Pahlavi cancelled

> **'THAT HE MAY BRING OUT** of the earth oil to make a cheerful countenance.'
>
> Dispatch from George Reynolds, quoting Psalm 104, after he had struck oil in southern Persia in 1908.

Just when they were about to give up, engineer George Reynolds (left), a man made of 'solid English oak', and his team discovered oil in Persia in 1908, opening up the Pandora's Box of oil in the Middle East.

the Anglo-Persian concession in 1932, he almost literally had Cadman, the company and the British government over a barrel. Cadman renegotiated the concession and renamed Anglo-Persian the Anglo-Iranian Oil Company (Persia became Iran in 1935). Anglo-Iranian, backed by the British government, also secured a 50 per cent stake with Gulf Oil of America in the new Kuwait Oil Company.

PLAYING POLITICS

After the Second World War, with the world divided between the two superpowers, the USA and USSR, Anglo-Iranian (as it was now known) was locked out of Saudi Arabia by the Americans.

'THERE IS NO OIL in Arabia.'
John Cadman, head of the Anglo-Persian
Oil Company in the 1930s

However, it remained in Kuwait, and appeared unassailable on the northern side of the Gulf. Nevertheless, Washington, possibly under the pretext of concern for Iran's vulnerability to Soviet influence, increased pressure on Britain and Anglo-Iranian to make a better deal with the nationalist prime minister of Iran, Mohammed Mossadeq. At the same time, relations between the British government and the company in which it held a majority stake were becoming strained.

In 1951 Mossadeq nationalized the company's assets and became a local hero. But in 1953 Mossadeq, having been *Time* magazine's 'Man of the Year', was toppled by the CIA after the British convinced the Americans he was a Soviet agent of influence. British Petroleum, as the company was renamed, became a 40 per cent shareholder in a consortium of Western oil companies in Iran. After the 1956 Suez Crisis, BP continued to derive revenues from Kuwait and Iran, but looked to reduce its dependence on the Middle East.

PASTURES NEW

Britannic House, the company's headquarters, opened in the City of London in 1967, towering over an old well head from D'Arcy's Persian oil fields. The glass and marble building – together with the Jaguars of the senior executives – exuded a sense of power, privilege and pirates in pinstripes. In the same year, after Sinclair Oil and BP had six expensive drilling failures in Alaska, one last shot at Prudhoe Bay on the north coast by ARCO struck the largest oil field ever discovered in North America. In 1969 BP bought the Alaskan Valdez terminal for $1 from the Chugach people, and became part of the Trans-Alaskan pipeline consortium. Local environmental opposition proved so effective that a delay of four years in production meant that the British and American oil companies would be unable to counter the effects of the 1973–4 OPEC Middle Eastern oil shocks with Alaskan oil.

BP and other oil companies were also prospecting elsewhere. Wells had been drilled onshore for oil and gas in western Europe since the 1920s, and in the North Sea since the early 1960s. BP had first discovered gas off the coast of Britain in 1965,

A dry hole

In 1983 BP's Sohio affiliate drilling on the cusp of the Beaufort Sea and the Arctic Ocean off Alaska found that it had thrown $2 billion down what turned out to be a dry hole. 'We drilled in the right place,' insisted the president of Sohio. 'We were simply 30 million years too late.'

and in 1970, shortly after a find by the American Phillips company in the Ekofisk field on the Norwegian side of the North Sea, BP announced the discovery of the Forties field on the British side. Finds by Exxon and Shell in the Brent field followed, and the North Sea oil rush was on. The nationalization of oil assets in Kuwait and the 1979 fall of the shah of Iran only served to reinforce the need to reduce dependence on the Middle East. So ended over 80 years of involvement by BP and its predecessors in Persia/Iran.

The extraordinary technical challenges of North Sea oil exploration were complicated by the then Labour government's suspicion of free-market capitalism and oil companies in particular. The North Sea enterprise cost, in financial terms, more than NASA paid to put a man on the moon. The British taxpayer lost billions in oil revenues, compared with Norway, in under-priced concessions and bad deals favouring foreign, particularly American, contractors over competent British suppliers. By 1983 the North Sea was producing more than Nigeria, Libya and Algeria combined.

'BEYOND PETROLEUM'

Between 1984 and 1987, the British government under Margaret Thatcher, as part of its policy of privatization, sold off its 70-year holding in BP, but subsequently blocked an attempt by the Kuwait Investment Office to gain control of the company. Sir Bob Horton took charge of the company in 1989, trimmed head office staff and downsized the headquarters. His successor, Sir (now Lord) John Browne, a lifelong employee of the company, 'left the church of the oil industry' in 1998 by endorsing the Kyoto Protocol on reducing carbon emissions, and in 1999 accepted a UN award for environmental leadership. Under Browne's stewardship BP bought up Amoco, ARCO and Castrol, making it the second-largest oil company in the world.

An explosion at Prudhoe Bay in 2002 highlighted safety concerns for BP. A female member of the Arctic caribou-hunting Gwich'in nation travelled from Alaska to attend BP's annual general meeting in protest at the environmental threat to the herds' migration routes and feeding grounds. Another explosion in 2005, killing 15 people and seriously injuring 180 at the Texas City refinery, was the worst industrial accident in the USA in a decade. This was followed in 2006 by an oil spill from corroded pipes at Prudhoe Bay that shut down half of North America's largest oil field. These incidents undid much of Browne's work in trying to improve BP's reputation for corporate responsibility. Browne's own fall from grace in 2007 after newspaper reports surrounding his private life was an undignified end to an exceptional career.

1901
William Knox D'Arcy is offered oil concessions in Persia.

1902
D'Arcy's operation, under **George Reynolds**, begins drilling.

1905
D'Arcy, near bankruptcy, is **refinanced** by the Scottish Burmah Oil Company.

1909
Incorporation of the **Anglo-Persian Oil Company**.

1914
The **British government buys** a 51 per cent stake in Anglo-Persian.

1929
The company becomes a partner in the **Iraq Petroleum Company**.

1930s
Anglo-Persian becomes Anglo-Iranian, and secures a 50 per cent stake in the **Kuwait Oil Company**.

1951
The Iranian prime minister, Mohammed Mossadeq, **nationalizes** the company's assets.

1953
A CIA-backed **military coup** overthrows Mossadeq.

1960s
BP opens up **new fields in Alaska and the North Sea**, which come on stream in the 1970s.

1984–7
The **British government sells off** its interest in BP.

1995
Sir (now Lord) **John Browne** steers the company along a more environmentally-aware path.

2007
Browne resigns.

BP today is a $300 billion company with 1.2 million shareholders, employing 100,000 people in six continents and 100 countries, operating refineries and service stations around the world. North Sea production fell nearly 13 per cent in 2005, leaving Britain a net importer for first time in decades. Production was expected to fall to one-third of its peak by 2020. Beleaguered by a record $400 million in fines over alleged propane price fixing and lawsuits following the Texas City disaster, the company has announced it is scaling down operations in Alaska, and has entered into oil and gas partnerships in Russia. BP's 'Beyond Petroleum' initiative aims to continue Lord Browne's commitment with an $8 billion investment over ten years in post-hydrocarbon energy sources, such as hydrogen, solar and wind power. Could BP one day stand for 'Beyond Petroleum'?

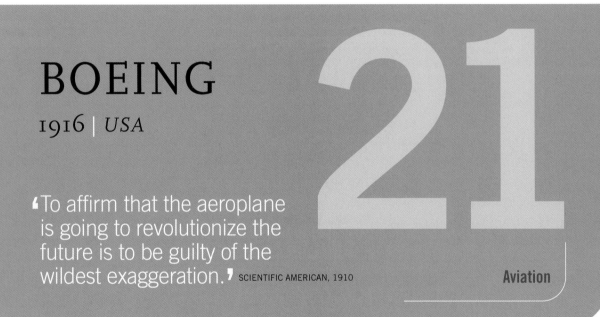

BOEING

1916 | USA

21

'To affirm that the aeroplane is going to revolutionize the future is to be guilty of the wildest exaggeration.' SCIENTIFIC AMERICAN, 1910

Aviation

The Boeing Company is the largest exporter in the United States, and the biggest aircraft manufacturer by revenue in the world. It began in 1915 when the company founder built a seaplane in a boathouse in Seattle. Two more years would pass before Boeing won its first order. The company today is a $60 billion combination of the corporations that have defined American aviation: Boeing, the Douglas Aircraft Company, the McDonnell Aircraft Corporation, North American Aviation and Hughes Aircraft.

William E. 'Bill' Boeing was born to an American mother and a successful German mining engineer who also became a logging entrepreneur. Young Boeing briefly studied engineering at Yale before making a fortune trading timber in Washington State – an experience that gave him a knowledge of wooden structures. The Wright Brothers' pioneering flight at Kitty Hawk in 1903

Seattle, 1962: the new Boeing 727 expanded on the revolutionary design of the 707 and the 'Dash-80'. As many as 1300 Boeing 727s would still be in service around the world nearly 40 years later.

was still fresh in Boeing's mind when in 1910 he travelled to the first American aeronautical meeting in Los Angeles determined to fly aboard one of the new aeroplanes. None of the aviators there would oblige – as another later told him: 'Mostly they come out to see us crash.'

BOEING'S FIRST AIRCRAFT

Back home in Seattle Boeing befriended George Conrad Westerveld, a navy engineer who had studied aeronautics. The two men flew in an early Curtiss biplane that required the pilot and passenger to sit on the wing – 'I never could find any definite answer as to why it held together,' Westerveld wrote. Convinced they could do better, Boeing and Westerveld designed and began to build the B&W twin-float seaplane in Boeing's Lake Union boathouse, and when Westerveld was posted east Boeing completed construction of two aircraft. The pilot Boeing had hired arrived just in time to see Boeing take the controls himself, taxi to the end of the lake, turn and lift off for a quarter-mile flight. On 15 July 1916, following the maiden flight, Boeing incorporated the Pacific Aero Products Company; a year later he changed the name to the Boeing Airplane Company.

With no sales, Boeing personally guaranteed a loan to cover the payroll. His first aeronautical engineer was Tsu Wong, a Chinese immigrant and MIT graduate. It was Tsu who designed the Boeing Model C seaplane, the plane that won the company's first order – for 50 wartime training aircraft – from the US Navy. The payroll rose from 28 to 337 people. While war made the company, peace almost unmade it – a pattern that was to be repeated more than once in Boeing's history. With the end of the First World War, military orders ceased. Boeing found himself competing in a market flooded with war-surplus biplanes, and the company only survived by building flat-bottomed boats, phonograph cases, and dressers, counters and furniture for a confectioner's store and a corset company.

AIRMAIL AND PASSENGER TRANSPORT

Throughout the first half of the 1920s, Boeing manufactured biplanes for other aircraft companies. He also delivered the first airmail and became the first pilot to fly over Mount Rainier. He may have made history, but he failed to make much in the way of profits. This began to change with his Model 15 pursuit fighter, and in 1927 Boeing's Model 40A mailplane won the US Post Office contract to deliver mail between San Francisco and Chicago. Boeing's brother-in-law, Thorpe Hiscock, also developed the first two-way radio for use on Boeing mailplanes. Most significantly, Boeing Air Transport (BAT) was formed to run the new airline, making the company its own supplier.

The airmail routes opened up the possibility of passenger flight, and BAT carried nearly 2000 passengers in its first year. In 1929 Boeing introduced the first dedicated passenger transport, the 12-seater Model 80 biplane. Shortly afterwards Boeing integrated with a supplier, the engine manufacturer Pratt & Whitney, and formed the United Aircraft and Transport Corporation (UATC). The new corporation swiftly absorbed half a dozen more manufacturers and airlines, only to be stopped in its tracks by the 1934 anti-trust legislation that forbade airplane manufacturers from owning mail-carrying airlines. UATC was broken up into three entities: United Airlines, United Aircraft and the Boeing Aeroplane Company. William E. Boeing retired and sold his stockholding.

Claire Egtvedt, his colleague and successor, saw the future in the 'Big Boeings' already in development that would transport both prosperity and destruction around the world. The Model 314 Clipper flying boat made the first scheduled transatlantic flight in 1939, and the Model 307 Stratoliner, which first flew in 1938, was the first pressurized airliner, capable of cruising at 20,000 feet – above most weather disturbances.

> ## Recognizing the pioneers
>
> WILLIAM E. BOEING RETIRED in 1934 to pursue his timber interests, engage in philanthropy, and breed horses and cattle. He died in 1956, having suffered a heart attack aboard his yacht. In 1966 he was memorialized in the Aviation Hall of Fame in Dayton, Ohio. Tsu Wong, Boeing's first aeronautical engineer, became instrumental in Chinese and Taiwanese aviation and died in 1965. Largely unmentioned by the company, he is acknowledged as a pioneering Asian American by the Museum of Flight in Seattle.

BIG BOMBERS AND JET AIRLINERS

Boeing is famous for its contribution to the Allied effort in the Second World War. The iconic B-17 Flying Fortress (commemorated in movies such as *Memphis Belle*) flew thousands of missions over occupied Europe, while the massive B-29 Superfortress dropped the atomic bombs on Hiroshima and Nagasaki, bringing the conflict to an end. William E. Boeing himself advised the company during the war. In a giant factory in Seattle camouflaged from the air by burlap houses and chicken-wire lawns, and at another factory in Kansas, thousands of bombers were assembled by women workers whose husbands were away at the war – such women were celebrated by the US government's poster girl, Rosie the Riveter, accompanied by the slogan 'We can do it.' With the coming of peace, 70,000 Boeing employees lost their jobs.

Wind-tunnel data discovered by Allied scientists in the ruins of a secret aeronautical research establishment in Germany revealed the superior aerodynamic qualities of the 'swept-back' wing. Boeing's chief aerodynamicist George Schairer scribbled a drawing and key mathematical formulae in a letter and mailed it marked 'censored' back to the United States. This single act made the fuel-hungry jet engine feasible for long-range passenger flight, and led to the development programme of the large-scale jet aircraft christened the Dash-80. In 1955 the new aircraft was unveiled in an aerial display, during which test pilot Tex Johnston barrel-rolled the plane over Lake Washington.

Out of the Dash-80 emerged the Boeing 707, delivery of which was begun in 1958. The 707, a four-engined 156-passenger jet airliner, was Boeing's response to Britain's De Havilland Comet, the French Sud Aviation Caravelle and the Russian Tupolev Tu-104. In 1959 American Airlines introduced the first 707 non-stop coast-to-coast flights across America, cutting the time to five hours – piston aircraft had taken eight, while travelling by railroad took four days. The $5 million 707 could carry as many passengers across the Atlantic in a year as the $30 million Queen Mary ocean liner – using one-tenth of the fuel. It also reduced the flight time from New York to London to six hours from twelve. Subsequent variants included the 720 and 727: 1300 of the latter were still in service around the world at the turn of the millennium.

WAR AND PEACE

Boeing was first rescued by war in 1917, and conflict has influenced its fortunes ever since. The Second World War, the Cold War, Korea, Vietnam, the Gulf, Afghanistan, Iraq – the demand generated by these and other conflicts has at times enriched and at other times destabilized the company. As the arms race with the Soviet Union crossed into the space race, Boeing deployed its pilotless technology in the likes of the Minuteman missile, the Saturn 5 rocket booster, satellites, the lunar orbiter for the Apollo programme and the Mariner 10 probe sent to Venus and Mercury. The cancellation of Apollo and a recession in aviation at the beginning of the 1970s saw the company go 18 months without an order, and the workforce more than halved from 80,000 to 37,000. A billboard on the outskirts of the city read: 'Will the last person leaving Seattle turn out the lights.'

The intercontinental 747 and further models saw Boeing through the oil shocks and recessions of the 1970s and into the booming 1980s. Competition increased from the European Airbus in the 1990s, and the terror attacks of 2001 were followed by something of a collapse in the big jet market. Boeing has, however, made substantial sales to long-term Airbus buyers such as Air India and Air Canada. Better customer focus, acknowledgement of the competition and use of the 'lean production' assembly techniques pioneered by carmaker Toyota 50 years earlier have all reinvigorated the company. Another contribution to this revival has been the new super-efficient 787 Dreamliner, the world's longest-range passenger aircraft and the fastest-selling wide-body airliner in history.

TIMELINE

—— 1881 ——
Birth of **William E. Boeing**.

—— 1916 ——
Maiden flight of Boeing's first aircraft.

—— 1917 ——
America's entry into the **First World War** brings an order for 50 aircraft.

—— 1927 ——
Boeing wins the **US Post Office** contract to deliver airmail between San Francisco and Chicago using its own planes, and soon begins to carry passengers.

—— 1929 ——
Boeing introduces its **first dedicated passenger plane**, the Model 80.

—— 1934 ——
Anti-trust legislation forbids airplane manufacturers from owning mail-carrying airlines. William Boeing retires.

—— 1938 ——
Boeing introduces the **first pressurized airliner**, the 307 Stratoliner.

—— 1939 ——
Boeing's 314 Clipper makes the **first scheduled transatlantic flight**.

—— 1945 ——
Boeing B-29 Stratofortresses drop **atomic bombs** on Hiroshima and Nagasaki.

—— 1956 ——
Death of **William Boeing**.

—— 1958 ——
First delivery of the **Boeing 707 jet airliner**.

—— 1969 ——
Maiden flight of the **Boeing 747 'Jumbo Jet'**.

—— 2008 ——
Boeing 787 Dreamliner scheduled to enter service.

In 2006, in spite of a $615 million government fine over a purchasing scandal, Boeing took 55 per cent of global commercial aircraft orders for the first time since 2000. Its customer list includes British Airways, Virgin, Air India, Air Canada, Air France, Lufthansa, Japan Airlines, Qantas, Gulf Air, Malaysian Airlines and Ariana (Afghanistan), as well as hundreds of corporate customers and private individuals.

Aerospace is a high-investment, low-margin industry. Boeing is probably the only company in the world capable of operating NASA's Space Shuttle and International Space Station. Back on earth, America's 13th-largest corporate producer of air pollution is working to reduce the fuel consumption and noise levels that add up to an enormous carbon footprint. Today the company, whose headquarters are now in Chicago, Illinois, employs 150,000 people in the USA and 70 other countries. Boeing has nearly 12,000 commercial jetliners in service – approximately 75 per cent of the worldwide fleet.

DISNEY

1923 | USA

22

‘We don't even let the word "art" be used around the studio. If anyone begins to get arty, we knock them down.’ WALT DISNEY, 1940

Media
Mass entertainment

The Walt Disney Company began life as the Disney Brothers Cartoon Studio, founded by Walt and Roy Disney and the animator Ub Iwerks on 16 October 1923. Today the company – one of 30 that make up the Dow Jones Industrial Average – is a $34 billion media and entertainment corporation, one of the largest in the world. The company is a barometer of corporate America and American sensitivity about the shallowness (or depth) of its arts. Disney has created at least one masterpiece, and a visual grammar that has reached out to billions of children and adults alike.

Walter Elias Disney was born of Irish-Canadian and German-American parents in Chicago on 5 December 1901. His early life was defined by his relationships with his elder brother Roy, and with an unloving father who believed boys should learn the value of hard work. He spent several years on a farm in Marceline, Missouri, where aged seven he sold his first drawing (of a horse) for 25 cents. During his schooldays in Chicago he slept through classes and sketched figures in his exercise books, flipping the pages so that they appeared to move. On one occasion he drew cartoons for a barber shop in return for a haircut, and his first proper job was drawing

slides for a Kansas City advertising agency. In these slides Disney created idealized versions of the animals he had known on the farm of his boyhood: horses performed heroic feats, cows munched dreamily, hens laid mountains of eggs after eating Non-such Miracle Henfood. At night in his 'studio' over a garage he spent hours coaxing a pair of real-life mice out of their holes onto his drawing board. His was an introverted, obsessive talent that was always going to succeed or fail on a spectacular scale.

MICKEY AND FRIENDS

Disney's first venture making animated films went bankrupt. When his family moved to the Pacific coast he remained in Kansas City and worked as a baby photographer. In 1923 Roy was selling vacuum cleaners in Los Angeles and lent Walt enough money to join him. Walt travelled to California dressed in an old sweater and trousers, carrying nothing but a suitcase full of drawing materials. The Disney Brothers Cartoon Studio – renamed in 1925 at Walt's insistence as Walt Disney Studios – made a series of *Alice in Wonderland* silent pictures in which human beings appeared with cartoon characters. But it was a struggle, and the brothers often had to get by on one square meal a day, shared between the two of them. They picked up a contract to animate *Oswald the Rabbit*, but lost this when the New York distributor rejected Disney's ideas for improvements. On the overnight train journey back from New York he came up with a character based on a mouse that lived in the Disney offices. Disney called him Mortimer; his wife Lillian suggested a less formal alternative.

'**MICKEY MOUSE IS UNDERSTOOD** all over the world because he does not talk.' *Time* magazine, 1931

Disney's first two pictures featuring Mickey, a mouse who behaved like a man, were ignored by Hollywood. The third, *Steamboat Willie*, was also a silent picture; but sound was coming to the movies and the brothers raised the money to add sequences including a dishpan concert and a xylophone solo on the teeth of a surprised cow. The picture opened in New York City on 19 September 1928 and caused a sensation. By the end of 1929 Disney had made 15 Mickey Mouse features and begun a new series called *Silly Symphonies*. This was also the last year in which Disney drew his own pictures. Henceforth,

Walt Disney in his studio in Burbank, California, 1955. On the drawing board is the mouse that was his first and most famous creation.

once the gag writers had agreed the story, a team of 'animators' drew the beginning and end of each action, 'in-betweeners' drew the subtle changes that made the movement, and 'inkers' placed a square of celluloid on each drawing and outlined it in ink. The action was created by super-imposing thousands of these transparent drawings over painted backgrounds to be photographed by camera. None of this painstaking labour on the part of others would be acknowledged until years later. As *Time* magazine observed in 1931: 'Cartoonist Walter Disney, 30, thin and dark, gives his collaborators no publicity. He is the originator and so far as the world knows the sole creator of Mickey Mouse's doings.'

Disney had struggled a long time and was not about to disagree when American censors insisted his cartoon cow had to have smaller udders, or when *Time* declared: 'Mickey Mouse ... can reach inside a bull's mouth, pull out his teeth and use them for castanets. He can lead a band or play violin solos; his ingenuity is limitless; he never fails.' Above all, 'Mickey Mouse is understood all over the world because he does not talk.' Mickey's fans soon included Franklin D. Roosevelt, the Italian dictator Benito Mussolini, and King George V of Britain, who was reputed to attend a movie theatre only if Mickey was on the bill. The irrepressible mouse was soon joined by Goofy, the faithful and long-suffering hound Pluto, and the irascible yet inimitable Donald Duck, allegedly an amalgam of all the people his creator had ever disliked.

SNOW WHITE AND FANTASIA

Disney was an investor in technology – he was one of the first customers of the electronic pioneers Bill Hewlett and Dave Packard. He was also an astute reader of industry trends, and a calculated risk-taker on an epic scale. His first full-length animated feature, *Snow White and the Seven Dwarfs*, took hundreds of staff three years to draw and photograph its 250,000 pictures and cost $1.6 million. Rivals referred to it as 'Disney's folly'. Even Roy Disney, who managed the company finances, observed, 'We've bought the

'GEE! This'll *make* Beethoven.'

Walt Disney on his animated version of Beethoven's Sixth Symphony in *Fantasia*.

whole damned sweepstakes.' In 1937 *Snow White* became the highest-grossing movie of all time until 1939's *Gone With the Wind*. Frank Churchill's memorable score played a key part in this success.

Disney himself nursed a desire to animate a 'serious' opera, and as far back as 1929 he had turned Saint-Saens' *Danse Macabre* into a Silly Symphony. When the legendary Leopold Stokowski begged to be allowed to conduct the music for a Mickey Mouse short, *The Sorcerer's Apprentice*, Disney agreed. Many of the 1200 staff at the new $3 million Disney studio in Burbank (most of whom had never been to a classical concert) were turned over to the production of *Fantasia*, a surreal, astonishing, at times outrageous animated stereophonic widescreen rendition of great works of classical music. Disney himself was insensitive to cultural history – 'Gee! This'll *make* Beethoven,' he exclaimed when adapting the latter's Sixth Symphony – but his animators' golden touch with Bach, Wagner, Beethoven, Schubert, Dukas, Mussorgsky and even Stravinsky left audiences gasping: 'Critics may deplore Disney's lapses of taste,' *Time* noted of the premiere in 1940, 'but he trips, Mickey-like, into an art form that immortals from Aeschylus to Richard Wagner have always dreamed of.' *Fantasia* was his masterpiece and proof of his remark that 'Art is never conscious. Things that have lived were seldom planned that way.'

THE GREAT POPULIST

The cost of *Fantasia*, combined with the high costs of *Pinocchio*, *Bambi* and *Dumbo*, left the company heavily in debt. When Disney halved his workforce in 1941, an animators' strike and lockout embittered its founder. Disney had incorporated anti-union sentiments in *Alice's Eggplant* as early as 1925; later he would testify against left-wing influence in the unions. An America Firster to rival Henry Ford, only after Pearl Harbor did he allow the studio to make propaganda films for the government.

The studio might have closed for good had it not been for the war work. With the outbreak of peace, Disney, still smarting from his near-brush with insolvency, declared: 'We're through with caviar. From now on it's mashed potatoes and gravy.' The period until his death in 1966 saw Disney and the company at their most prolific and populist, with a mixture of animations, live-action adventures and nature documentaries such as *Cinderella*, *Peter Pan*, *Lady and the Tramp*, *The Living Desert*, *Treasure Island*, *Swiss Family Robinson*, *20,000 Leagues Under the Sea* and *The Incredible Journey*.

By the mid-1950s more than one-third of the world's population had seen at least one of Disney's 657 films, most of which were dubbed into 14 languages. All these movies contributed to the explosion in sales of Disney merchandize around the world. Disneyland, a theme

1901
Birth of **Walt Disney**.

1923
Foundation of the **Disney Brothers Cartoon Studio**.

1925
The company changes its name to **Walt Disney Studios**.

1928
Disney's third Mickey Mouse film, ***Steamboat Willie***, becomes a hit.

1937
Release of Disney's first full-length animated film, ***Snow White and the Seven Dwarfs***.

1940
Release of ***Fantasia***, regarded by some as Disney's masterpiece.

1955
Opening of **Disneyland** in southern California.

1957
The company goes **public**.

1966
Death of **Walt Disney**.

1971
Opening of **Disney World** in Florida.

1984
Michael Eisner becomes CEO, and halts a period of decline.

1994
Release of ***The Lion King***, which becomes the second-highest grossing film of all time.

1995
Release of ***Toy Story***, the first computer-animated feature.

2005
Eisner is replaced as CEO by **Robert Iger**.

park conceived as early as 1936, opened in Anaheim, southern California, in 1955, and within two years had received its 10 millionth visitor. In the same year, 1957, the company went public. In 1960 *Sleeping Beauty* failed at the box office, but five years later *Mary Poppins*, starring Julie Andrews, broke box-office records worldwide. When Disney himself died on 15 December 1966, there were rumours that his body was cryogenically frozen in readiness for his return.

DISNEY SINCE WALT

Since the death of the founder and driving force of the company, Disney has been faced with the question as to whether it should try to sustain the uniqueness and unanimity of his vision – and, if so, how. In 1971, the year Disney World opened in Florida, Roy Disney died, and over the next 13 years the company had three chief executive officers. Roy Disney's son, Roy Edward, resigned from the company, citing issues with management and a decline in quality. By 1980 Disney was conspicuously lacking successes: 'Some of us are in the film business,' the saying went, 'and some work for Disney.' In 1984 the company narrowly saw off a hostile takeover by Saul Steinberg, and in the same year Roy Edward Disney, still a powerful stockholder, removed Walt Disney's son-in-law Ron W. Miller as CEO and replaced him with Michael Eisner. In the same year Touchstone Films

> **'WE'RE THROUGH WITH CAVIAR.** From now on it's mashed potatoes and gravy.'
> Walt Disney, on his post-1945 attitude to movie making.

was created and made its first adult movie, *Splash*, followed in 1986 by the smash hit *Down and Out in Beverly Hills*. At the same time, old Disney classics were shrewdly reissued on video.

Disney under Eisner was back on track. 1989's *The Little Mermaid* was followed in 1991 by *Beauty and the Beast*, and the following year Euro Disney (now Disneyland Resort Paris) opened in France. *Aladdin*, the hit of 1993, starred Robin Williams, an inspired choice to play the voice of the Genie; by this time Eisner was the world's highest-paid executive. *The Lion King*, released in 1994, became the highest-grossing traditionally animated film in history, and the second-highest grossing film of all time.

And so it goes on. In 1995 *Toy Story*, the first computer-animated feature, became the year's top-grossing movie. In 1996 the company bought ABC TV for $19 billion, and in 2001 acquired Fox Family programming and cable network for $3 billion. In 2005 Michael Eisner was ousted, Robert Iger took over as CEO and Roy E. Disney rejoined the company. The following year Disney bought Pixar for $7.4 billion, *Pirates of the Caribbean: Dead Man's Chest* became only the third film in history to gross over $1 billion, and Apple's Steve Jobs became Disney's largest individual shareholder.

Disney – whether you love it for its cute disingenuousness or hate it for its cultural homogenization – is unique in the entertainment industry worldwide, and a corporate phenomenon. Unlike their creator Walt, who was in fact cremated, his characters will never die.

THE SHENANDOAH CORPORATION

(GOLDMAN SACHS)

1929 | USA

23

Crash and burn

The Shenandoah Corporation was a closed-end fund or investment trust launched by one of America's leading investment banks in July 1929, at the height of a stock market boom. Its collapse in the aftermath of the Wall Street Crash revealed a pyramid of leveraged funds created by Goldman Sachs, which tarnished the reputation of the banking house for several years and brought about the Glass-Steagall Acts and the establishment of the Securities and Exchange Commission.

The booming investment climate of the 1920s had been fuelled by the technological advances of the telegraph, railroad, automobile and utility companies. Vast fortunes had been made by the likes of Rockefeller, the du Ponts, Vanderbilt, Ford, Morgan and Whitney, and new stock issues encouraged the public to regard share ownership as a form of saving. Flotations of companies such as Sears Roebuck, S.H. Kress, United Biscuit and American Cities Power & Light undoubtedly enabled these companies to grow, and also contributed to the wealth of the individual stockholder. However, an industry had also grown up alongside in which investment companies – created by investment banks such as Dillon, Read and Goldman Sachs – aimed to attract the savings of the salaried worker and small-business owner. These closed-end funds or investment trusts were aggressively marketed by advertising campaigns and by sales forces dependent on commission, with the small investor encouraged by instalment plans and the promise that they too could 'make money while they slept', as their closely supervised shares accumulated in value in the manner enjoyed by the rich.

> **'THE FUTURE APPEARS BRILLIANT** ... We have the greatest and soundest prosperity, and the best material prospects of any country in the world.'
>
> Thomas J. Lamont to President Herbert Hoover, 22 October 1929.

THE BUBBLE INFLATES

Between 1921 and 1929 investment mania saw the number of these investment companies in the United States rise from around 40 to 700: 250 were created in 1929 alone. For the investment companies, every new closed-end fund meant income from commissions and increases in share values in a rising market; as this market rose and rose, there was a growth in the scale and exposure of cross-holdings between the investment companies themselves and the investment banks that sponsored them. While the base investment of a new closed-end fund would be real – in other words a holding in a utility company or chain-store retailer that was trading – the upper layers of the fund would consist of holdings in other investment companies whose base shareholdings were similarly real but whose upper layers consisted of cross-holdings in other investment companies.

Each of these transactions generated internal fee income for the companies in question. There was no obligation on the part of the investment company to disclose the nature of its investment portfolio; indeed fund promoters claimed that to do so would jeopardize the interests of the private investor by allowing others to 'copy' the fund's portfolio and so avoid paying a management fee. Likewise, the partners in the investment bank not only received millions of dollars in underwriting fees for every new issue, but also frequently received thousands of dollars' worth of heavily touted new stock for a few dollars, or even a few cents, a share.

This lack of transparency enabled the banks and companies to trade on margins without accountability or regulatory oversight, and meant that while the members of the New York Stock Exchange and Wall Street investment community could pick and choose when to cash in and get out, the mass of small investors would be the last to know. Given the boom and bust nature of the American economy since the days of the telegraph, the 'railroads crisis' of 1873 and the Knickerbocker Trust of 1907, the next downturn was only a matter of time.

A HOUSE OF CARDS

By 1929 Goldman Sachs was riding high. The investment bank that had begun life as a buyer of commercial paper had underwritten a string of successful share issues in manufacturers and retailers. Sydney Weinburg and Waddill Catchings were coming men on Wall Street. Weinburg was a celebrated 'picker' of likely issues; Catchings was a Harvard law graduate with executive experience in industry. Weinburg and Catchings had already formed the Goldman Sachs Trading Corporation, and, together with Harrison Williams of Central States Electric Corporation, they launched the Shenandoah Corporation. Goldman Sachs held common stock in Shenandoah and sold common and preferred stock to the public.

As *Time* magazine noted on Monday 5 August 1929: 'Last week a select portion of the US public was permitted to buy stock in Shenandoah Corp., a newborn investment trust which

> ### How many lightbulbs ... ?
> One of the founders of the Shenandoah Corporation was Harrison Williams of Central States Electric Corporation. It was said that, were his interests to fold, one in every ten American light bulbs would go out.

came into being with a silver spoon of $102,000,000 resources in its mouth. Eager, the public snapped up 1 million shares of common, 1 million shares of preferred, paying up to 42 for common offered at 17½ and up to 60 for preferred offered at 50. By mid-afternoon of the first day's sale there was no ... stock available.'

The Shenandoah Corporation was empowered to 'buy, sell, trade in and hold stocks and securities of any kind ... participate in syndicates and underwritings ... exercise such other of its charter powers as its Board of Directors may from time to time determine'. Weinburg, Catchings and Williams had already determined that one-third of Shenandoah's stock should be in Goldman Sachs Trading Corporation; they now determined that Shenandoah should set up the Blue Ridge Corporation, another investment trust, in which it held common stock and sold preferred shares to the public; this was the second level of leverage, whereby the shareholding structure was such that any gain in the value of Blue Ridge would flow back to Shenandoah, and these gains would multiply as they flowed back to Goldman Sachs.

Blue Ridge was a major holder of stock in Harrison Williams's Central States Electric Corporation, which in turn held controlling shares in the American Cities Power and Light Company, which in turn held controlling shares in Chain Stores Inc., which held controlling shares in a company that was actually trading: Metropolitan Chain Stores. Of course, if the value of Blue Ridge fell, this fall would be magnified before it hit Shenandoah, and magnified again before it hit Goldman Sachs.

THE WALL STREET CRASH

Meanwhile the overheating economy had to reach meltdown. On 'Black Thursday' – 24 October 1929 – 12.9 million shares were traded on the New York Stock Exchange, signalling the end of a five-year bull market.

Crowds in Wall Street, New York, following news of the stock market crash. The ruin of thousands of small investors led to the first effective investment legislation in America.

TIMELINE

——— *1929* ———
July: Formation of the **Shenandoah Corporation**, an investment trust, by Goldman Sachs.

August: Shares in the Shenandoah Corporation are **offered to the public**.

October: The **Wall Street Crash** wipes $30 billion off the value of shares in one week.

——— *1932* ———
Shares in the Goldman Sachs Trading Company, **issued at $104 a share, trade at $1.75.**

——— *1933* ———
The **Glass-Steagall Act**, the first of a number of pieces of legislation regulating investment practices.

——— *1934* ———
The **Securities Exchange Act**.

——— *1935* ———
The **Public Utility Holding Company Act**.

——— *1940* ———
The **Investment Company Act**.

On 'Black Tuesday' – 29 October – 12.4 million shares were traded. In one week the market had lost $30 billion, ten times the annual budget of the federal government and more than the entire US spending in the First World War. Thousands were ruined amid scenes of panic, mayhem and suicide that seared themselves into the American consciousness.

Among the companies that failed was Metropolitan Chain Stores, the company at the base of the pyramid of investment companies at whose apex was Goldman Sachs. When the profits of Metropolitan Chain Stores proved insufficient to pay dividends, the losses magnified through the companies that were pyramided onto it. Blue Ridge stock fell from an opening premium of 46 per cent to a discount of 24.5 per cent by 1930. Shenandoah, which had opened at a 103 per cent premium, was wiped out. By 1932 Goldman Sachs Trading Company stock, issued to 40,000 investors for $104 a share, was trading at $1.75.

> **'I LOST $250,000 – I would have lost more, but that was all I had.'** Groucho Marx

Among the 'select' investors to whom Shenandoah had been carefully touted was the legendary comedian Groucho Marx. 'I lost $250,000,' he later quipped. 'I would have lost more, but that was all I had.' The total value of Wall Street investment companies fell from $8 billion in 1929 to less than $2 billion in 1932.

REGULATING THE INVESTMENT HISTORY

Amid public outrage, the legislative response was swift. The 1933 Glass-Steagall Act, the 1934 Securities Exchange Act, the 1935 Public Utility Holding Company Act and the 1940 Investment Company Act introduced laws to control investment practices, in particular requiring directors of investment companies to be independent of sponsoring investment banks. Mutual funds, whereby salaried workers and other small investors could more safely save and redeem their shareholdings, would dwarf the closed-end funds over the next four decades. In the short term, the small investor was to a degree reassured that a stock market that had fallen in value from $90 billion to $16 billion between 1929 and 1932 was not rigged by financial professionals. Nonetheless, the damage to the New York Stock Exchange was such that it did not regain its pre-Crash high until November 1954. Goldman Sachs likewise took some years to achieve recovery of its reputation, which was redeemed by its successful initial public offering for the Ford Motor Company in 1956.

Groucho Marx never recovered entirely from his losses, but he kept his sense of humour: 'Hey Groucho,' asked a trader on the New York Stock Exchange, 'where do you keep your money?' 'I keep them in Treasury Bonds.' 'They don't make you much money.' 'They do if you have enough of them,' came the reply.

Sydney Weinburg of Goldman Sachs was asked at the time why his company had formed so many closed-end funds. 'Well,' he replied, 'the people want them.' Of its role in the 1920s, however, its website only says: 'The first to hire MBAs on Wall Street.'

UNILEVER

1930 | UK / Netherlands

Now wash your hands

Manufacturing

Unilever was created by the union of a British soap maker and a Dutch margarine producer. The result was a boom in palm oil production in the Congo and the Solomon Islands, and the world's first modern multinational company. Today Unilever manages 400 of the best-known local and global brands from headquarters in London and Rotterdam, and is the world's largest manufacturer of ice cream.

William Hesketh Lever and his brother James were wholesale family grocers when, in 1885, they bought a small soap works in the town of Warrington in northwest England. Soap had previously been made from tallow, or mutton and beef fat. The Lever brothers aimed to use glycerin and vegetable oils to produce a new, stronger-lathering 'Sunlight Soap' at a rate of 450 tons a week. James Lever suffered from ill health and subsequently played little part in the business. William Hesketh Lever's mission was 'to make cleanliness commonplace; to lessen work for women; to foster health and contribute to personal attractiveness, that life may be more enjoyable and rewarding for the people who use our products'. In 1888 Lever Brothers built a larger plant on the marshes at Bromborough Pool on the Wirral peninsula. They named it after their product: Port Sunlight.

PORT SUNLIGHT

Port Sunlight was an extraordinary, paternalistic experiment in employment practice and social engineering. The Sunlight Soap factory, and the town that grew up around it, centred on 'The Village' built by Lever Brothers for its employees, a cross between communistic idealism and an antecedent of the controlling practices of Henry Ford. Unlike Ford's vision, however, the employment policies of the Lever brothers never descended into repression and violence. Each of Port Sunlight's blocks of houses was designed by a different architect, and the properties allotted to employees and their families.

The company's gospel of hygiene spread rapidly, and Lever Brothers prospered both at home and via the trade routes of the British Empire. By 1900 Lever Brothers was a public company and 'Lifebuoy' soap, 'Lux' washing flakes and 'Vim' cleaning agent were household names throughout Britain and its colonies. Hundreds of Port Sunlight families enjoyed above-average wages and a decent standard of living – all of which they would forfeit if they lost their jobs – and subsidiaries of Lever Brothers were established in the United States, Canada, Australia and mainland Europe. The company's paternalistic attitude towards its employees was matched by its zealous concern for its reputation. In 1907, after the British *Daily Mail* newspaper had accused Lever Brothers and others of conducting a cartel, or 'Soap Trust', the company sued and won £50,000 in damages – an enormous sum for the time.

INTERESTS IN AFRICA AND ELSEWHERE

By 1911 Lever had personally secured supplies from palm-oil plantations in the Belgian Congo – savagely managed by Belgian colonialists and manned by forced local labour – and the Solomon Islands. Lever Brothers had also acquired a clutch of soap makers in northern England. After

Early brochures stressed the facilities provided by Lever Brothers for workers at its Port Sunlight plant. By 2008 the company owned the largest portfolio of brands on earth.

Lever's house was destroyed by a suffragette in 1911 – ironically, since he was in favour of women's suffrage – he built a new mansion, including a public zoo that featured yaks, a zebra and a lion cub. After the death of his wife he frequently slept in the open air. The outbreak of the First World War, by which time Lever Brothers was producing 135,000 tons of soap a year, brought government control of the oil and fats industry and saw the company move into the margarine market, which fell away after the war with the greater affordability of butter. In 1920 Lever Brothers gained control of the Niger Company, later the West Africa Company, and in 1922 the company bought Walls, manufacturer of a popular sausage, which had begun to make ice cream for the summer season when demand for sausages contracted. The same year, Lever became Viscount Leverhulme, choosing the name partly in honour of his late wife, Elizabeth Hulme.

By the time of his death in 1925 from pneumonia – indoors – Leverhulme was the archetypal British magnate, with his happy, toiling workers at Port Sunlight and a string of factories and plantations around the world, his splendid house in Hampstead and control of 60 per cent of British soap production. His private interests included ownership of Lewis and Harris in the Western Isles of Scotland, where, in order to handle the produce from his own estate, he established the MacFisheries business, later bought by Lever Brothers. Leverhulme eventually gave the island to the islanders, who were unappreciative, having objected to the purchase in the first place.

UNION WITH THE DUTCH

Lever Brothers' 1926 'Clean Hands Campaign' encouraged handwashing 'before breakfast, before dinner and after school'. As well as preaching the virtues of hygiene and awareness of germs, the campaign instilled the company's brands in the minds of children and their parents. By 1929, however, supplies of palm oil were becoming hotly fought over, and the following year Lever Brothers entered into an arrangement with the Dutch company Margarine Unie, a rival consumer of palm oil, with the object of preserving each other's sources of supply. The arrangement rapidly became a full-scale merger: they called it Unilever. This was the birth of the modern multinational company.

The 1930s and the Great Depression saw Unilever nonetheless expand into Latin America while experiencing competition from Procter & Gamble in the United Kingdom. In the Netherlands, the domestic market of Lever Brothers' new partner, the company drove the growth of 'enhanced' alternatives to butter such as Stork and Blue Band. On the home front during the Second World War, Unilever's Lifebuoy soap vans equipped with soap, hot water and towels toured the bombed areas of the country ministering to survivors of Luftwaffe air raids. In Germany and Japan the company's assets were frozen, and Unilever has not attracted the opprobrium aimed at the likes of DuPont, Ford, General Motors and IBM for their dealings with the Third Reich. After the end of hostilities, Unilever lost many of its interests in Soviet-dominated Eastern Europe, and, after the communist takeover in 1949, in China.

TIMELINE

——— *1851* ———
Birth of **William Hesketh Lever**.

——— *1885* ———
Lever and his brother James buy a **soap factory** in Warrington.

——— *1888* ———
The company builds a bigger soap factory and housing for employees at **Port Sunlight**.

——— *1900* ———
The company goes **public**.

——— *1922* ———
Acquisition of **Walls**.

——— *1925* ———
Death of **William Hesketh Lever**, now Viscount Leverhulme.

——— *1930* ———
Lever Brothers merges with Margarine Unie to form **Unilever**.

——— *1955* ———
The **first British TV advertisement** is for a Unilever product: Gibbs SR toothpaste.

THE WIND OF CHANGE

In the postwar era, as the British Empire was gradually dismantled, the so-called 'wind of change' might have blown away a less substantial institution than Unilever. But Unilever's United Africa Company simply rebranded itself and carried on as usual. At home, in 1955 the company paid for the first British TV commercial – for Gibbs SR toothpaste. Another TV commercial, for PG Tips tea, featuring chimpanzees from London Zoo, became a long-running national favourite. The greater range of processed meats and frozen foods – combined with Britain's closer political and commercial proximity to Europe and the increased prosperity of the United Kingdom in the 1960s – saw Unilever go from strength to strength, with bigger diversifications, unsuccessful merger attempts that left the company undamaged, and the first colour TV advertisements. In the 1970s the company responded to rampant inflation, flat sales and tough times in the UK by capitalizing on oil-driven growth in Nigeria and aggressively expanding its operations in the United States.

> ## Leverburgh
>
> After Lord Leverhulme bought Lewis and Harris in 1918, he selected the settlement of Obbe (*An T-ob* in Gaelic) as the site of a major fishing development. The name was changed to Leverburgh, but the proposed development never materialized, and the Gaelic name is returning to use.

The boom years of the 1980s saw Unilever become the world's 26th largest company, in which soap and personal-care products were no longer the principal sources of revenue. Following the fall of the Berlin Wall at the end of the decade, the new post-communist Eastern Europe beckoned, and the first modern multinational lapped up the opportunities. Acquisitions and divestments – such as Calvin Klein and Elizabeth Arden – became bigger and more prestigious. By 2001 the company had reduced its categories of operations from 50 to 13, and its brands from 1600 to 900.

THE WORLD'S BIGGEST BRAND PORTFOLIO

Today Unilever is a $50 billion conglomerate employing 180,000 people in operating companies and factories on every continent, with research laboratories in Britain, the Netherlands, the United States, India, Pakistan and China. The company's brands include Ben and Jerry's ice cream, Hellman's mayonnaise, PG Tips tea, Findus frozen foods, Bovril, Colman's mustard, Knorr sauces and stock cubes, Marmite, Cif cleaning fluid, Domestos, Signal, Omo, Persil, Sunsilk, Timotei, Pond's Creams and Q-Tips. Many of its other brands are region-specific, from Belgium to Brazil, from Poland to Peru. Unilever's Comfort is the top fabric conditioner in China; Rexona is the top deodorant in Ukraine. The company is also the world's largest manufacturer of ice cream. The company that predates global branding is today the proprietor of the biggest brand portfolio of them all.

In the early years of the 21st century Unilever began to address issues of sustainability and the environment. Like any other company, however, it is vulnerable to a 'bad news day': in 2007 Hindustan Unilever, the Indian arm of the company, was obliged to withdraw its television advertisements for 'Fair and Lovely' skin-lightening beauty cream, which showed previously depressed, dark-skinned women suddenly finding handsome boyfriends and successful careers.

THE LEVER HERITAGE

The Unilever houses at Port Sunlight in Cheshire remained occupied by Unilever employees and their families until the 1980s, and the 900 Grade II listed buildings are now a World Heritage Site. The Lady Lever Art Gallery in Port Sunlight, founded by Viscount Leverhulme in 1922, contains one of the finest collections of paintings and decorative arts in Britain.

Lever's personal legacy is also manifest in the Leverhulme Trust, which makes substantial donations to educational and research projects, funded by Unilever stock, and is administered by trustees drawn from the senior ranks of the company. The Hill, the garden of Viscount Leverhulme's mansion in Hampstead, has been a public park for Londoners since 1960. Lever House, the recently renovated 1950s skyscraper on New York's Park Avenue, has featured displays by artists including Damien Hirst and Keith Haring.

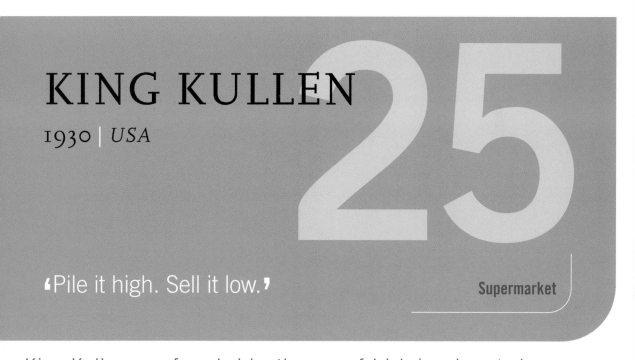

KING KULLEN

1930 | USA

'Pile it high. Sell it low.'

Supermarket

25

King Kullen was founded by the son of Irish immigrants in a vacant garage in the suburb of Queens, New York. Michael J. Cullen's previous employer had not bothered to reply to his letter suggesting a new kind of retailing. Within a day, people were coming from miles around to America's first supermarket.

The concept of self-service is attributed to Clarence Saunders, who opened his Piggly Wiggly store in 1916 in Memphis, Tennessee. Saunders saw the commercial advantage of allowing customers to pick from the shelves instead of ordering from clerks behind a counter. The method speeded up service by enabling the retailer to stack shelves with weighed and measured products at night, and the customer to bring their purchases to the front of the store by day. It also cut labour costs and allowed for bulk buying at lower prices. Saunders's store, for which he was awarded several patents, grew via franchising into the Piggly Wiggly chain, inspiring imitators and competitors, with the result that the self-service grocery store was a familiar sight on the main streets of North America and Canada by the 1920s. One of these was Kroger Stores in Herrin, Illinois, the general sales manager of which was Michael J. Cullen.

THE SUPERMARKET IS BORN

Cullen had joined the Great Atlantic & Pacific Tea Company as a clerk at the age of 18, and remained with A & P for 17 years before moving on to Kroger. In 1929 he wrote to the president of Kroger outlining a plan for five self-service, cash-and-carry 'supermarkets', 'monstrous in size', which he believed could generate much higher profits with much lower margins. Cullen's letter never reached the president and his idea was dismissed out of hand by a subordinate. Undeterred, Cullen quit his job and moved his family to Long Island, where, with a partner, he leased a 6000 square foot abandoned garage and parking lot a few blocks from the main shopping district on Jamaica Avenue in the suburb of Queens. Here, on 4 August 1930,

'**THE WORLD'S GREATEST** price wrecker.'

Accolade awarded to King Kullen in the 1930s.

they opened a giant self-service, cash-and-carry supermarket on the model of Cullen's letter. The store's slogan proclaimed 'Pile it high. Sell it low.' In the spirit of the movie *King Kong*, they called the store 'King Kullen'.

King Kullen grocery store, Rockville Center, Long Island, New York, 1940s. By this time the enterprise that began in a vacant garage ten years earlier had changed the face of family shopping.

King Kullen carried a range of approximately 1000 items, including automotive accessories and hardware as well as groceries. From the day of opening, customers flocked from up to 30 miles away, attracted by affordable prices, prominently advertised discounts, and free parking. With the deepening of the Great Depression, customers became more price-sensitive, and the King Kullen Grocery Company was soon generating 20 times the volume of its nearest competitor, winning the accolade of 'the World's Greatest Price Wrecker'. By the time of Michael Cullen's sudden death in 1935, 17 King Kullen supermarkets were collectively carrying out business worth $6 million a year. Cullen's widow Nan assumed leadership of the company, which led the way as an employer in the late 1930s with regular pay rises, insurance and vacations. Nan Cullen was supported by members of the Cullen family in the day-to-day running of the company, which by 1940 was established as New York's leading supermarket.

A FAMILY BUSINESS

By 1952 King Kullen employed 1000 people in 30 stores ranging from 10,000 to 15,000 square feet. In 1956 the company also became the first supermarket chain in the area to offer trading stamps. The Cullen family retained a controlling interest when the company went public in 1961; an employee stock-ownership plan was also introduced, and shares were offered over the counter of the supermarkets. Over the following few years the Cullen family rejected offers from two would-be purchasers. By this time meat was the core business of the company, on the grounds that meat was the basis of family dining and housewives would buy groceries where they bought meat. King Kullen's 'naturally aged beef' sold at a slight premium and proved the thesis right in so far as it accounted for 25 per cent of all revenues. The company also offered its own-label products, using such brands as 'King Kullen', 'Lady Nan' and 'High Chief'.

After Nan Cullen retired, President James A. Cullen saw the need to modernize, and gave his full support to a young management team led by Walter Miller. 'We had our heads in the sand for so long,' Miller told *Progressive Grocer*, 'we weren't really merchants any more ... Our methods were antiquated. We had lots of money, but we weren't spending it.' In 1969 King Kullen stopped offering trading stamps and simultaneously pegged certain staple items for three weeks at 1931 prices. Customers of the 40 stores in Brooklyn, Queens and across Long Island remained loyal, as in many cases their parents had done.

BEYOND GROCERIES

Walter Miller's leadership proved capable if hardly radical – the company was anything but broke and he and the Cullen family saw no need to fix it. Revenues climbed from $100 million to $200 million then $300 million, and warehouses and parking lots got bigger, as did the transport fleet. The company bought non-grocery products such as automotive goods, kitchenware, beauty aids, greetings cards and soft goods such as socks, underwear, pillows and slippers

1916
Clarence Saunders opens the **first self-service store**, in Memphis, Tennessee.

1930
Michael J. Cullen opens the **first King Kullen store** in Queens, New York, promoting the idea of the self-service store on a giant scale – the supermarket.

1935
After the death of Michael Cullen, his widow **Nan takes control** of the company.

1961
King Kullen goes **public**, but the Cullen family retains a controlling interest.

1983
The company reverts to **private** ownership.

1995
The company opens its **first organic 'Wild by Nature'** store.

from other merchandisers and stuck to its knitting. In its mentality and behaviour it resembled a British cooperative retail society, and in 1983, with employees holding one-third of the stock, the Cullen family trusts one-fifth, and around 300 stockholders in all, the company withdrew from Nasdaq and went private again. It has remained so ever since.

> ‘**WE HAD OUR HEADS IN THE SAND** for so long, we weren't really merchants any more ...’
>
> Walter Miller, who modernized the company in the 1960s.

King Kullen diversified in the recessionary early 1990s into non-food lines such as real estate, advertising and data processing, all of these activities acting vertically in the service of the company. In the first half of the same decade it yielded to competitive pressures and opened its 47 stores around the clock – except on Sundays. ATMs, fax machines, seafood, salad bars, snack bars and delicatessen counters became standard. In 1995, under pressure from Dana Conklin, daughter of the chairman of the board, King Kullen opened its first Wild By Nature store, dedicated to organic and natural foods and to cosmetics devoid of artificial colours, preservatives and flavours.

A TRUE ORIGINAL

North American and Canadian retailers are mainly regional rather than national. Safeway and Michael J. Cullen's former employer Krogers, after initially resisting Cullen's pioneering example, were among King Kullen's earliest imitators and competitors, along with Loblaw and Sobeys. In the United Kingdom, national chains such as Sainsbury, Tesco and ASDA use many of Cullen's techniques, and have grown controversial in their ability to dictate terms to suppliers, their carbon footprints and the potential threat they pose to communities. In the United States, these issues are probably best epitomized by the Wal-Mart phenomenon.

King Kullen today remains firmly under the control of the Cullen family, three generations of whom have served in and managed the company. It is a story of evolution rather than revolution. In 2007 *Supermarket News* rated King Kullen number 75 in the 'Top 75 North American Food Retailers', based on previous year sales of $800 million. By contrast with global brands whose local origins date from the 1930s and earlier, King Kullen has barely ventured beyond Long Island and Staten Island – in 1989 it dipped its toe in Suffern, New York, 20 miles north of New York City, and withdrew again quickly – yet it is the one-stop shop that changed the way we feed our families. The Smithsonian Institution officially designates King Kullen as America's first supermarket. Like the movie that inspired its name, it has been remade many times. But – as with the movie – for the loyal folks and families of Long Island and Staten Island, the innocence and purity of the original remain.

EMI
1931 | UK

Sound recording
Television
Music

The speed of sound

EMI (Electrical and Musical Industries Limited) was the result of the merger between two gramophone companies. Out of this came stereo sound, broadcast television, the secret device that helped defeat the Nazis and the CAT scanner. It also brought the world the Beatles, Pavarotti and Coldplay. Much of this was due to a genius of Anglo-German-Jewish extraction who first presented his credentials as an electrical engineer – to his mother – when he was seven.

The Gramophone Company was founded in London in 1897 by Emile Berliner, a German-born American. Berliner had invented the 'gramophone' method of recording and reproducing sound on shellac discs. Within a few years, Berliner had signed up the likes of Adelina Patti, Nellie Melba and the Italian tenor Enrico Caruso, generally considered to be one of the greatest singers of the 20th century. Caruso's first recording session, on 11 April 1902, lasted two hours, during which he recorded ten songs. The company would release some 240 Caruso records over his career, making him the world's most widely known and celebrated recording artist.

The year in which the Gramophone Company was founded also saw the birth of the London branch of the American Columbia Phonograph Company, which retailed wax cylinders instead of discs and 'graphophone' machines, which initially outsold recording discs.

THE BIRTH OF EMI

By the beginning of the First World War the Gramophone Company was selling 4 million records a year. By this time an estimated one-third of British households owned a gramophone. Both the Gramophone Company and Columbia were affected by the hostilities, with the former losing its substantial businesses in Germany (where the company operates to this day as Deutsche Grammophon) and, after the Revolution, in Russia.

Both companies grew rapidly again in the 1920s, with Columbia, having converted to shellac discs, contracting the likes of Igor Stravinsky and Sir Henry Wood. The Gramophone Company's roster included the Berlin and Vienna Philharmonic orchestras and Sir Edward Elgar. By the beginning of the 1930s, however, the Great Depression had decimated consumer spending around the world, slashing sales of gramophone records by over 80 per cent. Both companies had invested heavily in research and development and were faced with imminent extinction. To avoid this, in 1931 the two companies merged into a single recording organization under the name of Electrical and Musical Industries: EMI. In the same year EMI's new recording studios at Abbey Road in London were opened by Sir Edward Elgar.

THE GENIUS OF ALAN BLUMLEIN

EMI's combined research resources included Alan Blumlein, the son of a naturalized German immigrant. Blumlein, at the age of seven, had repaired the doorbell of the family home in London and presented his mother with an invoice signed 'Alan Blumlein, Electrical Engineer'. After attending Highgate School and graduating with distinction from City & Guilds College, he had worked on long-distance telephony for a division of Bell Laboratories – for which he was awarded a prize at the age of 23 – and then joined the Columbia Graphophone Company, as it was then called, where he invented a method of disc-cutting that circumvented the Bell patent.

Based at EMI's laboratories in Middlesex, Blumlein developed many of the ideas for 'binaural' or stereophonic sound recording used today. Attending a local cinema with his fiancée Doreen in 1931, he had been distracted by the monophonic sound system of the early 'talkies', whereby a single set of loudspeakers was used with the result that the actor was often on one side of the screen while his or her voice was on the other. Blumlein told Doreen that he had found a way to make the sound 'follow' the actor across the screen. The immediate application was in musical sound recording, and the first stereophonic discs were cut by EMI in 1933, although market costs would prohibit their general commercial availability until the late 1950s. Blumlein's determination to have 'the sound follow the actor' was realized in the few short test films he made for EMI, notably *The Walking and Talking Film* and *Trains at Hayes Station*.

Blumlein also invented the moving-coil microphones used in the EMI recording studios and by the BBC at Alexandra Palace. His work on the television camera and the 405-line high-definition Marconi-EMI television system, chosen by the British government over the John Logie Baird rival, would come to fruition in the landmark outside television broadcast by the BBC of the coronation procession of King George VI, linked by an 8-mile cable to the Alexandra Palace transmitter, for which Blumlein invented the resonant slot aerial.

"HIS MASTER'S VOICE"
REG. U.S. PAT. OFF.

'Nipper' the dog became one of the most famous trademarks in the world and symbol of 'the greatest recording organization' which encompassed an extraordinary technological diversity, from the first stereo discs to radar and colour television cameras.

CONTRIBUTION TO RADAR

Television-camera and radar technology shared the same origins, and in 1939 EMI developed a 60 MHz radar patented by Blumlein and E.L.C. White. By 1940 the system was being used in combat by the Bristol Beaufighter, and the following year Blumlein and others began work on the H2S radar system to help bombers find their targets. In June 1942 the Halifax bomber in which Blumlein was flying crashed during a test of the only prototype of the airborne H2S radar. Blumlein, two colleagues from EMI and the eight others on board were all killed. Blumlein was 38 years old.

The radar technology that Blumlein developed was introduced in 1943 and made a substantial contribution both to the strategic bombing campaign against Germany and to the detection of German U-boats and thus to the winning of the Battle of the Atlantic. It has often been said that the atomic bomb ended the Second World War, but it was radar that won it. Blumlein, in his short life, had been awarded an astonishing 128 patents, mostly between the years 1933 to 1940, and many of them concerning the EMI television system. Partly because of the intense secrecy that surrounded his wartime work – no obituary or other tribute appeared at the time – his remarkable life and achievements are revered within the world of electronic engineering, but little known in the wider world.

FROM SINATRA TO THE SEX PISTOLS

EMI regained the balance between music and technology in the immediate postwar years. The first 33 rpm vinyl long-playing records

TIMELINE

1897
Founding of the **Gramophone Company**.

1926
The Gramophone Company achieves its **first million-seller**, 'O For the Wings of a Dove'.

1931
The Gramophone Company merges with the Columbia Phonograph Company to form **EMI**.

1933
EMI cuts the **first stereophonic discs**, based on the invention of EMI engineer Alan Blumlein.

1937
Outside broadcast of the coronation of King George VI using the Marconi-EMI television system.

1939
EMI develops a **radar system** patented by Blumlein and E.L.C. White.

1942
Blumlein killed in an air crash.

1955
EMI acquires **Capitol Records**.

1958
EMI produces the **Emidec 1100**, Britain's first transistorized computer.

1962
EMI signs up the **Beatles**.

1979
EMI merges with THORN Electrical Industries to form **Thorn EMI**.

1992
EMI acquires **Virgin Music**.

1996
Demerger of Thorn EMI.

2007
EMI is bought by the British private equity firm **Terra Firma Capital Partners**.

and the 45 rpm 'single' became market standards. With the loss of many artists supplied under licence by the American Columbia company, in 1955 the company bought its own American roster in the form of Capitol Records, which included Frank Sinatra, Nat 'King' Cole and Peggy Lee. EMI also enjoyed a dozen British hits with Elvis Presley, starting with 'Heartbreak Hotel', under licence from RCA. It lost the licence in 1957, and attempted to 'clone' him in the form of Cliff Richard, who turned into one of popular music's most durable performers.

> ## 'WE DON'T LIKE THEIR SOUND, and guitar music is on the way out.'
> Spokesman for Decca in 1962, turning down the Beatles. The group was promptly snapped up by George Martin of EMI.

In 1962 George Martin, one of the company's first A&R ('artistes and repertoire') men, spotted the Beatles, who had just been turned down by Decca: 'We don't like their sound,' a spokesman said, 'and guitar music is on the way out.' Martin signed them to EMI's Parlophone label to record their first single, 'Love Me Do'. 'Please Please Me' followed, and in 1963 'From Me To You', 'She Loves You' and 'I Want To Hold Your Hand' all went to Number One. The Beatles would go on to sell an estimated 1 billion records, including the classic *Abbey Road*, named after the EMI recording studio. Throughout the 1970s the company also experienced phenomenal sales with Pink Floyd's *Dark Side of the Moon*, Queen's 'Bohemian Rhapsody' and the Rolling Stones, which enabled it to afford the mistake in 1976 of signing the Sex Pistols, whom it dropped and was rewarded with the ineffectual revenge single 'EMI'.

MISSILES, MEDICAL TECHNOLOGY AND MUSIC

This monolithic and in many ways conservative recording company was still one half of a two-headed creature. EMI had continued to be involved in other areas of electrical and electronic engineering, producing guided missiles and radar equipment, and, in 1958, the Emidec 1100, Britain's first transistorized computer. Geoffrey Hounsfield, who led the project, went on to develop the first CAT scanner, which revolutionized medical imaging, and for which he would be awarded a Nobel Prize. EMI colour television cameras, in particular the EMI 2001, became the staple of the BBC and ITV. In 1979 the merger with THORN Electrical Industries to form Thorn EMI created one of Europe's largest defence companies. This schizophrenia ended with the demerger of Thorn EMI in 1996. The music company had seen a decline in record sales in the 1980s, before the advent of compact-disc technology and its reinvigoration with the purchase of Virgin Music in 1992. Subsequently, performers such as Blur, the Verve, the Chemical Brothers, the Spice Girls, Mariah Carey and Robbie Williams all recorded with EMI labels. The company finally ceased in-house CD and DVD manufacturing altogether in 2004.

EMI today is exclusively a music company. In some respects it has reaped the harvest of its sometimes miserly treatment of artists from Ernest Lough to Marillion – the latter of whom pioneered a comeback deal on terms that demonstrated the greater negotiating power of acts with loyal fan bases in the internet age. The advent of digital piracy and internet downloading has decimated EMI's CD sales. In 2007, after a fruitless seven-year search for a merger partner, the company accepted a £4 billion takeover offer by the British private equity firm Terra Firma Capital Partners.

ALLEN LANE / PENGUIN

27

1935 | *UK*

The future is orange

Book publishing

Where once only the rich could afford to build their own libraries and benefit from the power of literacy, the advent of the inexpensive paperback brought all kinds of literature – from novels to history to science and philosophy – to a wider audience, thus changing both people and societies. This revolution was brought about by a company that began life in a quintessentially English way, in a church crypt. The company's logo – an amiable flightless bird – was designed by an office junior. But it was a logo that came to be recognized and respected around the world. Penguin is the principal reason so many millions came to know the authors named here, and many others.

The paperback book had existed since the late 19th century in the form of pamphlets, pornography, cheap foreign-language editions, 'dime' novels and 'railway' books, thus giving rise to its justifiably seamy reputation. 'Proper' clothbound and stitched hardback books were traditionally sold through bookshops, and neither bookshops nor private or public libraries made much if any space for the paperback. In 1931 the German publisher Albatross Books pioneered a paperback format for the mass market, but the venture soon failed commercially, in the spirit of the ill-omened bird. But it made an impression on the young managing editor of an English publishing house.

PENGUIN IS HATCHED

Allen Lane Williams – he and his family dropped the last name in order to retain ownership of the family company – had risen to the top of Bodley Head, founded by his uncle John Lane. Allen Lane was a man of forthright and progressive opinions, often at odds with other members of the board of directors. Returning from a visit to the English crime writer Agatha

A commuter reads *Lady Chatterley's Lover* on the London Underground, 3 November 1960 – the day Penguin's most notorious (and lucrative) book to date went on sale to the general public.

Christie in 1934, he found himself on a railway platform frustrated by his lack of decent reading material. Lane conceived the notion of a vending machine that could dispense afford-able quality books in the same manner as a packet of cigarettes. In conflict once more with the board of Bodley Head as to whether or not they should publish James Joyce's controversial masterpiece *Ulysses,* Lane left to set up his own list, initially under the Bodley Head umbrella. With capital of £100 he launched his own imprint from the crypt of the Holy Trinity Church on Marylebone Road in London. The books were piled in family vaults, and a fairground slide enabled deliveries from the street above.

Lane borrowed wholesale from the Albatross experiment of four years earlier. The covers featured bands of white and a colour to signify the genre: dark blue for biography, green for crime, orange for fiction. He also named his company after a bird: in

Lane and Pevsner

In 1951, with daily life in Britain still constricted by rationing, Allen Lane lent the German-Jewish refugee Nikolaus Pevsner a 1933 Wolseley Hornet car and a permit for 30 gallons of petrol. Pevsner's aim, during vacations from university teaching, was to research and write a 46-volume guide to the most significant buildings in England. This was the genesis of the classic *Pevsner Architectural Guides,* which would eventually extend to Scotland, Wales and Ireland, and which are regarded as *the* authoritative guides to the buildings of the British Isles. Pevsner also conceived and edited the *Pelican History of Art* series, beginning in 1953.

COMPANIES THAT CHANGED THE WORLD

this case the flightless yet indefatigable penguin. The Penguin logo and cover-look were designed by the 21-year-old office junior, Edward Young. The first Penguin list – all reprints of contemporary authors – included Ernest Hemingway, Eric Linklater, E. Arnot Robinson, Beverly Nichols, Mary Webb, Norman Douglas and André Maurois. The cover price was sixpence – the price of a packet of cigarettes. Lane bought paperback rights from publishers, placed large print orders and looked for non-literary retailers. The house of God became a temple of Mammon, and within ten months Lane had printed 1 million Penguin paperbacks, with André Maurois' *Ariel* as his top seller, and even traditional bookshops were stocking 'Penguins'. In 1936 Lane established Penguin Books as an independent company.

SHAKING UP A CONSERVATIVE INDUSTRY

Both publishers and authors were sceptical and alarmed by a genuinely 'disruptive' product, especially in terms of pricing – hardbacks sold for seven or eight shillings. Penguin's sudden and dramatic success was kick-started by a single major order from the (hitherto non-bookselling) high-street retail chain Woolworth, and helped by support in the press from influential authors such as George Orwell (whose *Animal Farm* and *1984* Penguin would publish). Imitators soon appeared in America, including Pocket Books (who published America's first mass-market pocket-sized paperback in the form of Pearl Buck's *The Good Earth*), Ace, Dell and Bantam. As the international situation deteriorated, Lane gave the new brand urgency and intellectual muscle with Penguin 'Specials' such as *Searchlight on Spain* and *What Hitler Wants*, which sold heavily. In 1937 he launched the Pelican imprint, which published original works addressing contemporary issues. In the same year the first 'Penguincubator' vending machine was installed on London's Charing Cross Road.

During the Second World War the cheap and portable Penguin format was suited both to wartime production strictures and to mass mobilization, and Penguin Specials such as *Aircraft Recognition* became bestsellers. Lane, with his brothers Dick and John, launched the King Penguin historical and decorative imprint, hiring Elizabeth Senior from the British Museum as first editor; she was killed in an air raid in 1942 and was succeeded by the architectural historian Nikolaus Pevsner. Puffin Books for children followed, and by the end of the war Penguin was distributing 1 million books a month in America. It also had operations in Australia. This helped fund Penguin Classics, which launched in 1946 with E.V. Rieu's translation of *The Odyssey*, a project he had initially undertaken for his wife, and which became Penguin's best-selling book. Penguin Classics soon became a major force in education worldwide.

———— *1902* ————
Birth of **Allen Lane**.

———— *1919* ————
Lane joins the **Bodley Head** publishing company.

———— *1931* ————
Albatross Books in Germany pioneers the mass-market paperback, but the venture fails.

———— *1936* ————
Lane leaves the Bodley Head to found **Penguin Books**.

———— *1937* ————
Launch of the **Pelican imprint**, featuring original works on contemporary issues.

———— *1946* ————
Launch of **Penguin Classics**.

———— *1952* ————
Lane is awarded a **knighthood**.

———— *1960* ————
Penguin Books found not guilty of obscenity after publishing *Lady Chatterley's Lover*.

———— *1961* ————
Penguin is **floated** on the London Stock Exchange.

———— *1965* ————
Lane falls out with Penguin chief editor **Tony Godwin**.

———— *1970* ————
Lane dies. Penguin sold to **Pearson**.

———— *1975* ————
Merger with the US publisher Viking.

———— *2000* ————
Dorling Kindersley bought by Pearson for the Penguin stable.

———— *2002* ————
Penguin completes purchase of **Rough Guides**.

CONFLICT AT THE TOP

By 1952, when Lane was knighted, Penguin had long overturned the 'intellectually cheap' image of the paperback book. Nevertheless, Lane's eye for publicity in the cause of profit was revealed by the 1960 trial under the archaic obscenity laws of Penguin's unexpurgated version of D.H. Lawrence's *Lady Chatterley's Lover*. The outcome of the trial, celebrated for the remark of the prosecuting counsel to the jury as to whether or not this was a book you would let your wife or servant read, marked out Penguin as a champion of liberty – and helped sell a further 3.5 million copies of the book. By the same year, dollar sales from paperbacks had surpassed those of hardcovers in the United States.

When Penguin floated on the London Stock Exchange in 1961, Lane's role was diminished. Tony Godwin, Penguin's *wunderkind* new chief editor, soon found himself playing to Lane the role Lane himself had played to his Bodley Head directors 30 years earlier. Godwin saw the effects of cheaper design and print technology in competitors such as Pan, who used full-colour covers, and hired art directors and designers such as Romek Marber and Germano Facetti. The Penguin Crime series stopped using the iconic striped cover design that had been the norm since 1935 and underwent a successful makeover. Facetti rolled out a design approach across Penguin that would become definitive in capturing intellectual thinking for generations of sixth-form and university students, for whom the Penguin edition assumed the status of the hardback of the 1930s.

The clash was inevitable and ultimately tragic. In 1965, when Godwin tried to oust Lane with the backing of the board of directors, the founder retaliated by stealing the print run of a controversial book by the cartoonist Siné and burning it. He launched the Allen Lane hardback imprint in 1967 in the very format he had originally challenged, and with which he had successfully competed. Godwin departed from Penguin and would die prematurely. Lane was diagnosed with cancer and retired shortly afterwards. Within only six weeks of Lane's death in 1970, a cash-strapped Penguin was sold to Pearson.

A CORPORATE BIRD

The changes that followed epitomized the crisis in British publishing, as decisions increasingly came to be made by accountants rather than editors. The merger with the US publisher Viking in 1975 brought American authors such as Arthur Miller, Saul Bellow and John Steinbeck into the combined list of a London-based, American-run conglomerate. Penguin's controversies of the 1970s and 1980s – encapsulated in Peter Wright's unreliable *Spycatcher* and Salman Rushdie's almost unreadable *The Satanic Verses* – smelled of corporate strategy rather than the human touch.

The conglomerate rumbled on, releasing audio books, buying the Rough Guide imprint, acquiring Dorling Kindersley and winning a lawsuit on behalf of its author Deborah Lipstadt against the Holocaust-denying historian David Irving. Penguin today in the USA and UK is a comparatively conventional corporate. Rather ironically, it behaves not unlike the publishers threatened by Allen Lane's disruptive new venture 70 years ago, when Penguin created a revolution and set an industry standard.

28

TOYOTA

1937 | Japan

'Business is war
– and war is business'

Toyota Motor Corporation – *Toyota Jidosha Kabushiki-gaisha* – was established in 1937 by Kiichiro Toyoda as an offshoot of Toyota Automatic Loom. The latter was part of his father's company, Toyota Industries, which began life in the 19th century with the help of technology transfer from Oldham in the north of England.

A lucky name トヨタ

The eight calligraphic strokes it takes to write *Toyota* are regarded as a lucky number.

The automotive division of Toyota Industries actually began life in 1933, encouraged by a Japanese government that needed domestic vehicle production in the face of worldwide recession and the Sino-Japanese War. Toyota produced the Type A engine in 1934, and a passenger car – the Model A1 – in 1935. In the same year the company also produced the G1 truck. Production of the Model AA passenger car started in 1936. These vehicles bore a strong resemblance to those manufactured by Dodge and Chevrolet, to the point where some parts were interchangeable with the American models. Japan had already become the first Asian country to emulate the West economically and industrially, and was characterized by a culture of hard work, education and a fanatical commitment to improving the quality of products and production.

MILITARY PRODUCTION

During the Second World War, Toyota's factories manufactured trucks for the Imperial Japanese Army. Material shortages meant that these vehicles were simple, with a single, centrally mounted headlight. Japan conceded defeat shortly before an Allied bombing raid was scheduled to destroy the Toyota plants, and unconditional surrender was followed by US military occupation. Japan was on its knees, dependent on American aid. By 1950 Toyota had managed to resume automobile production, but the company was on the brink of bankruptcy. One plant switched production to flour and bread simply to feed its workers.

Toyota was selling fewer than 300 trucks a month, and had stopped making cars altogether, when the CEO, Shotaro Kamiya, journeyed to the United States in the hope of striking a joint venture with the Ford Motor Company. Kamiya failed, not least because the US Defense Department felt the deal would undermine domestic American production. But by the time he returned to Japan, the Korean War had broken out and America was crying out for Japanese support. Kamiya was greeted with an order from the Pentagon for 1500 trucks a month.

'TOYOTA'S SALVATION'
CEO Shotaro Kamiya's description of the Korean War.

When the Korean War ended in 1953, 1 million Chinese, 600,000 Koreans and 54,246 Americans had been killed, and the disputed border between North and South Korea remained on the Thirty-eighth Parallel. The US Special Procurements Program had already pumped $3.5 billion into Japan, and to Kamiya the tragedy of Korea was 'Toyota's salvation' – although he felt a note of guilt that he was 'rejoicing over another country's war'. The governor of the Bank of Japan would go so far as to describe the Special Procurements Program as 'divine aid'.

NEW METHODS OF AUTOMOBILE MANUFACTURE

The profits from US investment in Japan enabled Eiji Toyoda, a descendant of the founder, to contemplate a return to car production. Toyoda travelled to Ford in Detroit and concluded that American methods – with their subordination of the individual worker, huge quantities of parts and inflexible mass-production line – were not the way. Other factors cited as influences on Toyoda at this time include the 'last-minute' distribution system of the Piggly-Wiggly self-service stores, and an education programme devised by the US Army.

'Just in time' – Toyota's revolutionary 'lean production' line saved the company from extinction in the aftermath of the Second World War and became the benchmark for all other automobile manufacturers.

Toyoda and his colleagues had to create a flexible system for the small and fragmented Japanese market. They modified second-hand American presses and told employees to turn out parts 'just in time'. Employees were also encouraged to halt the production line whenever a car was spotted with a defective or missing part. Initially the result was chaos, but as a team-building exercise the idea swiftly took on. Within a short time, Toyota was turning out more cars at a lower cost and higher quality than other Japanese carmakers. The 'Toyota Way' preached and practised continuous improvement and empowerment across the organization. They called it the Toyota Production System. Many years later, Westerners would christen it 'lean production'.

EXPORT SUCCESS

In 1957 the Toyota Crown, an uneasy combination of Western styling and Japanese engineering values, became the first Japanese automobile to be exported to the United States. By 1958 Toyota was still exporting fewer than 100 cars a year to America. However, Japanese manufacturing industry was booming, and the Vietnam War brought an injection of $3 billion in military orders from America between 1965 and 1970, further boosting the economy. In 1973 the first OPEC 'oil shock' had a massive inflationary effect on the West and on gasoline prices, illustrating the superiority of Japanese 'economy' cars over the American equivalents. In 1975 Toyota overtook Volkswagen and sold 800,000 cars in America. In 1979 the year of the second oil shock, Toyota sold 1.8 million vehicles in America.

Over the next decade Toyota established dealerships, service networks and then factories across the United States. American car manufacturers such as General Motors were meanwhile plunging into crisis, posting the largest losses in American corporate history and devastating automobile towns such as Flint, Michigan. In 1989 General Motors president Roger Smith admired a new car in a Detroit parking lot: 'What's that?' he asked the attendant. 'The new Mercedes-Benz?' 'No, sir,' came the reply, 'that's one of the new Japanese models.' The car was Toyota's Lexus. Twenty years on, Lexus would be the bestselling luxury marque in North America, and the division probably the most profitable of the entire Toyota Motor Corporation.

'AN ECONOMIC PEARL HARBOR'

The crisis in the American automobile industry at the beginning of the 1990s prompted questions in Washington and calls for punitive trade tariffs on the import of Japanese cars. One Democratic senator, Donald Riegle, went so far as to declare: 'This is an economic Pearl Harbor.' In 1992 President George Bush Sr, who had fought the Japanese as a Navy pilot in the Pacific War, took with him the heads of General Motors, Ford and Chrysler on a visit to Japan to press their hosts to buy more American automobiles. The initiative was a diplomatic and commercial failure, and perplexed the Japanese: 'President Bush's visit has produced much confusion and distress among the Japanese people,' noted a Japanese management consultant in the *Wall Street Journal*. 'Most of us don't understand why the President of the United States has taken up issues usually handled by assistants to Carla Hills [the US trade representative].'

The answer lay in American manufacturers – and foreign manufacturers in the United States such as BMW – embracing Japanese methods and values. Companies such as General Motors and Ford would have to redefine their corporate cultures, overhaul their dealer and service networks, and above all listen to the customer if they were ever to regain profitable market share in the industry they pioneered and of which they had long regarded themselves as world leaders.

TIMELINE

———*1894*———
Birth of **Kiichiro Toyoda**.

———*1933*———
Establishment of an **automotive division** within Toyota Industries.

———*1935*———
The first Toyota passenger car, the **Model A1**, is produced.

———*1937*———
Kiichiro Toyoda establishes the **Toyota Motor Corporation**.

———*1941–5*———
Toyota produces trucks for the **Imperial Japanese Army.**

———*1950*———
Outbreak of the **Korean War** brings big orders for military trucks from the USA.

———*1952*———
Death of **Kiichiro Toyoda**.

———*1957*———
The **Toyota Crown** becomes the first Japanese automobile to be exported to America.

———*1965–70*———
The **Vietnam War** brings more big US military orders.

———*1973*———
The **'oil shock'** leads to an increased demand in the USA for 'economy' cars.

———*1975*———
Toyota **sales overtake** those of **Volkswagen** in America.

———*1992*———
President **George Bush Sr** visits Japan with senior US automobile executives to press the Japanese to buy more American automobiles. The visit is not a success.

———*2007*———
Worldwide, Toyota **outsells General Motors**.

In 2007, although outsold by Honda in America, Toyota sold more cars and trucks worldwide than General Motors, ending the US group's 75-year reign as the world's largest carmaker. In the USA, the company operated assembly plants in Alabama, Kentucky (where it assembled the Toyota Camry, the best-selling car in America), Indiana, Texas, West Virginia and Mississippi. Toyota also manufactured locally for markets in the United Kingdom, Australia, Canada, France, Turkey, the Czech Republic, Indonesia, Poland, South Africa, Brazil, Pakistan, India, Argentina, Mexico, Malaysia, Thailand, China, Vietnam, Venezuela and the Philippines. Europeans in particular signed up for the hybrid Prius, which ran on gasoline, electricity or both. In the United States, with Ford and General Motors in full retreat, automobile-dependent Americans panicked by even modest gasoline price rises turned in ever-greater numbers to Toyota's fuel-efficient cars to carry them from the suburbs into work.

> **'DRIVE YOUR DREAMS'**
> Toyota slogan

VOLKSWAGENWERK

1938 | *Germany*

29

The vehicle of freedom
born of tyranny

Automobiles

Volkswagenwerk AG – the 'people's car company' – was the vision of the German Nazi leader Adolf Hitler. Hitler never learned to drive, but according to the *New York Times* in 1936 he was believed 'to reel off a higher annual motor mileage than any other ruler or head of state'. That same year he opened the Berlin Motor Show and announced that Germany had 'effectively solved the problem of producing synthetic gasoline'. This claim was never substantiated, but he had launched a network of autobahns and highways across the country, which, he declared, would mark 'a turning point in the history of German automobile traffic'.

Volkswagenwerk general manager Heinz Nordhoff at the end of the 1950s stands in front of the Wolfsburg plant with the car that was stolen from a Czech, commissioned by Hitler and rescued by a Briton.

Hitler was galled by the fact that one in five Americans owned their own cars – the figure in Germany was barely one in fifty. He commissioned Dr Ferdinand Porsche and others to design a *volkswagen* or 'people's car'. It was to cost under 1000 Reichsmarks ($140 at the time), have a low-revving, high-geared air-cooled engine, and a top speed of 60 mph. The vehicle was intended for the great autobahns that the Fuhrer and his chief architect, Albert Speer, would stretch all the way from Berlin to Moscow. According to Dr Porsche, Hitler also said the car should 'look like a beetle'.

Dr Porsche was one of a number of people Hitler consulted about the people's car, prominent among these being Hans Ledwinka, the technical chief of one of the oldest surviving carmakers in the world, the Czech company Tatra. Hitler was an admirer of the powerful, air-cooled, rear-engined V-8 Tatra sedans, and made a point of greeting

> **'IT IS FOR THE BROAD MASSES** that this car has been built. Its purpose is to answer their transportation needs, and it is intended to give them joy.'
>
> Adolf Hitler, laying the cornerstone of the new Volkswagen plant, 1938.

Ledwinka respectfully at Berlin Motor Shows. Hitler invited Ledwinka and his son Erich to his private apartments, where they talked about the *volkswagen*. On one of these occasions Ledwinka gave Hitler a detailed drawing based on the prototype of a small, air-cooled, rear-engined car he had designed and built some years earlier. Hitler passed this drawing to Dr Porsche. At the outbreak of the Second World War, Ledwinka was forced by the Germans to convert the Tatra plant in Czechoslovakia to munitions. In 1945 he was arrested by the Russians and sentenced to six years' imprisonment for collaboration with the Nazis. Ledwinka, Tatra and the car he had designed would disappear behind the Iron Curtain.

JOY FOR THE MASSES

The original plan was that the Volkswagen factory should be built near Nuremberg so that customers could collect their cars after attending the Nazi Party rallies. Instead a gigantic factory and town – KdF-Stadt or Strength-Through-Joy Town – were to be built on Luneberg Heath in Lower Saxony (*Kraft durch Freude* – 'Strength through Joy' – was the Nazi leisure organization). The plant was modelled on the Ford factory at Rouge River, Detroit, financed with funds confiscated from German labour unions and built by Italian workers on loan from Mussolini. Hitler admired Henry Ford and *Der Fordismus* and, as we have seen, the feeling was mutual. In 1938, at a rally worthy of Nuremberg, Hitler laid the cornerstone of the plant and declared, 'It is for the broad masses that this car has been built. Its purpose is to answer their transportation needs, and it is intended to give them joy.' The Führer added that the vehicle was to be known as *der KdF (Kraft-durch-Freude)-Wagen* – the 'Strength-Through-Joy Car'. In 1938 a prototype was displayed for the first time at the Berlin Motor Show.

The German public were slow to respond to Hitler's initiative, so a savings scheme was developed to stimulate interest. Prospective customers could reserve a Strength-Through-Joy Car by paying 5 Reichsmarks a week. Once they had paid 990 Reichsmarks, they could take delivery of the car. Full payment would take four years, although extra payments could ensure earlier delivery. In an echo of Henry Ford, they could have any colour they wanted as long as it was grey-blue. A missed payment would result in cancellation of the agreement. Children could save 5 Reichsmarks a month, and by mid-1939, 336,668 people had paid 110 million Reichsmarks into a Berlin bank account. Volkswagenwerk would still be compensating some of them 30 years later.

> **'THIS VEHICLE IS QUITE UNATTRACTIVE** to the average buyer. It is too ugly and too noisy.'
>
> Lord Rootes, the British automobile manufacturer, on the VW Beetle, 1945.

On 1 September 1939 Germany invaded Poland. KdF-Stadt had produced only a handful of Strength-Through-Joy Cars, and the factory under Dr Porsche and his son Ferry was converted for wartime production. A few vehicles were produced as staff cars for Nazi Party officials. Many were converted to run on coal, coke, bottled gas, anthracite or even peat. KdF-Stadt – manned by slave labour recruited from concentration camps and camps for Russian prisoners of war – was turned over to manufacturing the fuselage and wings of the V-I flying bomb. In the spring of 1945 Hitler was driven by his chauffeur Erich Kempka on one last visit to the Eastern Front in a modified version of the KdF-Wagen, the Type 87 *Kommandeurwagen*, a four-wheel-drive vehicle fitted with a roller at the front. Six weeks after his return, Hitler and Eva Braun committed suicide in their bunker in Berlin. Fittingly, their corpses were doused with gasoline, also by the chauffeur, and ignited.

POSTWAR RECONSTRUCTION

At the end of the war KdF-Stadt, only 10 miles west of the new Soviet Zone, was scheduled to be dismantled and its plant and machinery seized as reparations by the Allies. This was in accordance with the Morgenthau Plan, which aimed to deprive Germany of its industrial capacity and revert it to an agricultural economy. Henry Ford, on being shown the plant on the map commented, 'What we are being offered here isn't worth a damn.' The town and plant were renamed Wolfsburg, after Count von Schulenburg of Wolfsburg, on whose estate it had been built, and came under the control of the military government of the British Zone. In the summer of 1945 a young British officer, Major Ivan Hirst, arrived at the plant.

The British disagreed with the Morgenthau Plan, regarding it as the kind of humiliation that had encouraged the rise of Nazism in the first place, and believed that a reconstructed Germany would provide a bulwark against Soviet expansionism. They also needed motor vehicles, and Hirst's mission was to get a vehicle into production. He and his colleagues unearthed the remains of the beetle-shaped car that some of Hirst's fellow-officers had admired at the 1938 Berlin Motor Show. They repaired it, painted it dark green and sent it for inspection to the army headquarters of the military government of the British Zone. Hirst and his ragged German workforce were then visited by Lord Rootes, the British automobile magnate. 'This vehicle,' Lord Rootes told him, 'is quite unattractive to the average buyer. It is too ugly and too noisy. If you think you're going to build cars in this place, young man, you're a bloody fool.' Shortly afterwards, a message came back from the military government of the British Zone to Wolfsburg. They wanted 20,000 cars as soon as possible and advanced 20 million marks as working capital.

In spite of appalling conditions, and with the help of German prisoners of war, Hirst got the plant back into production, and by the end of 1945 they had manufactured 58 cars. The following year it was announced that no repairs could be made to the plant and that it would be dismantled if production did not rise to 1000 vehicles a month. Hirst's colleague Richard Berryman, a Royal Air Force officer, had worked for General Motors. He managed to obtain more food and blankets for the workforce, added meat to their lunchtime soup and ensured they slept more soundly in their huts. The workforce responded by increasing production to 1003 cars a month. In 1947 the first cars were shipped to the Netherlands, marking the rebirth of Germany as an exporting nation. Hirst handed over the plant to a German manager, Heinrich Nordhoff, and went home to England. Control of Wolfsburg passed to the federal government in Bonn, and thence to the state of Lower Saxony. The Morgenthau Plan gave way to the Marshall Plan, under which Germany received billions of dollars in the cause of reconstruction and the fight against communism. With the replacement of the Reichsmark by the Deutschmark at a rate of 15 to 1, Wolfsburg was flooded with orders for the car. They called it the Volkswagen Type One, but it was known simply as the Volkswagen.

THE BEST-SELLING CAR IN HISTORY

By 1953 a handful of Volkswagens were being imported into the United States. In 1959, in one of the most successful advertising campaigns ever mounted, Doyle Dane Bernbach played against the pretensions of General Motors and sold the Volkswagen as a well-built, dependable, classless – and affordable – alternative. By 1960, the 500,000th car had arrived in the

<aside>
TIMELINE

1938
Construction begins in Lower Saxony on what becomes the **VW plant**.

1939
A prototype of the **'Strength-Through-Joy Car'** is displayed at the Berlin Motor Show.

1945
After the defeat of Germany, the VW plant is returned to the production of what becomes known as the **'Beetle'**.

1947
VW begins to **export** the Beetle.

1960
By this year, **half a million Beetles have been exported to the USA.**

1972
The Beetle becomes the **best-selling car in history**.

1978
Production of the Beetle ends in Germany.

2007
Porsche rumoured to be increasing its 31 per cent stake in a **takeover bid** for the company.
</aside>

United States, and the 'Beetle' had captured the imagination of youthful America. On 19 January 1978 Volkswagen number 16,255,500 – the last of its line – left Wolfsburg. Six years earlier it had overtaken the Model T Ford to become the best-selling car in history. Production of the car would continue in Australia, Mexico and Nigeria.

Hans Ledwinka died in 1967, having failed to secure restitution for his lost fortune and patents. Porsche and Volkswagen made secret out-of-court settlements to the Ringhoffer family, who owned Tatra, for patent infringements relating to the people's car. Meanwhile, in a corner of the small Tatra museum in Koprivnice in the Czech Republic stands the prototype V750 rear-engined, air-cooled, beetle-shaped car in the drawing Ledwinka handed to Hitler. Designed and built by Ledwinka at least two years *before* the prototype built by Dr Porsche, this was the original 'people's car'. As for Volkswagenwerk, the company that went on to produce the Golf (Rabbit) and Passat, and took over Audi and Skoda – the latter in the Czech Republic after the fall of the Berlin Wall – the rest is history.

WONDERBRA / CANADELLE 30

1939 | *Canada*

'Even I get cleavage with them.' KATE MOSS

Women's clothing

The advent of the brassiere in the early 20th century marked the end of the 350-year tyranny of the corset, and the beginning of an era in which women took greater control over their own bodies. The Wonderbra itself began life in the 1930s, when it was first trademarked, patented and manufactured. In 2007 the Canadian Broadcasting Corporation (CBC) reported that respondents ranked the Wonderbra just after insulin and the telephone – and ahead of the cardiac pacemaker – in the top 50 'Greatest Canadian Inventions'.

The invention of the corset is attributed to Catherine de' Medici, Italian-born wife of King Henry II of France. In the 1550s she banned 'thick' waists at court, encouraging ladies to wear a whalebone and metal device tightened by lace pulleys and designed to reduce the waist by several inches. The inevitable result was competition among the ladies at court, and the beginning of 350 years of torture for half the human race. Nor did the innovation benefit its alleged creator, as Henry II took up with a French-born mistress.

THE ORIGIN OF THE BRASSIERE

As early as 1875, George Frost and George Phelps patented a boneless, lace-and-pulley-free supportive undergarment named the Union Under-Flannel. In 1889 the corset-maker Herminie Cadolle marketed the Bien-être ('well-being') shoulder-slung device as a health aid. Four years later Marie Tucek patented a 'breast supporter', which featured separate pockets for each breast and straps that reached over the shoulder. In 1907 *Vogue* magazine announced the arrival of the 'brassiere' as a breast-flattening alternative to the corset. The young Gabrielle ('Coco') Chanel was also designing loose-fitting dresses in reaction against the constrictions of whalebone and lace.

It was in 1913 that the New York socialite Mary Phelps Jacob, about to go out to a reception in a sheer evening gown, found that the whalebone of the traditional corset was unacceptably visible under the plunging neckline, disfiguring the texture of the fabric. She improvised with a pair of silk handkerchiefs and some red silk ribbon. Friends and family soon noticed and applauded the 'Backless Brassiere', which she patented in 1914.

A further impetus came during the First World War, when the US War Industries Board called on women to stop buying corsets, thus freeing up 28,000 tons of metal for the war effort. But running a company was not to Mary Phelps Jacob's liking, and she sold her patent for $1500 to the Warner Brothers Corset Company of Bridgeport, Connecticut. Over the next 30 years the company would make over $15 million from the patent.

'WE CARE ABOUT the shape you're in**'** Slogan for Wonderbra, 1970s

THE WONDERBRA IS BORN

In 1922 the Russian immigrant seamstress Ida Rosenthal and her husband founded the Maidenform company in Bayonne, New Jersey, producing brassieres that rebelled against the flat-chested conformity of the times. It was Ida Rosenthal who devised the system for categorizing women by bust size. Sara and Sam Stein's FayeMiss Lingerie Company (later the Bali Brassiere Company), founded in 1927, manufactured similar garments, and in 1935 New Yorker Israel Pilot improved on existing bra design and trademarked the 'Wonder-Bra'. In 1939 Moses ('Moe') Nadler, founder of the Canadian Lady Corset Company, licensed the trademark for the Canadian market.

> **'WHO CARES** if it's a bad hair day'** Slogan for Wonderbra, 1990s

Pilot's 1941 diagonal-slash patent subsequently became the basis for Nadler's small sewing shop in the centre of Montreal, where he manufactured a well-fitting, mid-priced quality bra that did not depend so much on elastic – a material that was rationed during the Second World War.

This gave Nadler and Canadian Lady a competitive advantage, one that he used to exploit the WonderBra brand (as it became known) to the full, with a range of lingerie and undergarments and sub-brands targeting different socio-economic sectors of the market. Yet in the United States, Israel Pilot's D'Amour company failed to penetrate the market with WonderBra and the patent expired in 1955. Sure of his instincts, Nadler ignored Pilot's demands that he cease using the designs and return the templates. Nadler launched a new line inspired by Christian Dior's 'New Look' and successfully acquired the rights to WonderBra for Canada, Europe and Asia. Ever forward-looking, in 1961, shortly before his death, he commissioned Louise Poirier to develop a deeply plunged, laced, push-up design numbered the 1300, which Canadian Lady licensed to Gossard. By the mid-1960s Canadian Lady was exporting and licensing the Wonderbra line (as it was by this time written) to western Europe, South Africa, Israel, Australia and the West Indies.

Eighty years after a New York socialite invented the 'backless brassiere', 'supermodel' Eva Herzigova raised eyebrows on New York's Times Square and allegedly caused motor accidents in Britain.

'LESS BRA' NOT 'NO BRA'

The sexual and fashion revolution of the late 1960s saw the girdle follow the corset into the dustbin of history. At the same time, burning one's bra became a symbolic gesture for radical feminists. While some companies cut back on bra marketing, Larry Nadler, who had inherited the company from his father, commissioned market research that identified new teenage market segments, and showed that most women wanted 'less bra' and not 'no bra' – they wanted to feel and look beautiful, and while some went bra-less, this was a fashion and not a political statement.

Canadian Lady – Canadelle as it became – pursued market share with TV advertising: 'We care about the shape you're in,' ran the slogan. Although the Canadian Broadcasting Corporation initially turned down the advert because it showed a woman in a bra, the explosion in sales that followed pushed the company to Number One. By 1980 Canadelle had 30 per cent of the Canadian market and $30 million in wholesale sales – in a country with only 10.3 million women and girls over 13.

'HELLO BOYS'

In 1992 the plunge-style push-up Gossard Wonderbra that had begun life as the 1300 suddenly become a hit with British women, and within two years it had claimed 12.5 per cent of the UK branded bra market. The 1994 relaunch of the Wonderbra in the United States by Sara Lee saw a $25 million campaign that included events with supermodel Eva Herzigova in New York's Times Square, and print and billboard advertising showing models wearing only the Wonderbra, accompanied by slogans such as 'Who cares if it's a bad hair day' and 'Look me in the eyes and tell me that you love me'. In the United Kingdom the campaign featured a series of billboard advertisements showing women modelling Wonderbras, with the caption 'Hello Boys'. 'I've got a couple of those Gossard Wonderbras,' supermodel Kate Moss told the *New York Times Magazine*. 'They are so brilliant, I swear, even I get cleavage with them.' A number of car accidents involving British (male) drivers were apocryphally attributed to the head-turning nature of the advertisements.

Sara Lee sold its 'intimate apparel' brands in 2006. The Wonderbra range remains a hugely popular brand around the world. The trademark is the property of Canadelle Limited Partnership of Canada, which is a wholly owned subsidiary of HanesBrands Inc. HanesBrands licenses and sells the Wonderbra range in all countries except the European Union, several other European states and South Africa; Wonderbra is licensed and sold in these markets by an affiliate of Sun Capital Partners under the Dim Branded Apparel Group, which is headquartered in Paris – a few kilometres and 450 years on from the court of Catherine de' Medici.

IKEA

1943 | *Sweden*

Design for living

Furniture

IKEA is the world's largest furniture and furnishings supplier, with 251 owned or franchised stores in 34 countries, ranging from Sweden to the United States, from the United Kingdom to Israel, Saudi Arabia, Russia and China.

IKEA was founded in 1943, near Almhult in neutral wartime Sweden, by a young entrepreneur called Ingvar Kamprad. The name is an acronym of '*I*ngvar *K*amprad, *E*lmtaryd, *A*gunnaryd', referring to the founder and the house and village in which he grew up. Whether by accident or design, the word is similar to the Greek *oikia* ('home') and the Finnish *oikea* ('correct, right'). The company exerts perhaps the greatest influence of any retailer on the way we live, regardless of culture, class or religion.

A TEENAGE ENTREPRENEUR

When Kamprad founded IKEA he was only 17, his father having given him the seed capital as a reward for doing well at school. Kamprad's grandfather had killed himself with a shotgun when he was unable to pay the mortgage on his farm, and this seems to have had a profound influence on the boy, who set about making money by any means available. At the age of five, he was bulk-buying matches from Stockholm and selling them to his neighbours by bicycle. The teenage Kamprad sold any kind of item for which there was a market and which he could discount – fish, pens, Christmas cards, seeds, wallets, table runners, picture frames, watches, jewellery, nylon stockings. He conducted his business from a shed on the family farm and later by mail order, using the local milk van for deliveries. He was also involved in the pro-Nazi New Swedish Movement (Nysvenska Rorelsen). When this was revealed in 1994, he refused to hide behind a PR machine, and instead publicly apologized to IKEA's employees of Jewish descent, describing the episode in his book *Leading by Design: The IKEA Story* as 'the greatest mistake of my life'.

> **Baby boom**
> One in ten Europeans is thought to be conceived in an IKEA bed.

By the age of 21, Kamprad was selling furniture and other goods from the first IKEA store, located in the southern Swedish town of Almhult. In 1951 he produced the first IKEA catalogue (Kamprad personally wrote the text of these until 1963) and from 1953 concentrated on furniture. Pressure from a competitor led him to open a showroom where the customer could see, touch and feel the quality of the goods. In 1955 he made the move into furniture design, in which Sweden was a world leader, and undercut the local cartel to the point where they 'persuaded' his suppliers to boycott the company. Kamprad's response was to look to Poland – where, incidentally, he also acquired a lifelong taste for vodka. In Poland he found manufacturers who could supply him with inexpensive components that could be assembled from flatpacks. This was the birth of IKEA as we know it today.

> **'HAPPINESS IS NOT** to reach one's goal but to be on the way.'
> Ingvar Kamprad, *A Furniture Dealer's Testament* (1976)

SWEDISH STYLE FOR ALL

Swedish design in the 1950s and 1960s was secular and modern, utilitarian yet stylish – and usually expensive. Kamprad demystified the aura surrounding the contemporary Scandinavian look, and brought it to the mass market with considerable flair and at prices that young people setting up their own homes could afford. He also 'democratized' the process of furniture shopping: the first IKEA warehouse store in Almhult combined the low margin/high volume and self-service of the supermarket with the IKEA brand and product range.

This became the model for all subsequent stores. The first of these outside Sweden opened in Asker, Norway, in 1963, and stores followed in many other countries, including Denmark in 1969, Switzerland in 1973, Germany and Japan in 1974, the United States in 1985, the United Kingdom in 1987, China in 1998, Russia in 2000 and Turkey in 2005.

'It's a question of good leadership.' Ingvar Kamprad's 'flat-pack' approach to design and management alike made IKEA one of the most successful retailers of the 20th and 21st centuries.

'IT IS OUR DUTY TO EXPAND'

Sweden's economic affluence and Kamprad's evangelical mission 'to create a better life for many' drove IKEA's expansion throughout the 1960s and 1970s. In 1976 he wrote and published *A Furniture Dealer's Testament*, which was required reading for new employees. In this he declared 'It is our duty to expand.' He appealed to the reader in motivational terms: 'Divide your life into 10-minute units and sacrifice as few as possible in meaningless activity... Wasting resources is a mortal sin ... Happiness is not to reach one's goal but to be on the way.'

> '**HOW THE HELL** can I ask people who work for me to travel cheaply if I am travelling in luxury? It's a question of good leadership.'
>
> Ingvar Kamprad, founder of IKEA and the richest man in Europe, who travels everywhere economy class.

Kamprad led by example, and his managers and workforce – who doubled as the models in IKEA catalogues – were willing disciples. During the 1980s IKEA-owned stores and franchises sprung up all around the world, transcending national, international and cultural frontiers – a process driven from within the company, enabled by the 'positive virtues' of the product, and anticipating by two decades the notion of building 'communities' of customers.

THE IKEA IDEA

IKEA stores typically conform to two or three designs, the largest of which is the 'blue box', which leads the customer 'the long natural way' through furniture showrooms and household wares, where the choices of purchase are made, to the warehouse where the flatpacks are collected, and from there to the cashier's station. Many stores include restaurants serving typical Swedish cuisine such as meatballs, blueberry cake and lingonberry jam, as well as local food.

The 12,000 products are designed in Sweden but manufactured by 1300 suppliers in 53 developing countries to keep down costs. Products are identified by single-word names of mainly Swedish, Danish, Finnish and Norwegian derivation and grouped by category: thus bookshelves, storage units and coffee tables are given Swedish place names; bathroom items are named after Scandinavian lakes, bays and rivers; children's toys and items are named after birds, mammals and adjectives (such as Duktig, meaning 'good' or 'well-behaved'). Like Henry Ford and Walt Disney, Kamprad is dyslexic and found names easier to remember than numbers. This has led to misunderstandings, such as with the Gutvik bedframe in Germany where the innocent Norwegian place name was pronounced *gut fick*, or 'good fuck'.

For the customer, the downsides of cost-saving 'interactivity' in collecting purchases, notoriously brief assembly instructions and sometimes lengthy self-assembly times are outweighed by the product. The annual IKEA catalogue is something of a phenomenon. It is all produced in IKEA's photo studio – the largest in northern Europe – in its home town of Almhult and published in 55 different editions, 27 languages and 35 countries, reaching more than 200 million people in Europe alone.

For the IKEA community of consumers, from Beijing to Bolingbrook, Illinois, the IKEA store is a one-stop sanctuary and treasure hall of affordable contemporary design. The cult and culture of the company is endlessly celebrated on websites and blogs around the world: 'Half my house is from IKEA – and the nearest store is six hours away' (USA), 'IKEA makes me free to become what I want to be' (Romania), 'Every time, it's trendy for less money' (Germany).

Consumer madness

The opening of a new IKEA store is a national event, which can sometimes lead to unexpected problems. In Emeryville, California, the traffic was so severe that police had to direct it manually for three months. In Edmonton, north London, a number of people were injured in the rush as it opened its doors and the store was closed after 30 minutes until the following day. In Saudi Arabia three people were crushed to death when IKEA offered a limited number of $150 gift vouchers.

THE COMPANY TODAY

IKEA today is a $15 billion business with 104,000 employees, controlled by a private holding structure owned by the Kamprad family and based in the Netherlands. The $36 billion foundation that protects IKEA from takeover has been estimated by the *Economist* as the world's wealthiest charity. The company structure is as flat as its furniture packs: titles and privileges are forbidden, suits and ties are absent, top managers fly economy class, and 'anti-bureaucracy weeks' see executives unloading trucks and tending the cash registers. IKEA has twice been named one of the 100 Best Companies for Working Mothers, and in 2006 was ranked 96 in *Fortune* magazine's 100 Best Companies to Work For.

Kamprad and his family have lived safe from Sweden's tax laws in Switzerland since 1976. Europe's richest man and one of the world's wealthiest – at one point displacing Bill Gates as Number One – maintains an estate in Sweden and a vineyard in France, but drives a second-hand Volvo, travels economy on trains, haggles in the local market, encourages IKEA employees to write on both sides of a piece of paper, and has been known to drop in to an IKEA store for a cheap meal. 'How the hell can I ask people who work for me to travel cheaply if I am travelling in luxury?' he says. 'It's a question of good leadership.' At the same time, IKEA has a strong tradition of charitable giving and philanthropy at local and international level. Kamprad is officially retired, but remains active in the company. In 2000 he cheerfully informed his three sons that whichever one most successfully ran his arm of Habitat, the upmarket retailer IKEA bought in 1992, would inherit IKEA and the $15 billion business when he was gone.

TIMELINE

1926
Birth of **Ingvar Kamprad**.

1943
Kamprad founds **IKEA**, aged only 17.

1951
The **first IKEA catalogue**.

1953
IKEA starts to focus on **furniture**.

1963
Opening of the **first IKEA store outside Sweden** (in Asker, Norway).

1969
The first IKEA store opens in **Denmark**.

1973
The first IKEA store opens in **Switzerland**.

1974
The first IKEA stores open in **Germany and Japan** (the company withdrew from Japan in 1986 but planned a return).

1985
The first IKEA store opens in the **USA**.

1987
The first IKEA store opens in the **UK**.

1992
IKEA buys **Habitat**.

1994
Kamprad **apologizes** for his wartime involvement with pro-Nazis in Sweden.

1998
The first IKEA store opens in **China**.

1999
Kamprad publishes (with Bertil Torekull) ***Leading by Design: The IKEA Story***.

2000
The first IKEA store opens in **Russia**.

2005
The first IKEA store opens in **Turkey**.

2006
IKEA is listed by *Fortune* magazine among the **100 Best Companies to Work For.**

SONY

1946 | *Japan*

Play it back

The Sony Corporation began in an abandoned department store in the ruins of postwar Tokyo. Out of the ashes came the tape recorder, transistor radio, television, Walkman, PlayStation – and the world's best-known Japanese citizen. Sony took Japan's innate technological capability from imitation to innovation and played back the pictures and soundtrack of our lives.

Masaru Ibuka was one of Japan's earliest shortwave 'ham' radio operators, and at the 1933 Paris Exhibition was awarded a prize for a modulated light transmission system of his own invention. He was already a gifted experimenter in sound, television and movie technology when, during the Second World War, he participated as a civilian in a project for the Japanese Imperial Navy to develop a heat-seeking missile. During the assignment he met a young officer called Akio Morita. In 1945 Ibuka started a radio repair shop in a bombed-out building in Tokyo. The following year Morita, the scion of a 300-year-old sake and soy sauce dynasty, joined him. He and Ibuka founded the *Tokyo Tsushin Kogyo K. K.*, or Tokyo Telecommunications Engineering Corporation, with $500 in capital and seven employees. Ibuka was managing director. Their first offices were in an abandoned department store. Their first product, an electric rice cooker, failed to sell.

Ibuka, in the words of his obituary, 'was a person of an entirely different dimension. In the middle of the desolation of postwar Japan, he set out a grand aim ... and then made unending efforts to create a company that could realize this fine goal. Every single employee from Akio Morita down worked to achieve Masaru Ibuka's dream.' Differences in age and rank between the two men were meaningless: Ibuka, the relentlessly curious engineer, and Morita, the effervescent marketing man,

> **'IF PHILIPS CAN DO IT,** perhaps we can also manage.'
>
> Akio Morita, writing to Masaru Ibuka in the 1950s.

were unswerving in their determination and symbiotic in their partnership. By 1949 they had developed their own magnetic recording tape, and, shortly afterwards, the Type-G, Japan's first tape recorder.

THE TRANSISTOR REVOLUTION

Ibuka had heard of the invention of the transistor by Bell Laboratories and was convinced of its enormous potential for consumer electronics in terms of miniaturization and energy efficiency. He travelled to the United States, where he persuaded Bell, which was besieged with requests for military applications, to grant him a licence. Within a year, in 1955, Ibuka, Morita and their small team had refined the transistor and produced Japan's first pocket-sized transistor radio. The product was an immediate success in a resurgent Japanese economy of which they would come to be the pre-eminent symbol.

Morita had also travelled to the United States, and had been overwhelmed by the scale and energy of the booming nation. How could he and Ibuka compete with American multi-nationals? He experienced similar emotions in Germany, but was reassured in the Netherlands, where he visited the home of the giant Philips electronics company in the old town of Eindhoven: 'If Philips can do it,' he wrote to Ibuka, 'perhaps we can also manage.' Returning to America in 1955 armed with the company's first tape recorder and transistor radio, he failed to win a significant order until he visited the Bulova watch company. The purchasing agent offered him an order for 100,000 miniature radios – more than the capitalization of Tokyo Telecommunications Engineering Corporation – on condition that Bulova marketed them under its own name. Ibuka and the board cabled that he should accept. Morita, determined to build the company into an international brand, turned the offer down. Later he was to describe the decision as the best of his career.

Tokyo Telecommunications Engineering Corporation's TR-63 'Sony' transistor radio was the smallest yet to enter commercial production, and came in four different colours. The name was derived from the Latin root of the word for 'sound', the English word 'sonny' and the Japanese slang term *sony-sony*, meaning 'whizz-kids'. In 1957 the Sony TR-63 cracked open the American youth market – driven by the new phenomenon of rock and roll – to such an extent that within a year (like Kodak nearly 70 years earlier) the success of the product led Morita to rename the company.

Small is beautiful – with its superior understanding of the American youth market, Sony's transistorized consumer electronics cracked it wide open. Sony became the first Japanese company to be listed on the New York Stock Exchange.

Morita wanted a Roman-alphabet name – this was most unusual for Japanese companies at the time. He also wanted one that would enable the brand to fly free of specific industrial ties. Ibuka and their bank, Mitsui, were among the objectors. Morita stood firm: the Sony Corporation was born.

MORITA IN AMERICA

Morita's strategy to make Sony a global company was centred on the United States. The Sony Corporation of America, established in 1960, distributed the transistor radio, the first transistor television and the first solid-state video recorder. The following year Sony became the first Japanese company to be listed on the New York Stock Exchange. By 1962 the *Economist* magazine was stating 'Apostles of conventional wisdom from the entire world should be coming to Japan to study just how to emulate it.'

Morita, meanwhile, had decided to make the move in the other direction. His reasoning was simple: if he was going to succeed in his ambition to build a dominant presence for Sony in America – a presence that had to appear local and not 'foreign' – he needed to know more about the people to whom he was selling. No Japanese company had ever sent its second-in-command to live abroad, and Ibuka was reluctant to agree, but Morita again prevailed, having promised Ibuka that he would return to Tokyo for a week every two months. Even though Morita's wife Yoshiko spoke no English, the Morita family uprooted themselves and took up residence in an apartment in Manhattan sublet from the violinist Nathan Milstein.

The dynamic, charismatic and approachable Morita, with his silver hair parted down the middle and his slate-grey eyes – rumoured to be the result of White Russian ancestry – became something of a phenomenon in America, and his Fifth Avenue apartment turned into a hub of New York society. By the mid-1960s, although again commuting from Tokyo, Morita was sealing the network of contacts that would make him the only Japanese on the international boards of companies such as Pan Am, IBM and Morgan Guaranty. His profile in the United States, and that of Sony, grew throughout the 1970s, fulfilling his strategy for the company and making him the best-known Japanese citizen in the world. But throughout his career his interests remained the interests of Ibuka and Sony. By 1968 Sony was selling 5 million transistor radios a year in America.

> ## Morita tells it how it is
>
> In 1992 Akio Morita, co-founder of Sony, made an appearance at the World Economic Forum in Davos, at a time when America was feeling particularly resentful of Japanese export success. The 71-year-old galvanized the $14,000-a-head audience of American chief executives with a speech assuring them that the Japanese market *was* open to them … if they had something to offer the Japanese consumer. He also pointed out that American competitiveness might improve if the likes of those present paid themselves less extravagantly. The audience rose and applauded as one.

'JOY AND FUN'

Ibuka for his part managed the single-gun, three-beam project that in 1967 became the Sony Trinitron television and later a range of computer monitors. His policy remained that Sony researched and developed its own standards and technologies. A string of products followed, such as the Walkman personal stereo, a classic product of the Morita/Ibuka partnership. Morita had noticed that the young wanted music around them all the time, so Ibuka inspired his designers to 'overreach' themselves and improve on the bulky 'portable' cassette players of the time. Other innovations included the Betamax video format (subsequently overtaken in the marketplace by JVC's VHS format, but retained in use by the film and television industries); the Betacam film and TV camera; the Discman portable CD player; the MiniDisc; and, in 1994, the PlayStation.

Ibuka's philosophy, remarkable for its clarity, consistency and longevity, was that Sony's products 'must bring joy and fun to users … [he] always asked himself what was at the core of "making things", and thought in broad terms of how these products could enhance people's lives and cultures'. He retired from day-to-day involvement in Sony in 1976, but remained honorary chairman and a significant presence in the company.

In 1993 Morita – who was 13 years younger than his old friend – suffered a stroke that confined him to a wheelchair and deprived him of the power of speech. Ibuka died in 1997. 'In good times and bad, we were always together,' Morita's wife said of him on her husband's behalf at the funeral. Two years later Morita himself died.

FACING THE FUTURE

The early 21st century saw Sony lose competitive edge in areas of innovation such as the Palmtop and iPod. It also experienced problems with digital-camera components and exploding laptop batteries (subsequently resolved). With 163,000 people employed across one of the world's largest media and entertainment conglomerates – Sony by this time included CBS Records, Columbia Pictures and MGM – it was too early to tell how the future might pan out. The open-mindedness and sense of innovation that have been Sony hallmarks were confirmed in 2005 when the British-born Howard Stringer was installed as the first foreigner to run a major Japanese electronics company.

Ibuka, Morita and Sony changed the face of Japanese industry, shifting it from a talent for imitation to a talent for innovation. Ibuka's personal legacy includes the Sony Fund for Education and his book *Kindergarten is Too Late*, in which he asserts that the most significant stage in a child's intellectual development takes place between the ages of nine months and three years. Morita was the first and is still the greatest Japanese business 'guru', a man who bridged two worlds in his business and domestic lives. In Sony, two men who had forged a lifelong and radiant friendship in the crucible of war created a global company synonymous with quality and style, setting a benchmark to which all would-be world-changing consumer electronics companies will have to aspire.

1908
Birth of **Masura Ibuka**.

1921
Birth of **Akio Morita**.

1946
Ibuka and Morita found the **Tokyo Telecommunications Engineering Corporation**.

1955
The company produces the **first Japanese pocket-sized transistor radio**.

1958
The company is renamed **Sony**, after its successful TR-63 Sony transistor radio.

1960
Establishment of the **Sony Corporation of America**.

1967
Launch of the Sony **Trinitron television**.

1979
Launch of the Sony **Walkman**.

1988
Sony acquires **CBS Records**.

1989
Sony acquires **Columbia Pictures**.

1994
Launch of the Sony **PlayStation**.

1997
Death of **Masura Ibuka**.

1999
Death of **Akio Morita**.

2005
A Sony-led consortium acquires **MGM**.

ARAMCO / TAPLINE

33

1948 | *USA / Saudi Arabia*

Pumping Middle Eastern oil

Infrastructure

The Tapline Company – the Trans-Arabian Pipeline – is probably the least-known and most influential infrastructure project of the 20th century. The oil it carried fuelled the recovery of Europe after the Second World War, transformed Saudi Arabia into one of the richest economies on earth, and underwrote the OPEC 'oil shocks' of the 1970s – which exerted a profound effect on everyday life in the West and influenced the fortunes of companies around the world.

In 1943 'Star' Rogers, chairman of Texaco, and Harry Collier, president of Socal (formerly Standard Oil of California), paid a visit in Washington to the secretary of the interior, Harold Ickes. The two oilmen were concerned about the security of their concession in Saudi Arabia. Washington meanwhile had become concerned about a shortage of oil for its armed forces. Ickes

> **'THE DEFENCE OF SAUDI ARABIA** is vital to the defence of the United States.'
>
> President F.D. Roosevelt, 1943

had recently been appointed petroleum administrator for war. Within a few days, President Roosevelt sent a letter to secretary of state Edward Stettinius authorizing lend-lease aid and declaring, 'I hereby find that the defence of Saudi Arabia is vital to the defence of the United States.'

STRATEGIC INTERESTS

Ickes's relations with Texaco and Socal soon succumbed to the longstanding distrust between government and the oil companies. However, when Ickes suggested that the US government construct a 1000-mile pipeline to carry Saudi Arabian oil to the Mediterranean, the two companies promptly signed up to the deal. The news that the United States intended to acquire an interest in Saudi oil and to finance a refinery and massive pipeline aroused a storm of protest from the British and from independent American oil producers – this was not the 'American way'. Instead Aramco – the Arabian-American Oil Company formed as a joint-venture by Texaco and Socal – would build the refinery and pipeline with the backing and political protection of the Truman administration, on the grounds that Middle Eastern oil supply was essential to the success of the Marshall Plan for rebuilding postwar Europe. As Socal's adviser and geologist in the region Karl Twitchell observed, 'It committed our government to a fixed foreign policy for at least twenty-five years.'

By the end of the Second World War, with the British displaced from the Saudi king's favours, Texaco and Socal were aware that the Saudi desert concealed more crude oil than the whole of the United States. In 1945 they incorporated the Trans-Arabian Pipeline Company, known as Tapline. Progress was delayed by wrangling in Congress, uncertainty over steel supplies and by the civil war in Palestine (soon to become Israel). But in 1948 Aramco, strengthened by investment from Esso and Mobil, began work on the eastern end of the 30-inch diameter, 1040-mile long pipeline – the world's longest – that was intended to stretch from Qatif on the Persian Gulf northwest across Saudi Arabia to the Jordanian border. Under the overall management of Bechtel, the giant San Francisco-based construction company, the aim was to link up with the Williams Brothers pipeline that was working down from Sidon on the Mediterranean shore of Lebanon. This extraordinarily ambitious project, if it succeeded, would cross the frontiers of Saudi Arabia, Jordan, Syria and Lebanon, and enable Saudi Arabia to export crude oil beyond its shores to Europe.

BUILDING THE PIPELINE

Over a quarter of a million tons of steel plate were ordered from the United States Steel Corporation in Geneva, Utah, and rolled by Consolidated Western Steel in Los Angeles. The pipe was shipped 9000 miles from California to the Persian Gulf, unloaded on to a manmade island 3 miles out in deep water and brought ashore in ten-ton loads to the new settlement of Ras Misha'ab by a 'Skyhook' overhead cable system based on a technique used by the logging industry. Giant Kenworth trucks and trailers capable of loads of 50 tons or more hauled the pipe to each location in three-joint lengths of 93 feet. The surveyors who had marked out the terrain and the drillers who put down wells for the proposed pumping stations were the first Westerners to set foot on many parts of the route, most of which was barren desert with an average rainfall of 3 inches a year and temperatures as high as 130 degrees Fahrenheit.

The pipeline was to be laid through the heart of the Muslim world, and the policy of the company was to employ as much local labour as possible. This also made commercial sense, as skilled Western labour had to be flown or shipped halfway round the world. Between 1948 and 1950 the Tapline workforce of Americans, Bahrainis and Palestinians – transported by Saudi Arabian truck drivers and serviced by the General Contracting Company under the Saudi entrepreneur Suliman Olayan – drove diggers, bulldozers

Watering the desert

Every year the Bedouin and their camel herds migrated hundreds of miles back and forth in search of grazing and water, many of the animals perishing en route. To the nomads, Tapline's wells provided a lifeline: one of the wells alone supplied water to 12,000 Bedouin, 20,000 camels and 40,000 sheep and goats. During the summer of 1950 it was estimated that Tapline was supplying free water to some 100,000 Bedouins, 150,000 camels and 300,000 head of livestock.

The Trans-Arabian Pipeline carried the 'black gold' drilled and transported by Americans, bringing an uneasy coalition between the world's greatest power and Saudi Arabia, the heart of Islam.

and trenchers, built camps, ran dining rooms, blasted rock, and welded and laid pipe above and below ground at a rate as high as 1 mile a day through the deserts of Saudi Arabia. At its height, Tapline employed 14,600 Arabs – including former pearl divers, farmers and Bedouin nomads – but fewer than 2000 Americans. Many of the Americans lived at Aramco head-quarters in Dhahran in neat compounds surrounded by desert but equipped with all the comforts of American home life, including a cinema and baseball park, secure behind a high barbed-wire fence.

Tapline 'towns' sprang up out of the featureless desert wherever the company established pumping stations. These maintenance bases and permanent camps for Tapline employees became a magnet for the local Bedouin, who would pitch their tents nearby, cover them with sheets of corrugated iron and build walls around them. These settlements became trading posts for sheep, cattle, tent ropes, cheap tyres imported from Iraq and cheap gasoline exported back across the Iraqi border. Tapline also built roads, schools and medical centres, supplied telecommunications and bottled gas, provided a police force and drilled wells.

GEOPOLITICAL CONSEQUENCES

When the final weld connected the eastern and western sections of the pipeline on 25 September 1950, a further two months were needed to fill the pipe. On 10 November the first Saudi oil began to arrive at Sidon in Lebanon, and the first tanker was loaded on 2 December. Tapline's 1040 miles of pipe replaced 3600 miles of sea journey from the Persian Gulf through the politically volatile Suez Canal to the Mediterranean. The annual output of the pipeline was the equivalent of 60 tankers in continuous operation, and the rate of throughput reached 600,000 barrels a day. The project did indeed fuel the Marshall Plan for the rebuilding of Europe and the economic development of Lebanon. Tapline also transformed the fortunes of everyone involved in its construction, from the Arab sub-contractors and Bedouin traders to the thousands of entrepreneurs encouraged by Aramco's Local Industrial Development Department and the likes of Suliman Olayan, who became one of the most successful private investors in America. Above all it transformed Saudi Arabia, once an impoverished desert kingdom, first into a grateful freeholder which leased oil reserves to Texaco, Socal, Exxon and Mobil, and then into a hydrocarbon super-power through which OPEC dictated much of world economics in the 1970s and 1980s. Aramco itself was fully owned by Saudi Arabia by 1980 and renamed Saudi Aramco. Today it is the largest oil corporation in the world.

Tapline was always vulnerable to the volatility of the frontiers it crossed. The 1967 Six-Day War saw the Golan Heights section come under Israeli control, although the Israelis permitted the pipeline to continue in operation. In 1976, after years of dispute between Saudi Arabia, Lebanon and Syria over transit fees, the line beyond Jordan ceased to carry oil. The rest of the line carried modest amounts until 1990, when the Saudis cut off the supply in response to Jordan's support for Iraq during the first Gulf War. The line is currently unfit for oil transport, but recent estimates have suggested that the cost of exporting via the Tapline through Haifa to Europe would be 40 per cent cheaper than shipping by tanker through the Suez Canal. In 2005 restoration of the Tapline was being considered by the Jordanian government.

By this time, the oil genie was long out of the box. Oil has fuelled coups or wars in Iran, Abu Dhabi, Libya, Oman and Iraq. Since the 1990s, Saudi Arabia's providential wealth – privately deployed by the likes of Osama bin Laden – has also bolstered Islamic fundamentalism, much of it fuelled by rage at the perceived corrupting affect the oil billions have brought to the kingdom. A portion of these very same billions has filtered through to the jihadists responsible for the 9/11 attacks on New York and the 7/7 attacks on London, and who are now resurgent in Iraq and Afghanistan. The black gold Roosevelt deemed so 'vital to the defence of the United States' has inextricably linked the fortunes of the world's greatest power with those of its most unstable region.

TIMELINE

1933
The Saudi government grants a concession to Socal (Standard Oil of California), which forms a subsidiary called **California-Arabian Standard Oil Company**.

1936
Texaco purchases a half share in the concession.

1938
Discovery of a productive well near **Dhahran**.

1943
President Roosevelt recognizes that America has vital strategic interests in **Saudi Arabia**.

1944
The California-Arabian Standard Oil Company becomes the Arabian American Oil Company – **Aramco**.

1945
Texaco and Socal incorporate the Trans-Arabian Pipeline Company – **Tapline**.

1948
Work begins on the construction of the oil pipeline from **Saudi Arabia to the Mediterranean**.

1950
Completion of the pipeline.

1980
The Saudi government brings Aramco completely under its ownership, renaming it **Saudi Aramco**.

BIC / BIRO

34

1950 | *France / Argentina*

Democratized handwriting

The ballpoint pen

Ladislao José Biró, born László József Bíró in Budapest, Hungary, in 1899, was visiting the printers of a magazine he edited for the Hungarian government in the 1930s when he noticed that the ink used in the printing shop dried quickly, leaving the paper clean and smudge-free. In an age when notes written by dip pen or fountain pen often smudged, and the pens themselves required regular refilling and often leaked, this was Bíró's eureka moment. Since 1950, Bic – which took up Bíró's invention – has sold more than 100 billion ballpoint pens, or 57 every second. The Bic Cristal has become a design classic and forms part of the permanent collection of the Museum of Modern Art in New York City.

The idea of the ballpoint was not new even in the 1930s – a primitive version was produced as early as 1895, and subsequent attempts had been made using ordinary ink in a pad stuffed down the barrel of the pen. Bíró's leap of imagination was to dispose of the nib in favour of a steel ball held in a brass casing; this was fed with a glutinous form of ink (developed by his chemist brother Georg) from a plastic tube contained within an outer barrel. The act of writing caused the ball to revolve, so transferring ink to the paper, where it dried virtually instantly. The moment the pen – and the pressure on the ballpoint – was lifted, the ink stopped flowing, no matter which way the pen was pointing.

FROM BUDAPEST TO BUENOS AIRES

Bíró was a journalist, artist, sculptor and amateur hypnotist. He was also a communist and a Jew, and at the outbreak of the Second World War he fled Budapest for Paris. With the German invasion of France he was forced to flee once again, this time to Argentina. Having developed and patented his invention there with the encouragement of the president, he was forced to spend most of his one-third share of the $80,000 seed capital of Biro Pens of Argentina on bringing the rest of his family across from Europe to safety in Buenos Aires. He also sold a licence for a reasonable if modest sum to an Englishman, Henry Martin.

Martin was aware that navigators in Royal Air Force bombers were hampered in their work by the use of pencils, which needed to be sharpened constantly, and by conventional fountain pens, which leaked ink over their maps and reacted unfavourably to changes in air pressure. The RAF tested the pen in combat and placed an order for 100,000 at a cost of £2.15s each – about half the average weekly wage. Martin went into partnership with the Miles Aircraft Company to form the Miles-Martin Pen Company. In a disused aircraft hangar near Reading, 20 young women manufactured ballpoint pens for the war effort.

Back in Buenos Aires, meanwhile, Bíró's invention was retailing for the equivalent of $40 or £25. He himself received far less than his original one-third share of the $2 million paid by Eversharp and Faber in 1944 for the exclusive rights to market the 'Birome' in North America. As he recalled many years later, 'I had sold most of my shares to buy lives.'

In Britain in 1945, during the run-up to the first peacetime Christmas since 1938, the Miles-Martin Pen Company marketed the 'Biro' as a luxury item costing 55 shillings, with the option of a 5-shilling refill and a guarantee dated by the retailer that if the pen ran out of ink within three months the customer could claim a free replacement: 'Writes an average of 200,000 words without refilling ... with a velvet touch and a smooth gliding action ... A boon to left-handed writers ... Does not leak at any altitude.' Within four years the Biro was outselling conventional fountain pens in the UK. When Gimbels in America launched a cheaper rival version in the same year, advertised as 'the first pen that writes under water', the New York store shifted nearly 10,000 at $12.50 each. Bíró, who had neglected to register the patent in America, received not a cent.

THE BIRTH OF *LE BIC*

The Miles-Martin Pen Company took its short-term profits and sold out to a new company, Biro-Swan, which in turn sold out to the Maybe Todd Corporation. The Biro in its luxury UK form subsequently disappeared. In 1950, however, the French businessman Baron Marcel Bich had bought the patent rights from László Bíró himself with a very different application in mind. Bich had founded the Bic company (the 'h' was dropped to avoid an inappropriate English pronunciation of the name) in 1945 with Edouard Buffard and set up a factory to manufacture parts for mechanical pencils

TIMELINE

——— *1899* ———
Birth of **László József Bíró**.

——— *1931* ———
Bíró exhibits his **first ballpoint pen** at the Budapest World Fair.

——— *1940* ———
Bíró leaves Europe for Argentina, where he **patents** his pen.

——— *1944* ———
Eversharp and Faber acquire rights to market the 'Birome' in North America.

——— *1945* ———
In the UK, the **Miles-Martin Pen Company** market the 'Biro' as a luxury item.

——— *1950* ———
The **Bic** company in France, founded by Baron Marcel Bich, buys the patent rights from László Bíró.

——— *1953* ———
Bic launches the classic **Cristal**.

——— *1960* ———
Bic starts to market its pen in the **USA**.

——— *1985* ———
Death of **László József Bíró**.

——— *1994* ———
Death of **Baron Bich**.

> **'WRITES AN AVERAGE** of 200,000 words without refilling ... with a velvet touch and a smooth gliding action ...'
>
> Advertising copy for the Biro in Britain, 1945

Status item 1950s-style – invented by a Hungarian émigré to Argentina and tested in combat by the RAF, the new 'ballpoint' pen was an immediate success in postwar Britain and America.

and fountain pens. Bich's plan was to harness Bíró's technology for mass production of an inexpensive, reliable, disposable ballpoint. Bic's Décolletage Plastique design team came up with a transparent polystyrene barrel, polypropylene cap, tungsten-carbide ball and brass/nickel silver tip with the ink and cap in four colours: blue, black, red and green. Later versions of the cap would feature a small hole to prevent asphyxiation if swallowed. The non-refillable, non-renewable Bic pen had a point size of one millimetre and contained ink made to a secret, solvent-based formula that could write for a distance equivalent to between two and three kilometres.

Bic launched the Cristal in France in 1953, and it soon became the main product of the company. Also known as the Bic Stic, it was launched in Britain in 1957. Schoolteachers frowned on the pen when it appeared and claimed – with some justification – that children could not learn to write properly with them. As sales of fountain pens slipped, however, the economical and reliable new pen became accepted as an alternative in many quarters. Two years later, in 1960, the Bic was released in the United States, where the Bic company had taken over the Waterman Pen Corporation of Milford, Connecticut. Market resistance was stiff at first, but Bic sold the pens for 29 cents each with a television advertising campaign using the slogan 'Writes first, every time.' Within a year, Bic had dropped the price to 10 cents, and by 1969 the Waterman-Bic Pen Corporation was selling 330 million ballpoints a year and had captured half the American market. Waterman-Bic also pushed its 19-cent throwaways and 49-cent retractables into Canada. Its sales force was noted for the ability to sell to owners of Mom-and-Pop shops, supermarkets and department stores on the basis of marketing ideas such as a fistful of pens in a bright display pocket, with three pens for 49 cents and eight for a dollar. Television commercials featured a Bic ballpoint being buried by a bulldozer, stamped on by the boot of a flamenco dancer and shot from a rifle, only to write again perfectly.

THE SOCIÉTÉ BIC

By the beginning of the 1970s, Société Bic's 18 plants were selling 1 billion ballpoints a year in 96 countries. Baron Bich himself kept a low profile, giving a rare 'face to face' interview with *L'Expansion* magazine but refusing to be photographed. He spent much of his time aboard his 12-metre yacht *Sovereign* (in the ballpoint industry he was known as *roi*, or 'king') and drove around Paris in his black Bentley – the trunk of which was held ajar by a telephone directory so that his Irish setter inside could breathe properly. He died in 1994, the fifth-richest man in France.

Today Société Bic, based in Clichy, France, is still controlled by the Bich family, who own 42 per cent of its stock and control 55 per cent of its voting power. The company has sold more than 100 billion disposable ballpoints, making it the world's bestselling pen. The pen and other stationery items are the lead products in a range that includes lighters, razors and surfboards. Bic is the third most-recognized brand in France and the best-known French brand in the United States, where, regardless of manufacturer, ballpoints are frequently referred to as 'Bics'.

Ballpoint pens are still known as 'biros' in many countries including the United Kingdom, Australia and New Zealand. In Argentina, regardless of manufacturer, they are known as 'biromes'. László Bíró himself withdrew from the business in 1947 to concentrate on painting. He also continued to invent, and among other things developed a pick-proof lock, a wrist dial that taped a record of blood temperature and a heat-proof tile. He died a wealthy man in Buenos Aires in 1985.

> **'WRITES FIRST,** every time'
> Bic advertising slogan in the USA, 1960

Argentina's Inventor's Day is celebrated on Bíró's birthday, 29 September. In the United States he was inducted into the Inventors Hall of Fame in Akron, Ohio, on 4 May 2007.

SEARLE

1961 | *USA*

35

'Welcome to the post-pill paradise.' JOHN UPDIKE

The oral contraceptive

The pharmaceutical company G.D. Searle was founded in Omaha, Nebraska, in 1888 by Gideon Daniel Searle. Its better-known products have included Metamucil, the first bulk laxative; Dramamine, a drug to counter motion sickness; and NutraSweet, an artificial sweetener. But towering above these was the product it launched in 1961, a product that had the potential to change the lives of half the world's population – and the lives of the other half too.

> **'NO WOMAN CAN CALL HERSELF FREE** who cannot choose the time to be a mother or not as she sees fit.'
>
> Margaret Sanger, *The Case for Birth Control* (1917)

It is unthinkable today in Western societies that a woman should not be able to control her own fertility; yet this was the case until less than half a century ago. Post-natal mortality, pre-emptive abortion and fear of pregnancy clouded marriages and relationships. The evolution of the contraceptive pill was no scientific accident, neither was it the work of God or the Devil. Rather it was the outcome of a thirty-year journey, one that gave women greater ownership of their bodies, and the ability to decide when they would accept the gift of a child.

THE STRUGGLE FOR FAMILY PLANNING

In 1916 the American nurse and women's health campaigner Margaret Sanger, together with her sister Ethel Byrne and Fania Mindel, opened the first birth-control clinic in America, in Brownsville, New York. Their mission was to provide contraceptive advice to hundreds of impoverished immigrant women; the latter demonstrated their need by queuing for hours before the clinic opened. Not unexpectedly, Sanger, Byrne and Mindell were arrested under the 1873 Comstock Laws, which defined contraceptive information as obscene and forbade its dissemination through the US Mail. Sanger, author of publications such as *The Woman Rebel* and *What Every Girl Should Know*, had already been indicted for the offence. The clinic was closed down within a few days, and two of the three women were jailed. Byrne staged a hunger and thirst strike and became the first woman to be force-fed in an American prison.

Throughout the 1920s and 1930s the birth-control movement gained worldwide support from educated women and men attracted by Sanger's lectures. Her foundation of *The Birth Control Review* and the American Birth Control League also addressed issues such as population growth and famine.

The enfranchisement of women on both sides of the Atlantic furthered the cause of a woman's right to determine when or whether to have a child, but powerful opposition remained from the Roman Catholic Church. In 1936 a landmark judgment by Judge Augustus Hand in the case of US vs. One Package of Japanese Pessaries ruled that, given data on the damages of unplanned pregnancy and the benefits of contraception, such advice could no longer be classified as

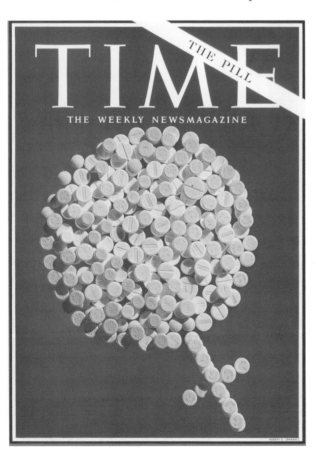

The cover of *Time* magazine, 7 April 1967 – the pill polarized America and eventually the world in the argument for and against a woman's right to control her biological destiny.

obscene. Margaret Sanger herself initiated the case by leaking information about her own contraceptive supplies to the postal authorities. The judgment applied only to New York, Connecticut and Vermont; nearly 30 years would pass before married couples across the country could obtain contraceptives from physicians.

HORMONE RESEARCH

Meanwhile, scientists had determined the structure of the steroid hormones – the sex hormones oestrogen, progesterone and testosterone – and by 1937 discovered that high doses of progesterone suppressed ovulation in rabbits. Progesterone was initially only obtainable from European pharmaceutical companies at prohibitive cost. Only when Russell Marker, a professor of organic chemistry at Pennsylvania State University (and subsequently co-founder of Syntex), developed methods of synthesizing progesterone did the price of steroid hormones fall – almost 200-fold over the 1940s.

In 1951 the hormone researcher Gregory Pincus of the Worcester Foundation for Experimental Biology met Margaret Sanger at a Manhattan dinner hosted by Abraham Stone, medical director and vice president of the Planned Parenthood Federation of America (PPFA). Stone helped Pincus to obtain a small grant from the PPFA to conduct research into a hormonal contraceptive that could be administered by injection or pill. Pincus's research expanded on the 1937 rabbit ovulation findings, and he approached G.D. Searle & Company for funding. They turned him down. Among the reasons cited were that Pincus's previous research for them had been 'a lamentable failure'. In addition, none of the Searle management – who were all men – believed a woman would ever take a pill every day simply for the purpose of contraception. The anti-birth-control laws were still on the statute books in 30 states, they pointed out, and the pharmaceutical companies feared a backlash from Catholics, who comprised 25 per cent of the American population. Many Searle employees were also Catholics. The company did however retain Pincus as a consultant, and provided him with chemical compounds.

TOWARDS THE PILL

With Pincus's work on hold for lack of funding, unknown either to Pincus or Sanger, the chemist Carl Djerassi and others working for Syntex in Mexico City had developed an effective progesterone pill. At Searle, Frank Colton had developed an effective oral compound that also worked as an anti-ovulent, called norethynodrel. Pincus, meanwhile, discovered that gynaecologist John Rock at Harvard had been successfully testing what amounted to an oral contraceptive. Again, the key figure, then 74 years old, was Margaret Sanger. Sanger introduced Pincus to her long-time friend and supporter Katharine Dexter McCormack, an heiress and suffragist, and the first woman to graduate with a science degree from Massachusetts Institute of Technology. McCormack, like

1873
US Comstock Laws define contraceptive information as **obscene**.

1888
Foundation of **G.D. Searle & Company**.

1916
Margaret Sanger opens the first birth-control clinic in America.

1936
Judge Augustus Hand rules that birth-control information is not obscene.

1937
Scientists establish that high doses of progesterone suppressed ovulation in rabbits.

1951
Gregory Pincus starts to develop a hormonal contraceptive.

1954
Pincus begins to test **norethynedrol** supplied by Searle as a contraceptive pill.

1960
The US Food and Drug Administration approves the **sale of contraceptive pills**.

1961
Searle starts to market **Enovid** as an oral contraceptive.

1968
Pope Paul VI issues an encyclical condemning 'artificial' contraception.

many, was outraged by the revelations in the Kinsey Report that 22 per cent of married women in America had been forced to endure an abortion, and that abortion ended 90 per cent of pregnancies outside marriage. McCormack wrote a cheque for $40,000 to Pincus, who joined forces with Rock. In 1954, under the guise of a fertility study, the two men began the first tests of the contraceptive pill on 50 women in Brookline, Massachusetts, a state with extremely restrictive anti-birth-control laws. The pills themselves were norethynedrol provided by Searle.

The Brookline trials proved conclusive. Not one of the 50 women ovulated while on the drug. Pincus and Rock further refined the pill and gave it the proprietary name Enovid. Subsequent trials took place in Puerto Rico (which was outside the anti-birth-control laws), Haiti, Mexico and Los Angeles. With word of the drug reaching the public and Enovid going on sale as a therapy for menstrual disorders with the warning that it would prevent ovulation, over half a million American married women mysteriously developed these disorders and asked their physicians for the drug.

The role of Rumsfeld

Searle's workforce was decimated in the 1970s and 1980s by a new CEO, a certain Donald Rumsfeld. He subsequently engineered the sale of the company to Monsanto, reputedly making millions. Searle later became part of Pfizer.

A QUIET REVOLUTION

On 9 May 1960, in the year the world population reached 3 billion, the American Food and Drug Administration approved the sale of oral steroid pills for contraception. Searle first officially marketed Enovid to physicians as an oral contraceptive pill on 11 May 1961. In the same year, Dr C. Lee Buxton of Yale Medical School and Estelle Griswold of Connecticut Planned Parenthood opened four Planned Parenthood clinics. In an echo of what had happened to Margaret Sanger nearly 50 years earlier, they were arrested – but this time the case brought to national attention the anachronistic nature of the anti-birth-control laws. By the time Searle's exclusive licence to market Enovid expired in 1962, 1.2 million American women were taking Enovid, and many remained loyal to Searle and its product. By 1965 one out of every four married women in America was 'on the Pill', and could choose from a range of products offered by major pharmaceutical companies – including Syntex, which marketed the Ortho Novum pill developed in the 1950s by Carl Djerassi.

Margaret Sanger died aged 86 in 1966. Gregory Pincus died aged 64 the following year of a blood disease thought to have been caused by exposure to laboratory chemicals. The man who never received a cent in royalties is today regarded as the pioneer of sex-hormone research and oncology – and one of the most influential scientists of the 20th century. Katharine Dexter McCormack, who donated over $2 million to enable this research, also died in 1967, aged 92. No major newspaper ran her obituary, and her contribution to the Pill went unmarked at the time. In 1998 she featured as a character in T.C. Boyle's novel *Riven Rock*; in 2000 she was inducted into the Michigan Women's Hall of Fame. John Rock died aged 94 in 1984. Carl Djerassi was made wealthy from Syntex and became an influential author and philanthropist.

SOCIAL AND ECONOMIC CONSEQUENCES

The social and economic consequences of the Pill have been immense. The principal effects have been to give women unprecedented control over their own fertility, and to distinguish procreation from sexual expression. In spite of many Catholics' expectations that the Church would take a more enlightened attitude to contraception, Pope Paul VI's *Humanae Vitae* in 1968 ignored the recommendations of the Papal Commission and condemned all 'artificial' forms of birth control. By 1970 two-thirds of all Catholic women were nonetheless using contraception, and 28 per cent were on the Pill. Feminists in the 1970s criticized the Pill as a male invention and a possible source of breast cancer; these debates are ongoing, but the Pill in its many contemporary forms is generally regarded as safe by governments, the medical establishment and the public.

It is not only the Catholic hierarchy who abhor the Pill as a threat to their control over human sexuality – the same attitude prevails in other patriarchal societies, in Islamic countries and elsewhere. Nevertheless, today over 100 million married and single women around the world are on the Pill and take for granted their right to determine their biological destinies in a manner punishable by law fewer than 50 years ago.

YVES SAINT LAURENT

1962 | *France*

36

'Fashions fade, but style is eternal.' YVES SAINT LAURENT

Haute couture
Ready-to-wear fashion

Yves Saint Laurent (YSL) is the most famous fashion brand in the world, and for four decades its founder reigned as the most influential fashion designer in the world. The story of Yves Saint Laurent is that of a brilliantly gifted outsider who, at the age of 21, rescued the fortunes of the greatest French *haute couture* house, set up his own label and became the first designer to democratize high fashion and bring its trends to ready-to-wear (*prêt-à-porter*) clothing. He thus transformed the way that women dressed, and in the process built a new kind of global luxury goods group.

Yves-Henri-Donat-Mathieu Saint Laurent was born on 1 August 1936 in Oran, Algeria, where his parents were *pieds noirs* – French settlers. The brilliant colours and dark undercurrents of Arab culture patterned his upbringing as the only son of a possessive mother and distant father. The young Yves lived doubly 'forbidden' lives as the child of foreign colonialists and as an artistic and homosexual teenager bullied at school. He found furtive if willing outlets for his desires with Arab men, for whom there was no shame in sex with a Westerner as long as the Arab adopted the dominant role.

THE REALIZATION OF A VOCATION

Saint Laurent initially wanted to be a theatrical designer, but soon the fashion pages of his mother's copies of *Vogue* and *Paris-Match* attracted his attention. In 1953, aged 17, his three black-and-white sketches of a coat, a dress and a suit won him third prize in a prestigious contest organized by the International Wool Secretariat in Paris. Accompanied by his mother he made his first visit to the French capital, where she ordered a new gown from the *haute couture* house of Jean Patou and secured for Yves an introduction to Michel de Brunhoff, editor-in-chief of French *Vogue*. De Brunhoff encouraged Yves to enrol in an industry design course at the Chambre Syndicale de la Couture. In Paris the shy, bespectacled boy embraced metropolitan life, won three out of seven prizes in the following year's competition – and acknowledged his ambition to become a famous *couturier*. His opportunity came at the age of 19 in 1955, when he was offered a job as a junior assistant with the greatest designer of the day, Christian Dior.

> '**SAINT LAURENT** has saved France!'
>
> The French press greet Saint Laurent's first collection.

Belle de jour – French movie star Catherine Deneuve and designer Yves Saint Laurent at the opening of the first Rive Gauche *prêt-à-porter* boutique in Paris, 1966. It took $24,000 on the first day.

Dior was more than a designer: he was the guardian of French national pride whose 'New Look' had single-handedly restored femininity to women after the austerity and rigours of the Second World War. Dior gave Saint Laurent an elegant, alluring environment in which to demonstrate his gifts. In 1957, when Dior suddenly died, Saint Laurent, at 21, was named the *dauphin* or heir apparent of the most influential fashion house in the world. In his first collection he was determined to create his own combination of elegance and wearability within the classic Dior style. The 'trapeze'-line dress caused a sensation, and the French press proclaimed: 'Saint Laurent has saved France!' The *New York Times* declared: 'Today's collection has made a French national hero out of Dior's successor, Yves Saint Laurent.' This was also the beginning of a treadmill on which he would be expected to repeat this success every six months in the face of fierce competition.

GOING IT ALONE

Saint Laurent's subsequent collections dropped the hem more than the conventional two inches per season and then lifted it to reveal the knees. This outraged some sections of the British press, but broadened the appeal of Dior from its middle-aged client base towards younger women attracted to American movies and the 'beatnik' street culture of the Left Bank. While the press and his employers expressed joy and alarm at this, Saint Laurent's life was overturned when he was drafted for military service in 1960 to fight in Algeria. After 20 days' training in France he suffered a severe nervous breakdown. He slowly recovered, only to find his job at Dior taken by his assistant Marc Bohan. Saint Laurent, encouraged by his lover Pierre Berge, sued and won damages that went some way towards the cost of opening their own small *couture* house, in which the couple were joined by two of his former Dior colleagues. Berge was becoming desperate for funds to launch the business when he found an unlikely saviour in the 'American Uncle', J. Mack Robinson, a self-made millionaire from second-hand car dealerships and motor-loan companies. With Robinson's backing they opened the house of Saint Laurent – YSL – in 1962. The collection of 104 outfits drew mixed reviews, but Berge orchestrated the occasion expertly and jealously – as he would the whole of Saint Laurent's career.

Saint Laurent's second collection combined stunning sophistication and street chic and established him as *the* couturier for the swinging sixties. J. Mack Robinson amicably sold his shareholding in YSL in 1965 to Richard Salomon, president of the American cosmetics company Charles of the Ritz. With the corporate side of the business driven by Berge and Salomon, Saint Laurent was able to concentrate on finding his full independent identity. He gathered around him a coterie of 'muses', including Clara Saint, Betty Catroux and movie star

Catherine Deneuve, and befriended the likes of Andy Warhol, incorporating his images, and those of other artists such as Mondrian, into his designs. Saint Laurent opened his first Rive Gauche boutique for women in 1966, in Paris; the shop took $24,000 on the first day.

By 1967 and the 'Summer of Love', Saint Laurent was the hippy *de luxe*, buying his first house with Berge in Marrakesh and hanging out with the Gettys. Saint Laurent would recall many years later 'Talitha and Paul Getty lying on a starlit terrace in Marrakesh, beautiful and damned, and a whole generation assembled as if for eternity where the curtain of the past seemed to lift before an extraordinary future.'

AN INTERNATIONAL BRAND

In 1968 YSL opened a Rive Gauche store on Madison Avenue in New York City and a similar boutique in London the following year, when the first men's range appeared. As the company grew in the early 1970s the success of the business was accompanied by a greater provocative-ness on the part of its creative genius. One of his models had already appeared bare-breasted under silk chiffon trimmed with ostrich feathers; in 1971 Saint Laurent himself posed for an iconic nude photograph wearing nothing but his spectacles. The subsequent controversy around the world helped to generate free publicity for the first YSL For Men perfume, and further fuelled the Saint Laurent myth. While the YSL empire grew to include *couture*, *prêt-à-porter*, sweaters, neckties, linens, children's clothes and fragrances, Berge sold licensing rights to YSL products, and Berge and Salomon orchestrated the buy-back of YSL from Charles of the Ritz's new owner, Squibb.

> **'YVES SAINT LAURENT ... will change the course of fashion around the world.'**
> *New York Times, 1976*

Saint Laurent played as hard as he worked, mixing drink and drugs not only as a lifestyle, but as a legacy of the medication given to him after his 1960 breakdown. By 1976 he and Berge had broken up as a couple, but the business partnership endured, and Saint Laurent combined designs for theatre with the classic *couture* styles that he would refine for the rest of his career. His 1976 collection – inspired by Leon Bakst's costume designs for the Ballets Russes in the early years of the 20th century – prompted the *New York Times* to declare on the front page: 'Yves Saint Laurent presented a fall *couture* collection today that will change the course of fashion around the world ... it is as stunning in its impact as the collection Christian Dior showed in 1947.'

A LIVING LEGEND

Often on the brink of collapse and even the subject of rumours of his death, an aura of fragility surrounded Saint Laurent through launch after launch. In 1983 he became the first living fashion designer to be the subject of an exhibition at the Metropolitan Museum in New York. The YSL retrospective was seen by 1 million people, and transferred to Beijing and Paris the following year, followed by Sydney and St Petersburg in 1987. In 1989 YSL went public at a value of $500 million; the flotation on the Paris stock exchange was heavily oversubscribed. In 1993 Sanofi paid $650 million in shares for YSL. The deal rebounded on Berge personally, when he was fined the following year for insider trading.

This proved to be the final flowering of Saint Laurent as a designer. In 1996, the year of his sixtieth birthday, he unveiled his July *haute couture* collection to rave reviews, and two years later he retired. Gucci subsequently bought the YSL brand, and Tom Ford designed its ready-to-wear collection. Showered with honours, Saint Laurent retreated to his house in Marrakesh where he has remained more or less ever since. Like the Left Bank hero of a *nouvelle vague* movie, he was always ultimately alone. In 2002 the *haute couture* house of Saint Laurent closed for good, but Gucci continues to use the YSL brand for its ready-to-wear range. In retirement, Saint Laurent and Berge created the Saint Laurent Museum in Paris, with a collection of 15,000 objects and 5000 pieces of clothing.

Saint Laurent's great talents included the ability to adapt from sources across the arts, and to feminize the male wardrobe while adapting many of its subtleties for women. He famously provided nine-to-five working women with an equivalent to men's business suits, in the form of severe trouser suits in tailored pinstripes, or dark double-breasted jackets to wear with matching skirts; there was also *le smoking* – the black tuxedo jacket for evening wear. He uniquely combined an understanding of printed textiles and luxurious materials such as silk, satin, chiffon and taffeta with a commitment to practical wearability. His legacy is one of unparalleled leadership, brilliant creativity, glamour, celebrity, commercial innovation and wealth. Above all, he created an exclusive yet accessible style for those who chose to embrace it. As he observed: 'Fashions fade, but style is eternal.'

NOKIA

1967 | *Finland*

Connecting people

Mobile telephony

Nokia owes its origins to a wood-pulp mill established in 1865 on the banks of a river in southern Finland. The telecommunications company that now has the name was initially an amalgam of timber mills, rubber works and manufacturers of telegraph and telephone cables. Today it is one of the world's most admired and successful companies – yet many people outside Finland have no idea where it is based.

Finland – a third of which lies to the north of the Arctic Circle – is bordered by Sweden, Norway and Russia. It is a land of forests, lakes and rivers, and the principal industries for centuries revolved around timber. In the 19th century Finland's fortunes were intimately connected with those of imperial Russia, of which it was effectively a colony.

PAPER, RUBBER AND CABLES

It was in 1865 that a mining engineer called Fredrik Idestam brought his improved method of paper manufacture to the banks of the Tammerkoski rapids in southern Finland and created the modern Finnish paper industry. While 15 per cent of Finland's population would die of famine the following year, Idestam and his wood-pulp mill flourished, and shortly thereafter he moved his operations to the town of Nokia on the Nokianverta River nearby, where there were better resources for hydropower production. In 1871 he established a company called Nokia Ab.

The company and the town grew rapidly, and by 1902 Nokia Ab had extended into electricity generation. From the early 1920s three jointly owned companies – Nokia Ab, Finnish Rubber Works and Finnish Cable Works (whose president was a former Olympic wrestler) – dominated the area. Finland's geographical remoteness, vast distances, low population and lack of many natural resources engendered a rugged entrepreneurialism in the Finns, and since independence in 1917 a spirit of strong nationalism has helped to generate a strong drive to build export markets for Finnish goods. This drive has been helped by a number of deep-water ports, and by the general economic growth in Scandinavia after the Second World War, in which technologically advanced market economies were encouraged by liberal governments and strong welfare systems.

KARI KAIRAMO AND THE NOKIA CORPORATION

In 1967 the three Finnish companies at Nokia were merged into a single conglomerate: the Nokia Corporation. Nokia Ab was in fact the smallest company in the group, whose first president was the head of Finnish Cable, Björn Westerlund. The collective businesses of the new Nokia Corporation were thus rubber (including bicycle and car tyres and Wellington boots), telephone and telegraph cables, electronics (including televisions and personal computers), power generation, and forestry and paper. It was from this last sector that Kari Kairamo joined the Nokia Corporation in its first year.

Kairamo was a dynamic, charismatic individual who rose up through the ranks with seemingly infinite energy and attention to detail. In 1974 he was appointed head of Nokia, and set out to build a multi-industry conglomerate that would compete in the international markets and bring Finland closer to Western Europe. He engineered a string of acquisitions and joint ventures to generate new products, especially in the growing field of telecommunications. Finnish Cable had already developed VHF radio for commercial and military use with the television company Salora Oy. After further mergers, the 1979 Mobira Oy radio telephone was followed in 1981 by Nordic Mobile Telephone, the world's first international roaming

A costly brick

Nokia's 1987 Mobira Cityman was the world's first handheld mobile telephone. In spite of weighing in at 1 lb 12 oz, and in spite of its £3000 price tag, it swiftly became a status item among 'yuppies' in the City of London and other leading European financial centres.

mobile telephone network. Nokia bought Salora Oy in 1984, and in the same year its Mobira Talkman became the first portable mobile telephone. Throughout the 1970s and early 1980s the company also developed the first digital switches for telephone exchanges.

Kairamo established close commercial and personal links with both the Soviet Union and Western Europe. In Finland he became a legend and a national hero. Nokia had become as synonymous with Finland as Volvo had with Sweden and General Motors was with America. However, Kairamo was an innately troubled soul, and when in 1988 his expansion programme – particularly in television and personal computers – brought financial problems commensurate with the size of the company, he committed suicide.

LEADING THE MOBILE REVOLUTION

Nokia had already been developing GSM (global system for mobile communications), which could carry data as well as voice traffic. With the deregulation of European telecommunications markets the company was perfectly positioned when GSM became the European standard. In 1991 the world's first GSM call was made over a Nokia

China's millions of Nokia mobile telephone users owe their ability to stay in touch to a product that began life in one of the world's least populated countries.

network on a Nokia telephone by Finnish prime minister Harri Holkeri. Kari Kairamo's successor Jorma Ollila had taken the decision to focus on telecommunications, and the rubber, cable and consumer electronics areas of the company were sold off during the course of the 1990s. The collapse of the Soviet Union badly damaged Finnish exports, bringing severe recession. But by 1993 the company and the country were beginning to recover, with an understandable commitment to a federal Europe. By this time the explosion in GSM mobiles in Europe, North America, South America and Asia exceeded even Ollila and Nokia's expectations, to the point where by the mid-1990s the company was struggling to meet demand.

By 1998 Nokia was the world leader in mobile telephony, supplying GSM systems to more than 90 operators around the world. The first internet mobile in 1999 was followed by the first 3G ('third generation') phone capable of music, video calls and web browsing, and a host of other innovations, including, in 2005, the Nseries telephone, video and multimedia device. In the same year the billionth Nokia phone was sold – in Nigeria.

A GLOBAL GIANT

Jorma Ollila presided over a long period of growth, although Nokia's reputation at home was somewhat tarnished in 2004 by a period of restructuring, lay-offs and bad publicity. In 2006 chief financial officer Olli-Pekka Kallasvuo took over as president, with a board of directors drawn from Finland, Britain, America, Germany, Sweden and India. Since then, Nokia's mobile-telephone digital cameras and music-download telephones have challenged Kodak and Apple, and Nokia has established research centres and programmes at the Massachusetts Institute of Technology and Stanford and Cambridge Universities. Its intellectual properties today include over 11,000 patent families. In 2007 Nokia and Siemens of Germany announced the merger of their networks and carrier operations, with the combined headquarters to be based in Helsinki. Nokia's global market share is around 36 per cent; its nearest rival is Motorola.

Nokia espouses a 'flat' corporate culture, and English is the company *lingua franca*. Its 68,000 employees represent 120 nationalities, and are based in countries ranging from Finland to the United States, China and Romania. Nokia's 850 million users express strong brand loyalty, and the company invests heavily in consumer and lifestyle research. Nokia also promotes ethical relationships with its suppliers and the environment, and has won numerous awards. These include, as of 2007, 20th place in *Fortune*'s 'World's Most Admired Companies', and 119th largest in *Fortune*'s Global 500. The previous year Nokia's revenues exceeded the size of the Finnish national economy, and the company accounts for around one-third of the market capitalization of the Helsinki Stock Exchange: this is unique in industrialized economies.

Finland, with 5 million people, is the sixth largest country by area in the European Union, yet the most sparsely populated. It has been assessed as the sixth happiest country in the world. Yet there is more to Finland than the popular image of reindeer, the hut by the lake and the well-stoked sauna, and Finland has frequently been voted the most competitive country in the world by the World Economic Forum. Nokia has proved to be one of its most competitive companies, a company that has connected the world with its mobile telephony.

NIKE

1968 | USA

Just do it

Nike Inc. is a global sports and fitness corporation that was originally founded by a college runner and his coach to import running shoes from Japan. Today the Nike 'swoosh' is one of the world's most recognized emblems, and Nike is a brand phenomenon. Its comfortable shoes have, however, also embodied the uncomfortable truths of global capitalism. It 'employs' 29,000 people worldwide, but those working on its products number twenty times that, in the form of non-stakeholding, low-paid labour in Nike-contracted factories in Asia, factories were described in the past as 'abusive sweatshops'.

In the late 1950s Philip Knight was an accountancy student and mile-runner at the University of Oregon, where his coach was Bill Bowerman, who had also trained numerous Olympic athletes. Knight graduated in 1959, and while at the Graduate School of Business

> **'I DON'T LOVE IT** but it will grow on me.'
>
> Philip Knight's first reaction when he saw the 'swoosh' logo in 1971.

at Stanford University he wrote a business plan entitled 'Can Japanese Sports Shoes Do to German Sports Shoes What Japanese Cameras Did to German Cameras?'

FROM BLUE RIBBON TO NIKE INC.

In 1964, on a handshake with Bowerman and an investment of $500 each, Knight started Blue Ribbon Sports Inc. from his mother's laundry room to distribute imported Onitsuka Tiger athletic footwear in the United States. Knight's postgraduate business plan came true, and while he managed the company Bowerman turned his attention to designing running shoes. Jeff Johnson, a Stanford runner and anthropology major, became the company's first employee in 1965 and sold Blue Ribbon shoes from the back of his van at high-school track meetings.

Johnson also opened the company's first retail outlet, in Santa Monica. In 1967, after visiting New Zealand, Bowerman wrote *Jogging*, the million-selling handbook that introduced the concept to the United States.

In 1968 Knight and Bowerman established Nike Inc. The name – that of the Greek winged goddess of victory – was chosen by Johnson. In 1971, with the company short of money and needing a shoe stripe logo for a Japanese presentation, Knight met design student Carolyn Davidson. He offered her $2 an hour to come up with a design that suggested movement. The result was the famous 'swoosh' over the company name. 'I don't love it but it will grow on me,' said Knight. She sent him an invoice for $35, which he paid; she was later retained and handsomely rewarded by the company.

SPONSORING ATHLETES

Knight, Bowerman and Johnson had the credibility to market Nike in the world of American athletics, but their first asset on the track was Steve Prefontaine, University of Oregon prodigy and one of the most charismatic runners in history. Prefontaine was a protégé of Bill Bowerman, and wore free Nike sportswear and shoes. He qualified while still a student for Bowerman's 1972 Munich Olympic team; his struggle with the Amateur Athletic Union, which demanded that athletes who wanted to remain amateur for the Olympics should not accept benefits, even from million-dollar athletics meetings, contributed to his heroic status. Bowerman shared Prefontaine's views, and had already designed the revolutionary 'Cortez' training shoe when he achieved a kind of legendary status for himself by using (and ruining) his wife's waffle iron to create a new kind of lightweight sole that would become the bestselling training shoe in the country.

Prefontaine, who held the American record for every event from 2000 metres to 10,000 metres, had attained the kind of celebrity and loyalty reserved for rock stars when he fatally crashed his MG B sports car following a party in 1975. He was just 24 years old. Nike had lost its celebrity endorser, but the lesson was clear – and the company leveraged the use of its track shoes by young athletes at the 1976 Olympics. In 1978, when Blue Ribbon officially changed its name to Nike, the company signed the brilliant and mercurial new tennis star John McEnroe to promote its sportswear. The following year, using technology developed for astronauts, Nike developed the pressurized gas 'air sole' cushioned shoes that runners and joggers loved. Sales took off into the stratosphere. Leading runners in distances ranging from 100 metres to the marathon endorsed Nike's products, and across America the running and jogging boom started by Bill Bowerman became a lifestyle for men and women of all ages. In 1980 Nike went public on the New York Stock Exchange and negotiated a contract to produce shoes in the People's Republic of China.

> **'NIKE, WE MADE YOU.** We can break you.'
>
> A 13-year-old boy from the Bronx protests in front of the TV cameras at Nike's reliance on sweatshops, *c.* 1998.

CELEBRITY ENDORSEMENT

By the mid-1980s the jogging craze had peaked, and Nike decided to become what Knight called 'the world's best sports and fitness company'. The identification of the brand was accordingly moved from the popular hero to the new phenomenon of the super-celebrity. Nike's choice of

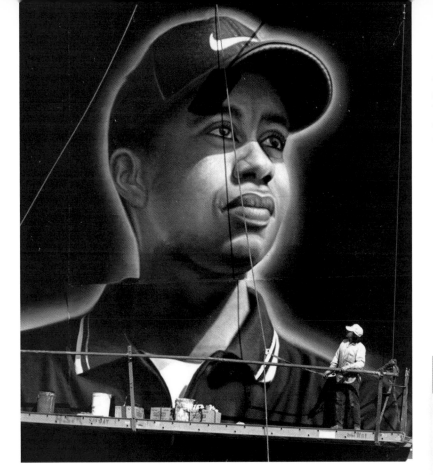

Painter Steve Sanchez admires his mural of golfer Tiger Woods on the side of a building in downtown Portland, Oregon, 1997. The mural is repainted periodically, but always features a Nike-sponsored athlete.

basketball player Michael Jordan made Nike what Tom Peters has called 'a pure player in brand brainware'. The prodigiously talented Jordan became a global superstar, conveying the 'idea' of sports as opposed to the prosaic fact of a tall African-American trying to get a ball into a net. The idea was embodied in the Nike strapline: 'Just do it.'

And it did. Between 1987 and 1993, through the recession that affected most Western economies, Nike went from a $750 million to a $4 billion company, and from sports shoes to street credibility. In 1992 Knight observed: 'For years we thought of ourselves as a production-oriented company ... But now we understand that the most important thing we do is market the product.'

CRITICISM OF THE COMPANY

As the anti-globalization movement gathered momentum, Nike became a prime target. The criticism that a $120 sports shoe was made for $6 in the Far East began to hurt the company, and Knight was branded a 'corporate villain' by Michael Moore in his 1997 film *The Big One*. Knight was the only one of 20 CEOs to agree to an interview for the film, and when Moore stated that pregnant women and 14-year-old girls were making shoes they could never afford for Nike in Indonesia, Knight replied that Nike did not own any of the factories. He continued with the proposition that if Moore were to invest in and build a factory in the USA that matched the quality and price of shoes made overseas, Nike would consider buying shoes from him. Nike was further taken to task in Naomi Klein's disingenuous but brilliant and essential polemic *No Logo*, published in 2000.

At the 1998 Nagano Winter Olympics CBS reporters were seen wearing Nike-emblazoned jackets. The fact that the company was the official sponsor of the network's coverage was no excuse in some eyes for breaching the sanctity of the Olympic brand, which itself had been inconspicuously sponsored since 1928 by Coca-Cola. Back home, things had gone from bad to worse: Nike's marketing campaign using the rapper Fat Boy Slim to endorse the brand went horribly wrong when youths were murdered for their sneakers, and word of the sweatshops led to protests by street kids outside Nike retail outlets in New York City: 'Nike, we made you. We can break you,' a 13-year-old boy from the Bronx told the TV cameras. The impact was felt all the way to the company's headquarters in Beaverton, Oregon, and in the New York Stock Exchange. After corporate efforts at damage limitation, Philip Knight decided to commit Nike to ethical supply and sourcing practices. It is a commitment to which the company has been held – perhaps excessively by the standards of other offenders – ever since.

THE IDEA OF SPORT

'A group of guys who had no reason to be in the shoe business,' Knight said in 2007, 'just got together and decided to try to build the best athletic brand in the world.' This is extreme disingenuousness, even given that branding requires the constant rewriting of history. The fact remains however that Nigel Bogle's observation that 'Global campaigns are born not made' fits Nike as perfectly as one of its shoes. Equally true is Naomi Klein's observation that Nike 'is a shoe company that is determined to unseat pro sports, the Olympics and even star athletes, to become the very definition of sports itself'.

Nike builds on the fact that anyone involved in sport will seek to connect with the greats. Golf's Tiger Woods, tennis's Roger Federer and Maria Sharapova and soccer's Wayne Rooney all embody 'the idea of sport' beyond their actual fields; yet their roots in a specific sport remain the key for both sponsor and sponsored. When Nike-sponsored American footballer Michael Vick became publicly associated with illegal gambling and dogfighting, the company terminated its endorsement.

Nike helped to create then rode the fitness phenomenon. History will show whether or not companies such as Nike contributed to or retarded the development of Asian countries; the answer is probably both. Nike's destiny may be to become the first post-superbrand company and market itself for what it is: a manufacturer of pretty good sports shoes and apparel, and a corporate citizen of Beaverton, Oregon.

In 2006 Philip Knight made a $105 million donation to Stanford Graduate Business School. In 2007 he announced that he and his wife Penny would be donating $100 million to the University of Oregon Athletics Legacy Fund. At the age of 70, he still owned 35 per cent of the company, which made him worth $8 billion and the 30th richest American. He could certainly afford to build the US mainland plant of which he spoke to Michael Moore. Just do it, Phil.

INTEL
1968 | USA

39

Give me five

The Intel Corporation is the world's largest semiconductor company, and the inventor of the x86 microprocessors used in personal computers. Its ubiquitous anonymity and invisible presence in millions of households are embodied in the Pentium chip and five-note start-up jingle written by a member of an obscure Austrian sampling band – and now heard millions of times a day around the world as people turn on their PCs.

The silicon memory chip evolved out of the ability of semiconductors to conduct electricity and their potential to store memory. Computers the size of a room with magnetic-core memory were the leading-edge technology by the mid-1960s, but physicist Robert Noyce was among those who believed the miniaturization of electronic circuitry onto a single silicon microchip was the way forward. Noyce had already co-invented the integrated circuit and pioneered silicon chip technology at Fairchild Semiconductor, where in 1965 his colleague Gordon Moore coined 'Moore's Law', which stated that the number of transistors that could be placed on a computer chip would double every year. Moore would be proved correct in this prediction every year for the next three decades.

THE HEART OF A REVOLUTION

In 1968 the two men left Fairchild and set up their own company. They wanted to call it the 'Moore Noyce Corporation' until somebody pointed out the unsuitability of the name for the electronics industry, where 'noise' is synonymous with interference. After a year as NM Electronics they adopted the name Integrated Electronics, or Intel.

Intel's aim – to create and exploit commercial applications for their memory-chip technology – was ambitious in so far as silicon memory was a hundred times more expensive than magnetic core, and at first only modestly successful. In 1971 the Japanese manufacturer Busicom asked the company to design for its range of high-end calculators a set of logic chips. While memory chips store instructions and data, logic chips perform calculations and execute programmes. Traditionally, such chips had always been discretely designed for each customer. However, Intel engineer Ted Hoff rejected Busicom's proposed design as unwieldy, and with his colleagues created a more compact device that included its own memory. This processor not only met Busicom's requirements, but had the capability to bring intelligence to any number of other 'dumb' machines.

Hoff and his colleagues, including Moore and Noyce, immediately saw the unlimited applications. Busicom, as their client, owned the rights, but either did not see the potential, or, if it did, could not afford to retain the rights at the time. The financially strapped Japanese company accepted Intel's offer to buy back its $60,000 investment. The decision would put Intel at the heart of the revolution in information technology.

THE INVENTION OF THE MICROPROCESSOR

Intel's 4004 chip or microcomputer set (the term 'microprocessor' would come later) was released into the market at the end of 1971. The $200 device carried the same power as ENIAC, America's first electronic computer, had done 25 years earlier. However, where the 3000-cubic-foot ENIAC had relied on 18,000 vacuum tubes, the 4004 was smaller than a thumbnail and contained 2300 transistors that could carry out 60,000 operations per second. Intel's chip as created by Hoff and his colleagues marked the invention of the microprocessor that would in time drive the personal computer; a brilliant solution for which they would be jointly credited after a near-simultaneous breakthrough by Texas Instruments.

Yet, for the next decade, the company would grow not through personal computing but rather on the strength of its semiconductors, and in particular its range of static random access memory chips, which were increasingly applied to all types of products and services – from digital grocery scales to medical instruments, from 'intelligent' traffic lights and inventories in fast-food restaurants to airline reservation systems and pinball arcades.

POWERING THE PC

By 1981 just two of Intel's range of chips were powering some 2500 applications a year. One of these assignments was commissioned by the business-machines giant IBM, and was conducted with extraordinary secretiveness on IBM's part. As an Intel engineer recalled, 'When we went in to provide technical support, they'd have our technical people on one side of a black curtain and theirs on the other side, with the prototype product. We'd ask questions, they'd tell us what was happening and we'd have to try to solve the problem literally in the dark. If we were lucky, they'd let us reach a hand through the curtain and grope around a bit to try figure out what

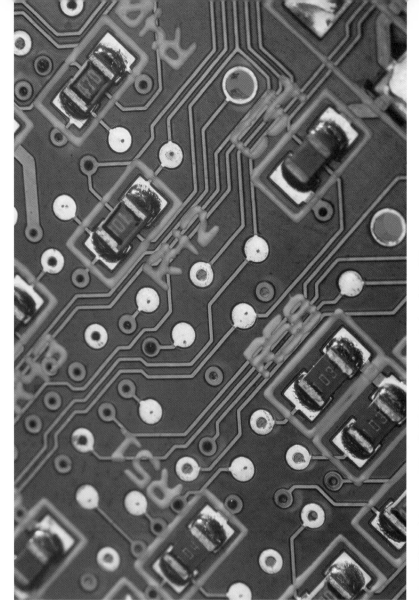

The abstract expressionist qualities of the integrated circuit board were probably irrelevant to Intel's Gordon Moore and Robert Noyce. To many, however, the integrated circuit board represents the perfect meeting of art and science.

TIMELINE

————1968————
Robert Noyce and Gordon Moore found **NM Electronics**.

————1969————
NM Electronics becomes Integrated Electronics – **Intel**.

————1971————
Intel develops a combined logic-and-memory chip, the **4004 microprocessor**.

————1981————
IBM uses Intel microprocessors in the PC.

————1985————
Compaq uses Intel's 386 chip in its PC clone.

————1991————
Launch of the Intel **start-up jingle**.

————1993————
Introduction of the **first Pentium chip**.

————2006————
Apple completes conversion of its product range to Intel processors.

the problem was.' The product for which IBM had chosen Intel as its first external microprocessor supplier was an idea that had failed to convince Gordon Moore a few years earlier: the first personal computer (see 'Missing the Boat?'). IBM's benchmark PC/AT machine a year later was powered by Intel's revolutionary new 286 processor, three times more powerful than any other chip of the time.

The success of the IBM PC and IBM 'clones' such as Compaq, coupled with increased pressure from Japanese chip manufacturers, prompted Intel's CEO Andy Grove to make microprocessors for personal computers the core business of the company. In 1985 Compaq's DESKPRO386 was the first machine to be based on Intel's 386 chip, which could perform more than 5 million instructions per second. Throughout the late 1980s and the 1990s, as personal computer sales soared, the company's plants in Santa Clara, California, Hillsboro, Oregon, and Phoenix, Arizona, developed and manufactured the 486 processor, the ever-more-powerful Pentium range, and the Celeron for laptops, desktops and servers. By 1991 Intel was the Number One manufacturer in the world; the 1994

'Pentium flaw' incident and recall only served to raise the company's profile and reputation. As Andy Grove, who authored the book *Only the Paranoid Survive*, remarked: 'Bad companies are destroyed by crises, good companies survive them, great companies are improved by them.' The company also manufactured mother boards and complete 'white box' systems for 'clone' manufacturers, thus at one point in the mid-1990s making 15 per cent of all personal computers. This ubiquitous anonymity was made instantly identifiable in 1990 by the phenomenally successful 'Intel inside' branding campaign, and in 1991 by the five-note PC Intel start-up jingle, written by Walter Werzowa from the 1980s Austrian sampling band Edelweiss.

PAST, PRESENT AND FUTURE

Intel has enjoyed an ambivalent and often controversial relationship with Microsoft, whose Windows 95, 98, 2000 and Vista operating systems have successively raised the bar for microprocessor power. In 2006 Apple completed the changeover of its entire product line to Intel processors. Intel adopted a new logo and slogan – 'Leap ahead' – in 2005, and the following years saw layoffs of 10,500 people or 10 per cent of the workforce, and the closure of a research laboratory at Cambridge University.

Intel is a Fortune 500 Nasdaq-traded company whose stock is widely held. It has nearly 100,000 employees and 200 facilities worldwide. It has been the Number One manufacturer of microprocessors in the world ever since 1991. Two engineers developed the first 4004 microprocessor in nine months; today, hundreds of people using computer-aided design map out each phase and portion of a new chip. The first Pentium in 1993 was already 1500 times faster than the first 4004 just over 20 years earlier. Andy Grove recalled of the 1970s: 'The fab [fabrication] area looked like Willy Wonka's factory, with hoses and wires and contraptions chugging along – the semiconductor equivalent of the Wright Brothers' jury-rigged airplane. It was state-of-the-art manufacturing at the time, but by today's standards it was unbelievably crude.' Even in the mid-1980s, fewer than 50 per cent of Intel's chips were functional at the end of the manufacturing line.

> **'BAD COMPANIES ARE DESTROYED BY CRISES**, good companies survive them, great companies are improved by them.'
>
> Intel CEO Andy Grove, in his 1996 book *Only the Paranoid Survive*.

The current generation of Intel 64 Mb chips are manufactured by robots and can store 3555 pages of text in a space the size of a ten-cent piece. A child using a Pentium-based PC today has more computing power at their disposal than NASA had to send men to the moon. The pace of change is such that Gordon Moore, who updated his own celebrated law regarding transistors to every two years instead of one, has observed: 'If the auto industry advanced as rapidly as the semiconductor industry, a Rolls-Royce would get half a million miles per gallon, and it would be cheaper to throw it away than park it.' Increased post-dotcom bubble competition in the lower reaches of the market, allegations of anti-trust activities by the EU and industrial espionage (against and not on behalf of the company) are all features of the Intel story. The memory chip has with justification been called the crude oil of the 21st century. To this day, Intel promotes widely from within and rewards work generously, and no one has an office. Moore and Noyce must rank among the great inventor-entrepreneurs of all time.

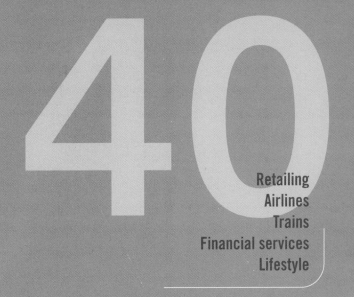

VIRGIN

1969 | *UK*

40

Retailing
Airlines
Trains
Financial services
Lifestyle

The smiling face of capitalism

The Virgin Group was incorporated in 1989, but its business and philosophy originated in London in the late 1960s when the English public-school dropout Richard Branson started a magazine called *Student*. The magazine was a critical success and a commercial failure, but in the mould of the true entrepreneur Branson was undaunted – he already had two failed ventures behind him, one growing Christmas trees and another raising budgerigars. Spotting a gap in the market, he started Britain's first discount mail-order record business.

Retail price maintenance – whereby the manufacturer forced the retailer to sell at a certain minimum price – had been abolished in Britain, but the popular music industry still behaved as a cartel adhering to an anti-competitive price structure. Many new records sold in conventional shops had also been played by browsing customers. Branson bought new unplayed LPs from suppliers in Britain and mainland Europe, then sold them at prices that undercut the traditional retailers, either from the boot of his car or through advertisements in the rock-music press. On an unplayed record the membrane across the hole in the centre of the disc is still intact – hence the company name: Virgin. Orders soon flooded in and an advertisement placed in *The Times* for extra staff declared 'Easy work, good money'.

> **'EASY WORK**, good money.'
>
> Richard Branson advertises for new staff for Virgin Records, *c.* 1970.

AN UNORTHODOX APPROACH

By 1971 Virgin Records was an effective if unorthodox corporate whose senior staff drew equal salaries of £50 a week and drove Volvo cars – in those days both nonconformist statements. Branson's business partner and boyhood friend Nik Powell oversaw the day-to-day running of

the business while Branson, who like IKEA's Ingvar Kamprad and Body Shop's Anita Roddick is dyslexic, demonstrated a flair for negotiation and publicity and above all for inspiring personal loyalty in what would now be termed 'transformational leadership'. When a postal strike threatened the mail-order record business, Branson suggested to his new associate and South African cousin Simon Draper that they open a Virgin shop and start up a Virgin record label. A first-floor room in Oxford Street became the first retail outlet, and Shipton Manor in Oxfordshire, complete with swimming pool and croquet lawns – and purchased with a loan from his aunt and a mortgage from Coutts, the Queen's bankers – became the Virgin Records recording studio.

With the mail-order business beginning to suffer from competition from other discounters, Branson's plans for the record label were put on hold – and the entire enterprise was threatened with collapse when Branson was arrested and charged with defrauding HM Customs and Excise. The young entrepreneur had discovered a loophole. This particular one apparently allowed records to be exported abroad and the purchase tax reclaimed without proof that the merchandize had physically left the country. The goods in question could thus be driven in and out of Dover docks, tax exemption authorized, and then resold in London. This was strictly

Richard Branson in training for the Atlantic balloon crossing, 1987. Branson's genius for marketing the brand would keep Virgin's diverse companies in the public eye for over four decades.

illegal, and Branson and Virgin were only saved from bankruptcy when his mother Eve – a former dancer, actress and air stewardess – remortgaged the family house to make a down payment towards the tax and charges due, and by Customs and Excise themselves, who gave Branson three years to pay off the balance. This was still a substantial sum, which neither Branson himself nor Virgin Records looked likely to be able to find within the allotted time.

TUBULAR BELLS AND OTHER HITS

The unlikely saviour of Virgin's fortunes was a young guitarist called Mike Oldfield, who handed a demo tape to Tom Newman, the manager of the Manor recording studio. Newman liked what he heard, but Virgin was yet to start its own record label and he advised Oldfield to go elsewhere. By the time Branson's associate Simon Draper heard the tape, Oldfield had been turned down by nearly every record company in London. Draper too became infatuated with the hypnotic, multilayered instrumental sound, and Oldfield became Virgin Records' first signing. Oldfield's contract, personally negotiated with Branson, gave him a modest annual salary and a royalty of 5 per cent. In return Virgin received worldwide rights to the album, entitled *Tubular Bells*, and to a number of albums he might make after that. Within a few weeks of its release Branson had applied his energies to marketing the album to music papers, magazines and radio stations, including the all-important John Peel programme on BBC Radio 1. The record went to Number One in the United Kingdom album chart. Branson then flew to the United States and sold it to Atlantic Records, who in turn licensed it to the makers of the movie *The Exorcist*. The album got to Number Three in the US charts, and would sell more copies than any album except *The Sound of Music*.

Tubular Bells and subsequent albums such as Tangerine Dream's *Phaedra* transformed the fortunes of Virgin Records, establishing it as the core brand in rock. By the end of the 1970s the company's roster included Oldfield, Tangerine Dream, the German bands Faust and Can, and the Sex Pistols. Branson himself had personally opened up licensing agreements and found partners in Italy, France and Germany. The company was highly geared, and when recession and inflation hit Britain, record sales slumped, staff were sacked, artists dropped and a planned expansion of shops into America delayed. Coutts, the company's bankers, threatened to call in the overdraft.

Again an obscure loophole came to the rescue. Seven years earlier, with what seems like remarkable prescience, Branson and Powell had registered the Virgin trademark logo in an offshore trust in the Cayman Islands exempt from UK tax. The royalties from the use of the logo paid into the trust were sufficient for Branson to use them as security against a £1 million loan enabling Virgin to weather the recession. In the early and mid-1980s the company signed a string of acts – Genesis, Culture Club, Human League, Phil Collins and Japan – that would turn it into one of the world's most successful record labels and lead to one of the most extraordinary brand expansions of any decade, in the form of Virgin Atlantic.

TIMELINE

1950
Birth of **Richard Branson**.

Late 1960s
Branson sets up a **cut-price record business**.

1972
Virgin starts up its **own recording label**.

1984
Formation of **Virgin Atlantic**.

1986
Virgin goes **public**.

1988
Branson returns Virgin to **private ownership**.

1992
Sale of the Virgin Music Group to **Thorn EMI**.

1997
Virgin Trains wins the franchise for Britain's main west coast line.

1999
Launch of **Virgin Mobile**.

1999
Branson is awarded a **knighthood** for 'services to entrepreneurship'.

2007
Virgin America launches domestic US airline services.

2007
Virgin mounts an unsuccessful rescue bid for **Northern Rock**.

FLYING BY THE SEAT OF HIS PANTS

Randolph Fields had founded British Atlantic with plans for a people-friendly low-cost airline, but when he went to Richard Branson with a business plan and an investment proposal he came up against Branson at the height of his ruthless negotiating powers. Branson took majority control of what had originally been an equal partnership, and Fields was forced to take a back seat. The poker face that Branson showed to Fields also concealed the fact that Virgin's £3 million overdraft limit would be breached by the last-minute cost of a replacement engine for the airline's only Boeing 747. Returning from the extravagantly publicized maiden flight from London to New

York, Branson was enraged to find a Coutts bank manager threatening to bounce any further cheques – a particularly infuriating move given that Virgin by this time was showing profits of £10 million on turnover of £98 million. Coutts bounced a number of Virgin cheques before Branson established facilities with six different banks and a £30 million overdraft facility.

By this time the decision had been taken to float Virgin on the London Stock Exchange. The conventional reason – 'to grow the business' – masked Branson's desire to give Britain's 15th largest private company the leverage to launch his long and deeply held ambition: a hostile takeover of a giant of the British music, film and cinema business, ten times larger than Virgin: Thorn EMI.

WHEELING AND DEALING

The launch of Virgin Atlantic against the likes of British Airways – against whom Branson won a giant-killing lawsuit over price-fixing – combined with his (albeit unsuccessful) bid to cross the Atlantic in a powerboat made Branson a British national icon. But the flotation of Virgin perplexed the City of London. The group went public in November 1986 at 140p per share; less than a year later the stock market crash knocked the price back to 90p, and the Thorn EMI bid was abandoned. In 1988 Branson and senior colleagues borrowed money to buy out 600,000 shareholders who had invested in the flotation, taking the company private again at the original price of 140p per share. This marked the incorporation of today's Virgin Group.

In a loss of innocence worthy of the group's name, worse was to come. Fujisankei, the Japanese media group, had already bought 25 per cent of the music businesses; the 1990 Gulf War and rising oil prices brought the worst recession ever to the aviation industry, and forced Branson to sell the Japanese Seibu-Saison group 10 per cent of his airline. The following year, in 1992, Branson and Draper sold the Virgin Music Group – the 'jewel in the crown' – for £560 million, to none other than Thorn EMI. Branson reputedly wept, and amid recriminations from long-serving Virgin employees, senior members like Simon Draper departed with many millions of pounds. Branson became even richer and Virgin Atlantic survived to become the core business of the group.

SPREADING THE BRAND

It is testament to the enduring power of the Virgin brand that, nearly 40 years on, whatever the Virgin product – be it airline tickets, train travel, mobile telephony, internet services, soft drinks or condoms – music is the association that the customer subliminally makes to this day. Likewise, while most of these enterprises began life as wholly owned Virgin subsidiaries, each is a separate entity to which Branson may simply yet lucratively license the brand (as in the case of Virgin Music and Virgin Radio) or in which he holds a minority stake (as in the case of the Virgin Active chain of health clubs, Virgin Media – bruised by competition with Rupert Murdoch's Sky – and Virgin Retail, the cornerstone of the brand).

Branson's wealth, estimated at some $7.8 billion, is owned by a complicated series of offshore trusts and companies, exposing him to a relatively small UK tax liability. His predilection for daredevil feats continues to give him a mixed public profile and a sometimes

Going Galactic

A recent Branson venture is Virgin Galactic, which, in a deal in part financed by Microsoft co-founder Paul Allen, plans to take paying customers into suborbital space. Tickets are likely to cost $200,000.

ambivalent value to the brand, with varying commercial consequences. In 2007 Virgin America won a 17-month battle to launch domestic US airline services, partly because the company agreed to distance itself from Branson and the Virgin Group, the latter holding a 25 per cent stake. In the same year, Virgin launched a rescue package for the stricken UK mortgage lender Northern Rock.

Branson has leveraged the 'people's champion' image brilliantly for four decades, in a juggling act that has enabled Virgin to cruise from music to airlines and railways and from vodka to condoms. From its obscure origins, Virgin has grown into a multi-billion-pound brand trusted by millions. With the exception of record discounting, Virgin has never invented anything, but has successfully created and maintained a safe zone for its customers. The question being asked in the early years of the 21st century is whether its core values were beginning to lose their sheen. If you can brand anything, what does the name signify any more?

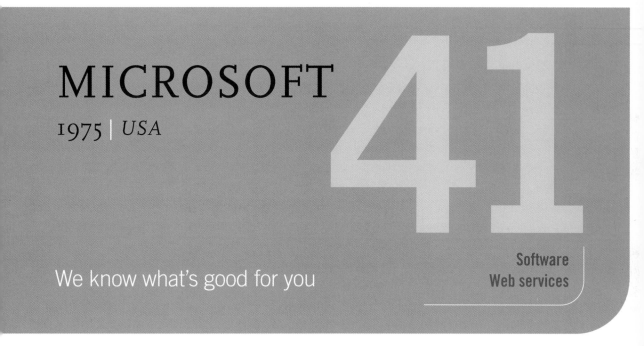

MICROSOFT

1975 | USA

41

Software
Web services

We know what's good for you

Microsoft Corporation is a pure American company. The remorseless march of product, the ongoing battles with anti-trust laws and the triumphalist logic of the principals locate it in the all-time capitalist pantheon. The many change and pass; the one remains.

William Henry Gates III was born in 1955 in Seattle to a family prominent in business and philanthropy. The young Bill excelled at mathematics and the sciences, and at the age of 13 he was enrolled in the exclusive Lakeside Preparatory School in Seattle. What changed the course of Bill III's life – and the world – was the Lakeside School mothers' rummage sale.

‘**A COMPUTER ON EVERY DESK** and in every home, running Microsoft software.’

The Microsoft mission, as enunciated in the early 1980s.

THE STUDENT PROGRAMMER

The mothers used the proceeds to buy a teletype terminal and time on a General Electric computer. Gates showed an aptitude for programming in BASIC – Beginners All-purpose Symbolic Instruction Code – and after the funds from the rummage sale ran out he and others, including Paul Allen (with whom Gates was to found Microsoft), continued on other computers until they were banned by Computer Center Corporation for exploiting bugs in its software system to obtain free computer time. When the ban was lifted, Gates offered to track down bugs in the company's system in return for access. CCC agreed, and the teenage Gates worked in their offices, learning programming in a number of computer languages. He also started a business with Allen to make traffic counters using the new Intel microprocessor, reputedly earning $20,000 in his first year, until his relative youth was discovered and business tailed off thereafter. He and other Lakeside students were also hired by another company to write a payroll programme in COBOL. This time the company paid both in computer time and royalties – a lesson Gates would remember.

> **'A FUNDAMENTAL NEW RULE** for business is that the Internet changes everything.'
> Bill Gates, *Business @ the Speed of Thought* (1999)

Gates enrolled at Harvard in 1973, and in due course met Steve Ballmer, who managed the college football team, and who was later to become CEO of Microsoft. Ballmer was studying maths and economics and had attended the muscular Detroit Country Day School. Gates for his part co-authored a paper on algorithms entitled 'Bounds for sorting by prefix reversal'. Paul Allen, meanwhile, had gone to Washington State University, dropped out and become a programmer for Honeywell in Boston.

THE BIRTH OF MICROSOFT

In 1975 Gates read an issue of *Popular Electronics* advertising the MITS (Micro Instrumentation and Telemetry Systems) Altair 8800 microcomputer kit, powered by Intel's new chip. Gates and Allen wrote to proprietor Ted Roberts offering a BASIC programming language for the machine. They neither had an Altair machine, nor had they written any code; they were simply testing his interest. When Roberts replied positively, they and Harvard graduate Monte Davidoff (usually omitted from the story) sat down to write a programme in BASIC using a PDP-10 minicomputer. Allen flew to Albuquerque with the 4K 'Altair BASIC' on a paper tape. The first time the programme ran, it crashed. At the second attempt, with a new paper tape, they typed in '2+2' and up came '4'. Allen was hired to work for MITS and persuaded Gates to take leave of absence from Harvard. Gates moved to Albuquerque and he and Allen christened their partnership 'Micro-Soft', in part after their first client. The following year, in 1976, they registered the name without the hyphen.

The success of the Altair 8800 made Microsoft's Altair BASIC popular with hobbyists. The absurdly youthful-looking Gates – the son of a lawyer – revealed his steel when free versions based on a leaked copy came onto the market. Gates, in a move that was unpopular with the computer hobbyists of the day, wrote in the MITS newsletter that software developers should receive payment. He and Allen distanced Microsoft from MITS (which would shortly go out of business) and concentrated on building the market for their software. Their small team soon included several highly talented programmers (the family of one of them had developed the Cabbage Patch dolls), a technical writer, and a chief mathematician who had been present at NASA's Mission Control during the first moon landing. Gates had the shortest hair, and in addition to overseeing the business he had final say over every line of code that was shipped, often rewriting it along the way. In 1979 the company moved to Bellevue, Seattle.

FROM QUICK AND DIRTY TO WINDOWS

In 1980, after failing to agree terms with another company, IBM awarded Microsoft the contract to supply a version of the CP/M operating system. Short of time, Paul Allen agreed a deal with Tim Paterson of Seattle Computer Products to buy the QDOS (Quick and Dirty Operating System) for $50,000, which he and Gates adapted as PC-DOS (Disk Operating System). This was to be the brain within IBM's first personal computer. Crucially, Gates and Allen retained the right to license PC-DOS to other manufacturers. When the IBM PC took off and spawned a flood of clones, Gates hired his Harvard friend Steve Ballmer, who had worked at Procter & Gamble. Microsoft's mission – 'a computer on every desk and in every home, running Microsoft software' – was anathema in some ways to the long-haired free spirits in the team who helped make this come true. Most of whom would leave, albeit as multimillionaires in terms of stock, by the mid-1980s: 'They beat the enthusiasm out of me,' said Jim Lane, who masterminded the Microsoft/Intel ('Wintel') partnership. The commune was becoming the corporate, with Gates, Ballmer and Allen at the top.

PC-DOS became MS-DOS, and with Microsoft's aggressive marketing in the face of competition from clones, MS-DOS became the all-powerful operating system in the personal computer world of IBM, Compaq and many others – Apple being the exception. In 1983 Paul Allen was diagnosed with Hodgkin's disease, and resigned from

Paul Allen (left) and Bill Gates, founders of Microsoft, 1981. The classic 'nerd' would reveal himself to be the Henry Ford of software and one of the most significant philanthropists of all time.

Microsoft for medical treatment. Allen recovered, but distanced himself from the day-to-day operations of the company. Fuelled by the PC boom, Microsoft introduced its first version of Windows as a graphical extension to MS-DOS, and introduced a new OS/2 operating system for IBM. The 1986 initial public offering of the company was one of the most successful ever, making Gates, Allen and Ballmer – and some of their early employees – instant multimillionaires. Henceforth the best and brightest who passed the Microsoft interview – 'Why is a manhole cover round' was a favourite question – could expect lucrative stock options and privileged status in a golden inner circle of programmers and software engineers.

'AN ABUSIVE MONOPOLY'?

The story of Microsoft throughout the 1990s is predominantly the story of the success of Microsoft Office and successive Windows operating systems, some controversially 'bundled' with web browsers such as Internet Explorer. In 1990 Windows 3.0 sold over 100,000 copies in two weeks, to the extent that Windows would replace OS/2 as the favoured PC software platform. Windows 95, MSN, MSNBC, Internet Explorer, Hotmail, Windows 98 and MSN Messenger are so familiar as products and services on the screens of desktops and laptops around the world as to be definitive and unquestioned. However, this verdict is not shared by some competitors, nor by the US Justice Department, which in 2000 declared the company 'an abusive monopoly'. The company was split into two units; lengthy appeals and complex settlements followed. European Union anti-trust regulators would also wade into the fray.

Meanwhile, the behemoth marched on, launching Windows XP, the Xbox gaming console, Windows Vista... In 2007 Microsoft decided not to outbid Google's $3.1 million for the online advertiser DoubleClick, but paid $6 billion for Aquantive and contemplated a merger with Yahoo that would make Microsoft's MSN search engine rival Google. The likely future shape of the company would encompass the old company determined to protect Windows and the new, cooler one competing as a brand in the youthful consumer electronics market.

> **'AMERICAN ANTI-INTELLECTUALISM** will never again be the same because of Bill Gates. Gates embodies what was supposed to be impossible – the practical intellectual.'
>
> Randall E. Stross, *The Microsoft Way* (1996)

By 2007 Microsoft was employing nearly 80,000 people in 102 countries. Its website receives more than 100 million hits a day. Microsoft has been simultaneously praised as an employer of women and racial and sexual minority groups, while elsewhere its working conditions have been described as a 'velvet sweatshop' with an inner circle of programmers ring-fenced by outsourcing and 'Microserfs'. A definitive American stock, it has created four billionaires and 12,000 millionaires among its employees over the years. Its rivalry and détente with Apple are legendary; its rivalry with Google is unbridled. The company also faces competition from open-source software such as Linux.

THE TRIUMVIRATE

Paul Allen remained on the board until 2000, and thereafter stayed on as an advisor and major shareholder. One of the richest men in the world, his holdings also include football and basketball teams, real estate, giant yachts and Jimi Hendrix memorabilia, including the guitar Hendrix played at Woodstock. Steve Ballmer is similarly rich, and noted for his extreme physical and vocal behaviour onstage at Microsoft events.

Bill Gates is worth $60 billion (his house alone is valued at $125 million), making him the world's richest man. This status testifies to but also obscures his extraordinary achievements. The boy who started his first venture as a teenager had by his mid-thirties made personal computing a reality. This book was written in Microsoft Word on a laptop operating Windows XP (powered by an Intel processor) and delivered by MSN Hotmail. As a person of influence he is unsurpassed in the 21st century and likely to remain as such. He has redefined philanthropy, and influenced others such as Warren Buffett to do likewise. In addition to the $210 million Gates Scholarships for the University of Cambridge, the Bill and Melinda Gates Foundation donates billions to otherwise neglected causes such as AIDS and other diseases in developing countries.

Bill Gates's email address is widely known, and he has received as many as 4 million emails a year. Many of these are 'spam' or junk mail offering advice on how to get rich quickly, or get out of debt: 'Which would be funny,' he has observed, 'if it weren't so irritating.'

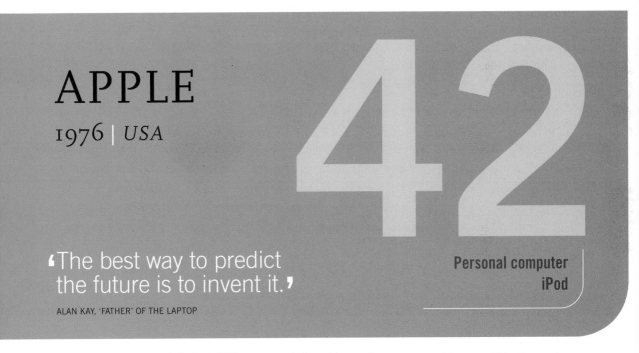

APPLE

1976 | *USA*

42

‘The best way to predict the future is to invent it.’

ALAN KAY, 'FATHER' OF THE LAPTOP

Personal computer
iPod

Apple Inc. is a $20 billion multinational corporation with headquarters at 1 Infinite Loop, Cupertino, California. Apple created the personal computer market, and the brand loyalty of its users is among the highest in the world. One co-founder sold out within two weeks; another resigned in despair; the third – Steve Jobs – sidelined by the man he appointed, founded Pixar Animations, then returned to Apple and is the largest private shareholder in Disney. The board of directors includes the CEO of Google and former US vice-president – and Nobel laureate – Al Gore.

'He was the first person I met who knew more about electronics than I did.' Apple Computer founders Steve Jobs (left) and Steve Wozniak between them created the 'personal' computer.

Born in 1955, the same year as Bill Gates, Steve Jobs was put up for adoption at the age of one week by his unmarried mother. He later dropped out of Reed College and experimented with a counter-cultural lifestyle and spiritual enlightenment in India before working on computer games for Atari. Here he met the other co-founders of Apple: Steve Wozniak and Ronald Wayne. Jobs called Wozniak 'the first person I met who knew more about electronics than I did'.

THE EARLY APPLES

Wozniak shared Jobs's vision of a 'personal' computer, and they designed the machine in Jobs's bedroom. Wozniak's Apple 1 was the first single-board model with a built-in video interface and on-board ROM, which told the computer how to load other programmes from an external source. The machine, like the Altair, had to be assembled from kit form and had neither keyboard nor monitor.

> **'I'M JUST A GUY** who probably should have been a semi-talented poet on the Left Bank. I got sort of sidetracked here.'
>
> Steve Jobs, quoted in *Fortune* magazine, 1984

Jobs marketed the machine for $666 to Wozniak's Homebrew Computer Club. When the Byte Shop, a local retailer, made an order, Jobs hustled parts from suppliers, and to raise the $1300 to go into production he sold his VW camper bus, while Wozniak sold his Hewlett-Packard calculator. On 1 April 1976 Jobs, Wozniak and Wayne formed Apple Computers, named after Jobs's favourite fruit, and with a pun intended on 'byte'. Wayne designed the first logo with Jobs and wrote the Apple 1 manual and the partnership agreement. After two weeks, however, uncomfortable with the idea of unlimited liability, Wayne sold his 10 per cent stockholding back to Jobs and Wozniak for $800. Wozniak, by contrast, threw in his job with Hewlett-Packard to join Jobs. The rainbow-coloured Apple logo as refined by Rob Janoff became the emblem of the company. The 'bite' out of the fruit is interpreted by many as a tribute to the British 'father of the computer', Alan Turing, who committed suicide in 1954 after his arrest for homosexual acts by biting into a cyanide-tainted apple.

They sold over 200 of the Apple 1, and in 1977 followed this with the Apple 2, which could interface with a colour monitor. Jobs encouraged programmers to develop applications, which eventually produced a 'library' of 16,000 software programmes. The Apple 2 featured a 'killer application' – the VisiCalc spreadsheet, which was intended to attract business customers: 'I threw in high-res,' Wozniak would recall. 'It was only two chips. I didn't know if people would use it.' Jobs brought in marketing and public relations expertise and was introduced to former Intel marketing manager and venture capitalist Mike Markkula. Markkula's investment would prove to be one of the most spectacularly successful in the history of Silicon Valley.

GRAPHICS, THE MOUSE AND DESKTOP PUBLISHING

In 1979 Jobs and other Apple engineers were allowed access to Xerox's Alto computer in return for $1 million of Apple stock. The Alto featured a graphical user interface (GUI), which enabled the user to manipulate images and 'widgets' on screen; Jobs became convinced that all computers would have to have the facility. The Apple 3, launched in 1980 without a cooling fan (at Jobs's insistence), had to be recalled in large numbers when they overheated. Apple was struggling against IBM, but the Apple 2 had given the company 700 per cent growth in three years. In 1980 the company went public and made Jobs, Wozniak and others millionaires many times over. The Apple Lisa, named after Jobs's daughter and launched in 1983, was the first mouse-controlled personal computer with a GUI; however, its $9995 price tag deterred buyers. Aware of the need to compete with IBM's Microsoft-brained, Intel-powered PCs, Jobs had a product in development called the Macintosh, and he challenged John Sculley, the CEO of Pepsi-Cola, to come on board to help him take on the PC. 'If you stay at Pepsi,' Jobs told Sculley, 'five years from now all you'll have accomplished is selling a lot more sugar water to kids. If you come to Apple you can change the world.'

In the early 1980s Jobs struck a deal with the education authorities in California whereby every public school in the state received a free Apple 2 and a LOGO software package. This paved the way for parental acceptance of the personal computer. The launch of the 128k Apple Macintosh – twice the power of the IBM PC and named after a variety of apple – was highlighted by Ridley Scott's giant-killing '1984' television commercial aired during the Super Bowl on 22 January. The release of the LaserWriter printer and PageMaker software harnessed the 'Mac's' advanced graphic capabilities, driving up sales and heralding the dawn of desktop publishing.

1955
Birth of **Steve Jobs**.

1976
Jobs and Steve Wozniak create the Apple 1 personal computer, and form **Apple Computers**.

1977
Launch of the **Apple 2**.

1980
Apple **goes public**.

1984
Introduction of the **Apple Macintosh**.

1984
Wozniak leaves Apple.

1985
Jobs resigns from Apple.

1991
The **Apple PowerBook** defines the modern laptop.

1997
Jobs returns to Apple.

1998
Launch of the **iMac**.

2001
Launch of the **iPod**.

2007
Launch of the **iPhone**.

A FAREWELL TO JOBS

Jobs's managerial techniques were abrasive, and his method of dividing and ruling by distinguishing 'corporate shirts' from 'pirates' to motivate development programmes alienated some. CEO John Sculley became convinced Jobs was harming the company. Sculley's voice carried the Apple board: in 1985 Jobs was marginalized, resigned, sold $20 million of Apple stock and drifted through Europe. His first post-Apple venture, NextStep, ran through $250 million; his second, Pixar Animation Studio, would sell for $7.4 billion and make Jobs the largest private shareholder in Disney.

Ironically the two co-founders of Apple were absent during its first 'Golden Age', from 1989 to 1991, when the Sony-assisted Powerbook 100 defined the modern laptop. This hardware distinguished Apple users in Levi's from PC users in suits. Apple could do no wrong in the eyes of analysts and consumers; this turned to hubris when the company sued Microsoft for theft of intellectual property. The lawsuit would drag on for years, before being thrown out of court, and rotted Apple from within. Meanwhile, Microsoft's 'killer app', Windows 95, driving PCs on the desk and in the lap, ate up Apple in the marketplace.

In 1996 Gil Amelio was appointed CEO of Apple. 'Apple is like a ship with a hole in the bottom,' said Amelio, 'and my job is to point the ship in the right direction.' Apple stock hit an all-time low, and after Steve Jobs sold all but one of his Apple shares in 1997 the company lost $708 million. Amelio was ousted and went on to success elsewhere. Michael Dell remarked that, if he was running Apple, he would have shut it down and given shareholders their money back. One who would not have benefited from this scenario was Ronald Wayne, whose original $800 stake would have been worth as much as $500 million. Wayne was rumoured to be working for a defence contractor in Salinas, California.

THE RETURN OF JOBS

Apple's purchase of NextStep in 1997 saw the return of Steve Jobs as acting CEO of the company. At that year's Macworld Conference and Expo, Jobs announced that the Apple Macintosh would be using Microsoft's Office software and Internet Explorer web browser: 'We have to let go of this notion that for Apple to win, Microsoft has to lose,' he told a stunned audience. When Bill Gates appeared on a large screen endorsing these sentiments, the reaction was akin to the appointment of King Herod to the board of Mothercare. Jobs and Gates won the day, and Microsoft acquired $150 million in non-voting Apple stock. Contrary to speculation, Apple was cash-rich at the time, and Microsoft later sold the stock for a healthy profit.

> **"WE HAVE TO LET GO OF THIS NOTION** that for Apple to win, Microsoft has to lose."
>
> Steve Jobs returns as CEO, 1997

In 1998 the translucent plastic iMac was produced by a team led by the British designer Jonathan Ive. Ive went on to create the definitive MP3 portable media player, the Apple iPod, of which over 100 million have been sold. In 2007 Jobs announced the renaming of the company from Apple Computer Inc. to Apple Inc. In the same year Apple stock passed $100 (from $6 in 2003) and overtook Dell.

LISTENING TO THE CUSTOMER – AND HAVING FUN

Genius, happenstance, pranks, blunders, egomania, infighting, counterculture, boardroom coups, pragmatism, creativity and awards all played their part in the Apple story. Steve Jobs remained CEO of Apple Inc. Steve 'Woz' Wozniak, his co-founder, crashed his Beechcraft Bonanza aircraft in 1981, lost his memory, married three times (once to an Olympic kayaker), returned to Apple and left in despair at a low point in 1984. He drives a Toyota Prius and a Hummer, claiming that the two cancel each other out on an environmental level. He has received numerous awards and honorary doctorates and is an active philanthropist and investor. In 2000 he was inducted into the National Inventors Hall of Fame. In 2006 he authored a book entitled *iWoz: from Computer Geek to Cult Icon: How I Invented the Personal Computer, Co-Founded Apple and Had Fun Doing It.*

'People talk about technology,' John Sculley has said, 'but Apple was a marketing company.' Sculley's achievements at Apple were notable, but this belies the importance of Jobs's and Wozniak's invention. Apple significantly extended the computer, personalized it for the home and workplace and emancipated the user. Software such as Mac OS, iLife and Final Cut is distinguished by its weightless, empowering capability. The Macintosh, iMac and iPod are design classics. The Apple iPhone was one of the most expensive and eagerly awaited devices of its kind ever to reach the market. Listen to the customer.

BODY SHOP 43

1976 | UK

'Being good is good business.' ANITA RODDICK

Ethical lifestyle
Beauty products

The Body Shop began life in the English coastal resort of Brighton. The store, which sold natural beauty products, was set up by a former hotelier and located next door to a funeral parlour. Anita Roddick's husband was trekking across America at the time, and when he returned he found she had sold half the business to a local garage owner, and hundreds of people were wanting to open Body Shop franchises. In 2006 the Roddicks sold the company to L'Oréal for £652 million.

Anita Perilli was born in 1942, the child of Italian immigrants who ran an American-style diner in the small English town of Littlehampton. Anita's family was loving if dysfunctional, and was dominated by her mother Gilda. It wasn't until she was 18 that Anita learned that her beloved 'step-father', who had died of tuberculosis when she was ten, was in fact her father.

REJECTING CONFORMITY

Anita had a wild childhood and a hippie adolescence, followed by a false start at drama school. She then trained to be a teacher, and spent time on a kibbutzim study scholarship in Israel. A brief and anarchic spell as a teacher was followed by other jobs – at one point the dyslexic Anita filed cuttings for the *International Herald Tribune* in Paris. She then hit the hippie trail through Tahiti, New Caledonia, Australia and South Africa, from where she was deported after breaking the apartheid laws by attending 'black' night at a jazz club. Brighton, the hardcore nonconformist enclave on the south coast of England, was always going to be her spiritual home.

> **'WORK IS MORE FUN** than fun.'
> Anita Roddick, quoted in Debbie Moore's *When a Woman Means Business* (1989)

It was in a Brighton club owned by Gilda that Anita met the poet and traveller Gordon Roddick: 'I looked at her and knew instantly we were going to be together,' he recalled, 'But I was young and free – the last thing I wanted was a permanent relationship. I said to the guy sitting next to me at the bar, "My life is over." I tried everything I could to be rude and put Anita off, but she wasn't having any of it.' One child and then another followed, and they got married. In 1970 they travelled to San Francisco, where on Telegraph Avenue they came across a store called The Body Shop. This sold shampoos, lotions and body creams while advocating environmental concerns and encouraging customers to bring their own recyclable containers. Back in England they opened a restaurant and small hotel, but after three years the lack of privacy and time for themselves proved too much and they struck an extraordinary deal. They sold up, and while Gordon set off to ride a horse from Buenos Aires to New York City, Anita stayed at home with their young daughters.

GREEN ENTERPRISE

Anita had noted during her travels that there was a lack of bath products in small or sample sizes. During the hot summer of 1976 she developed in her garage 15 natural products made from exotic ingredients such as jojoba oil and rhassoul mud sourced from local herbalists, and gave them names like Tea Tree Oil Facial Wash and Mango Dry Mist. These were first sold in unused bottles intended for urine samples. Anita painted the walls of her first shop green to hide the damp spots, and paid a local art student £20 to design the logo; the name was that of the store she had seen in San Francisco. For the opening, Anita perfumed the pavement outside the shop and hung potpourri inside. When the undertaker next door complained that this would be bad for his business, she retorted that she was a housewife trying to make a living and leaked the story to the press. With public interest ignited, the store took off, and she decided to open a second store in Chichester. The bank would not lend her the money and another business acquaintance also demurred; eventually a local garage owner, Ian McGlinn, offered her £4000 for a half share in the company. She wrote to Gordon for advice. His reply advising her against this arrived after she had accepted McGlinn's offer and opened the second shop.

Anita Roddick on her West Sussex estate. Her spirit, strength of character and uncompromising individuality infuriated the men in suits in the City of London and created the phenomenon of ethical retailing.

With Anita preoccupied with the business, her mother Gilda bore the brunt of bringing up the children. By the time Gordon returned, many customers themselves wanted to open shops – this was green enterprise for people to whom conventional capitalism was anathema. Gordon, with no prior knowledge of franchising, 'invented' the Body Shop model: there were no start-up or franchising fees; the franchisee financed the store in return for the use of the name; and Body Shop supplied the products. Most new franchisees were – and still are – women. 'What is your favourite flower?' Anita would ask prospective candidates, 'How would you like to die?' She took an equally clear line with staff: they had to be knowledgeable, avoid the hard sell, and wait for the customer to ask them for advice. The products were priced between the mass market and luxury brands, and never discounted. Customers who returned to refill containers would however receive a 15 per cent discount. Nor would Body Shop pay for advertising – the products were the advertising. Body Shop's mission, to which both Roddicks strongly adhered, was to combine profits with principles for social and environmental change.

> **'TO SUCCEED YOU HAVE TO BELIEVE** in something with such a passion that it becomes a reality.' Anita Roddick, *Body and Soul* (1991)

GROWTH AND FLOTATION

By the early 1980s Anita's evangelical zeal for the Body Shop, her talent for self-promotion and her husband's sound business sense had driven rapid growth – 50 per cent annually or two new openings a month – and Body Shop had created the UK market for ethical beauty products. Anita Roddick was a household name, and press attention was so great that she hired a public relations firm. The first overseas shop – a kiosk in Brussels – had opened in 1978; the Roddicks also bought the US rights to the name from the San Francisco store, which continued as a small chain called Body Time.

> **'I HATE THE BEAUTY BUSINESS.** It is a monster industry selling unattainable dreams. It lies. It cheats. It exploits women.'
>
> Anita Roddick

In 1984, in a booming economy, Body Shop was floated on the London Stock Exchange; two years later its stock had risen in value from 95p to 820p. Ian McGlinn's original £4000 investment had grown to over £100 million, and the Roddicks increasingly devoted their wealth and energies to campaigns such as the Community Trade initiative, Greenpeace, Friends of the Earth and Children on the Edge. These relationships were sometimes turbulent – as might be expected given Anita Roddick's mercurial character. Nevertheless, Body Shop has established important trade partnerships in over 24 countries around the world that would otherwise be neglected by local and global capital.

A CONFLICT OF VALUES

As the United Kingdom boom turned to recession in 1991, share prices fell sharply and Roddick's outspokenness in the causes of the environment and 'greener' capitalism placed her at odds with some City analysts, Body Shop shareholders and even Body Shop franchisees. Roddick herself came to regard the flotation of Body Shop as 'a pact with the devil' and longed to take the company private again. Expansion in the USA, where there were over 2500 franchise applications in the first year, 1990, proved problematic, with poor market research, loose franchise controls, and competition from the likes of Bath and Body Works. Nonetheless, the underlying strength of the brand and its values meant that unlike many 1980s flotations the company withstood the worst of the recession. In 1991 Anita Roddick was honoured with the World Vision Award for Development Initiative. The Body Shop Foundation and Gordon Roddick also co-founded the *Big Issue* magazine, which gives employment to its homeless sellers.

The Roddicks persevered with expansion and social activism in the USA, in spite of hostile press coverage alleging plagiarism over the original name and concept. In 1998 Anita stepped down as chief executive of the company in a move that partly resolved the conflict of values between the City of London and the Body Shop ethos. Recognition elsewhere of her achievements led to numerous further awards and decorations, culminating in her creation as Dame Anita Roddick by Her Majesty the Queen in 2003.

By 2006 there were 2045 Body Shop stores and 80 million customers in 50 countries, and the company was one of the most trusted brands in the world. That year the company was bought and de-listed by the French L'Oréal cosmetics group for £652 million. Criticism was inevitable, but ignored the fact that L'Oréal had long been keen to develop natural products of the kind pioneered by the Roddicks, both of whom were approaching their mid-sixties after 30 years with the company.

PIONEERS OF ETHICAL CONSUMERISM

Anita Roddick briefly remained a part-time advisor to L'Oréal. Her commitment to her principles endured, as did her belief in transparency and her extraordinary partnership with her husband. One of the few women in this book, and the only significant woman entrepreneur, she inspired thousands of women Body Shop franchisees and 'educated' millions of customers through her retail philosophy. Whether regarded as the architects of a product tied to a social cause for business gain, or as exponents of 'profits with principles', she and her husband were the most successful exponents of the principle that accountability can equal profits. One of the legacies of the Roddicks is that today's stakeholder expects a new kind of integrity.

The many contradictions in Anita's character and her freedom of spirit testify to an idealist who changed the nature of retailing. As one of her favourite sayings, emblazoned on the side of Body Shop trucks, reads: 'If you think you are too small to have an impact, try going to bed with a mosquito.' Her death at the age of 64 in 2007 robbed ethical retailing and the debate over globalization of one of its most credible, experienced, charismatic and important practitioners.

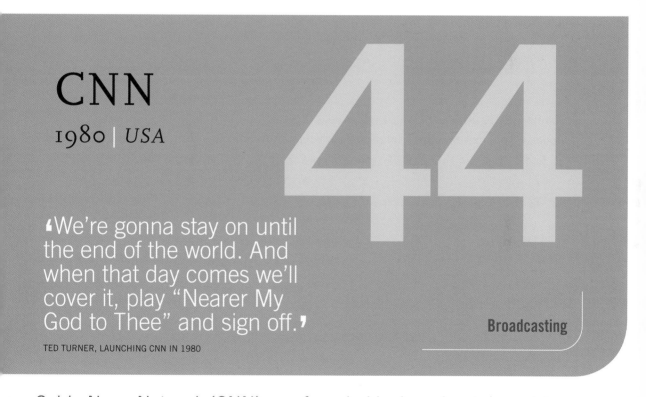

CNN
1980 | *USA*

44

‘We're gonna stay on until the end of the world. And when that day comes we'll cover it, play "Nearer My God to Thee" and sign off.’

TED TURNER, LAUNCHING CNN IN 1980

Broadcasting

Cable News Network (CNN) was founded by broadcaster, yachtsman, baseball fan and bison breeder Ted Turner as the first 24-hour live TV news network. Turner's father had mocked his son's choice of university course, and shortly afterwards committed suicide. Ted Turner married and divorced Hollywood actress Jane Fonda. Today CNN reaches 1.5 billion people in virtually every country in the world.

Robert Edward Turner III – a maverick character who has never been shy of publicity – attended Brown University, where his first choice of Classics made his father, in his own words, 'almost puke'. Turner switched to Economics, and was twice suspended from Brown for breaking dormitory rules, but eventually took his degree. He took over the Turner Outdoor Advertising billboard business in 1963, aged 24, after his father's death. The company was already worth

$1 million, and in 1970 Turner used the money to buy a broadcasting station in Atlanta, Georgia. He had spotted the potential of communications satellites and cable networks to boost the viewership and hence the advertising revenues of local broadcasters. This marked the beginning of the Turner Broadcasting System. In 1976 he bought the Atlanta Braves baseball team, giving WTBS, as it was known by this time, sports coverage and a profile in Major League Baseball.

'ALL THE NEWS, ALL THE TIME'

Turner launched Cable News Network (CNN) from a former country club on the outskirts of Atlanta at 5 p.m. on 1 June 1980. His unique selling point was 24-hour live coverage. The husband and wife team of David Walker and Lois Hart anchored the first broadcast. CNN's 24-hour live coverage swiftly became a must for all the millions who, like Turner, got home from work too late to watch the network news at 6.30 p.m. CNN meant it did not matter what time of day or night it was, the latest breaking news was there for *you*, to suit *you*, and the professionalism of its reporters soon put the network on the map.

> **'I'VE BEEN LEARNING HOW TO GIVE.** It's something you have to keep working on, because people like money the way they do their homes and their dogs.'
>
> Ted Turner

Unlike its bigger rivals, especially the BBC, CNN's international coverage often used local journalists, who were sometimes affected by the events they were reporting, thus conveying a greater sense of immediacy. The news channel that personalized news and the viewer itself began to make news, as CNN was attacked at home for being too 'liberal' or 'anti-American' and abroad, notably in the Middle East, for being too 'pro-American.' This played well with the typical liberal sophisticate news viewer in both constituencies.

EXPANSION INTO ENTERTAINMENT

Turner's creation and its audience grew, and in 1984 he launched Cable Music Channel as a rival to MTV, the phenomenally successful seamlessly self-repeating youth music and lifestyle cable network closest in style to CNN. The venture was unsuccessful, but Turner was never a man to be deterred, whatever the endeavour. Having failed in a bid to buy CBS, he promptly bought MGM/United Artists Entertainment for $1.5 billion, the volume of debt involved necessitating the disposal of all but MGM/UA's pre-merger film and TV library – a vast amount of material. Turner used this material and other assets to start new cable channels, including, in 1988, Turner Network Television, which he launched with a broadcast of *Gone With the Wind*.

'DO YOU KNOW what I want them to put on my tombstone? Do not disturb.**'** Ted Turner

By this time Turner had also purchased and reinvigorated the struggling Omni International development in downtown Atlanta, renaming it the CNN Center and buying the Atlanta Hawks baseball team from the developer into the bargain. As he had done with the Atlanta Braves, Turner turned ownership of the team and TV channel into mutually beneficial assets, and in the process created the 'Goodwill Games' as an arena for peace through sport.

BEING THERE

CNN's coverage of the *Challenger* space shuttle disaster in 1986 became the definitive unfolding story. The vivid imagery of the immediate aftermath of the disaster, the iconic, unbelievable and yet inescapable sequence of events, together with the tangibility of the human loss, made this effectively the first interactive tragedy in which the viewer was all but drawn alongside the disbelieving family and friends of the astronauts watching the drama come to its conclusion.

With the outbreak in 1991 of the First Gulf War, CNN scooped the 'big three' US networks – CBS, NBC and ABC – when Peter Arnett, Bernard Shaw and John Holliman became the only news reporters able to broadcast live from Baghdad as America began its bombing campaign. The resulting images helped to democratize information about the conflict. After the 'Black Hawk Down' helicopter disaster involving US troops in Somalia, Pentagon officials coined the phrase 'the CNN effect' in reference to the effects of real-time, uncensored coverage of the consequences of US foreign policy on public opinion, and on the policymakers.

CNN's reporters were becoming celebrities to match Ted Turner and his wife Jane Fonda, the movie star and activist to whom he was married from 1991 to 2001. Christiane Amanpour's exploits in Iraq made her one of the most highly paid reporters in television, caricatured as Adriana Cruz in the 1999 movie *Three Kings*. Turner himself had already merged CNN with Time Warner and was now something of a media mogul. CNN's coverage of the events of 9/11 only cemented its status as America's unshootable messenger.

In 2005 the network celebrated its 25th anniversary. Today it maintains networks that are watched by more than a quarter of the world's population. Many of the images that have shaped the world in the late 20th and early 21st centuries were first seen on CNN. CNN.com is now one of the most popular news websites on earth.

TIMELINE

1938
Birth of **Ted Turner**.

1963
Takes over his father's **advertising business**.

1970
Acquires a **broadcasting station** in Atlanta, Georgia.

1976
Buys the **Atlanta Braves** baseball team.

1980
Launches **CNN**.

1986
Buys **MGM/United Artists Entertainment**.

1988
Launches **Turner Network Television**.

1991
CNN scoops the coverage of the **First Gulf War**.

1991
Turner **marries** Jane Fonda.

1996
Merger of CNN with Time Warner.

2001
Divorces Jane Fonda.

2005
25th anniversary of CNN.

Breaking news – a CNN reporter after the terror attack on the twin towers of the World Trade Center, New York, 11 September 2001. Today the network reaches people in virtually every country on earth.

THE 'MOUTH FROM THE SOUTH'

Turner has been labelled the 'Mouth from the South' for his general ebullience and outspokenness. 'We have 28,000 – why can't they have 10?' he has said of Iran's alleged aspirations to obtain nuclear weapons. On another occasion he has stated that 'Men should be barred from public office for 100 years ... Let's give it to the women.' Turner, the largest private landowner in the US and the world's fifth-largest bison breeder, is also a major force in efforts to conserve the environment in America. Ted's Montana Grill, a restaurant chain he started with George McKerrow Jr, serves bison burgers across 18 states and proclaims 'Eat great. Do good.'

> **'THIS IS JUST IN.** You are looking at obviously a very disturbing live shot here. That is the World Trade Center, and we have unconfirmed reports this morning that a plane has crashed into one of the towers ...'
>
> Carol Lin, CNN, 8.49 a.m., 11 September 2001

Turner's truly American personality has undertaken the roles of both corporate executive and entrepreneur. Unlike the bison, his may be a dying breed, yet his example is likely to endure as an inspiration after his death. The question of whether or not his father would have approved might well be what has driven him all along.

SWATCH

1983 | *Switzerland*

45

Changing the face of our time

Watches
Automobiles

The Swatch Group is a *mezze* of companies founded by a Lebanese-American émigré to Switzerland who led the Swiss watch industry's counterattack against the Japanese. In the process he rescued Switzerland's national day, reinvented the timepiece and came up with the Smart Car.

By the early 1980s the rise of Japanese manufacturers had brought Swiss watchmaking to breaking point. The watches made by great names such as Omega and Longines had been supplanted by the digital quartz watches made by Seiko, Citizen and Casio in Japan and Hong Kong. Sales of Swiss watches had fallen to 15 per cent of the world market, and dropped by 25 per cent in a single year. In this dismal climate the liquidation of the Swiss watchmakers ASUAG and SSIH was called for by their bankers. The man chosen to administer the last rites to the two companies was Nicolas Hayek.

Hayek was born to a Lebanese mother and American father in Beirut, Lebanon, the cosmopolitan and commercial city that was once known as the 'Paris of the Orient.' When he was seven his family moved to Switzerland, and Hayek subsequently studied mathematics, physics and chemistry at the University of Lyon in France. In his capacity as head of his own business consulting firm, Hayek was brought in to oversee the liquidation of the two Swiss companies. Instead, with what would become his trademark panache, he set about the seemingly hopeless task of turning them around.

FACING DOWN THE JAPANESE – WITH FLAIR

Hayek was not alone in realizing that the traditional Swiss reputation for high quality was no longer enough to compete with the Japanese. Nevertheless, this reputation – enhanced by more efficient manufacturing processes, more advanced technology, fewer parts and lower production costs – could be sustained and leveraged where it would hurt the competition. As Hayek put it, 'The Japanese thought we would withdraw from there and concentrate on the production of expensive, high-class watches. They were totally flabbergasted when we

SWATCH

183

suddenly started our counterattack in the lower end of the market, and chose a head-on confrontation with their products.'

Under Hayek's guidance, the production line was automated, and the number of components reduced from 91 to 51. He introduced new, contemporary, even cheeky designs, offering high quality at aggressively competitive prices, and marketed the product to a mass audience with flair and drive. Hayek also began to unleash an un-Swiss penchant for self-publicity, though tempered with a hard business head. Switzerland, the land of penknives, neutrality and chocolate, was suddenly about to become interesting.

CREATING A COOL ACCESSORY RANGE

The first collection of 12 'Swatch' watches was launched on 1 March 1983. The name was assumed to stand for 'Swiss watch', but Hayek would always insist it was a contraction of 'second watch', denoting a fashion accessory. The implicit disposability of the watch, as opposed to the traditional trusty model kept for life and handed down the generations, encouraged huge repeat demand for further models. The retail price initially ranged between 39.9 and 49.9 Swiss francs, before being standardized at 50 francs. The target of 1 million sales in the first year was followed by 2.5 million in 1984. By this time the Swatches were a smash hit, to the extent that people began buying up more than one model, wearing two models at a time, either with one on each wrist or with one on one wrist and the other as a pony tail band.

> '**THE JAPANESE THOUGHT WE WOULD** ... concentrate on the production of expensive, high-class watches. They were totally flabbergasted when we suddenly started our counter-attack in the lower end of the market ...' Nicolas Hayek

Hayek and SMH, as the merged companies were renamed, had created the marketing dream of a new brand and a community of users, which, during the booming mid-1980s, spread rapidly beyond Switzerland across Europe to the United States of America. Many a suited 'yuppie', well able to afford a traditional watch ten times the price, sported an inexpensive, highly coloured Swatch as a clue to their 'real' personality. The first collection itself became a collector's item, which, in common with subsequent complete collections, thereafter changed hands for vast prices. Partnerships between Swatch and New York 'street' artists such as Keith Haring further drove the 'exclusivity' and cutting-edge lifestyle imagery of the brand. By 1993 SMH and the Swatch watches had taken Switzerland to over 50 per cent of the world market. Hayek was a national hero, and he built on the success of the Swatch brand by expanding research into plastics, battery innovation and electronic-motor technology.

THE SWATCHMOBILES

The Swiss had long lacked an indigenous automobile industry, and Swatch went into partnership with Volkswagen, then Daimler-Benz, in a venture to develop an entirely new kind of vehicle. The project echoed that of an earlier Middle Eastern émigré, Alec Issigonis, who 35 years previously had designed the world's most fashionable small car, the Mini.

Hayek and Daimler-Benz unveiled the first 'Swatchmobiles', the Eco-Sprinter and Eco-Speedster, in Stuttgart in 1994. The vehicles were 95 inches long and 55 inches wide, and could

The flamboyant Nicolas G. Hayek, founder and president of Swatch, the company that took the battle to keep time to the Japanese and won. Hayek went on to pioneer the hybrid-powered Smart Car automobile.

TIMELINE

———1928———
Birth of **Nicolas Hayek**.

———1983———
Hayek merges the Swiss watchmakers ASUAG and SSIH into a single entity, later known as SMH, and launches the **Swatch**.

———1993———
Switzerland takes more than **50 per cent of the world watch market**, thanks to Swatch.

———1994———
Hayek and Daimler-Benz unveil the first 'Swatchmobiles' or **Smart Cars**.

———1998———
SMH becomes the **Swatch Group**.

———2005———
Swatch pulls out of the Smart Car.

———2007———
Hayek enters into a new partnership to develop a **hybrid engine**.

park at right angles to the pavement, yet carry two adults and shopping through city traffic. The petro-electric hybrid power unit under the floor had a range of 350 miles and could generate a top speed of 90 miles per hour. The body was made from lightweight plastic, yet could withstand considerable impact. By the following summer, Daimler-Benz was besieged with orders from potential dealers and customers, and in 1997 construction began at Hambach, a small town in France near the German and Swiss borders, of a $450 million plant that would employ 2000 people and produce 200,000 cars a year.

Hayek, the Swatch Group (as SMH was renamed in 1998) and Daimler-Benz had created in the 'Smart (Swatch Mercedes Art) Car' the most revolutionary vehicle since the Mini. There were some problems: critics pointed to its high retail cost and small front crumple zone, and the engine development proved more expensive than expected. In 2005 Swatch pulled out. However, the underlying concept was irresistible, and the vehicles went on to sell to nearly 1 million customers in various forms in 25 countries, predominantly in Europe and North America.

THE RESTORATION OF NATIONAL PRIDE

Swatch today is still best known for its watches: having claimed the low ground, Swatch brands have also reclaimed the high ground with Breguet, Blancpain, Omega and Longines; and the middle ground, with Tissot, Calvin Klein and Pierre Balmain. Perhaps Hayek's most important legacy, however, will prove to have been in the field of post-hydrocarbon automobile propulsion. Hayek had always been disappointed that the Smart Cars eventually carried a conventional engine: 'I want to do everything within my powers to accelerate the development of alternative and renewable energy,' he told *Hebdo* magazine in 2007. In the same year he entered into partnership with Swiss Group E to develop an electric engine running on energy released by a hydrogen fuel cell.

Hayek, his son Nick and daughter Nayla remained active in the company. In 2007 Hayek learned that the Swiss national celebrations in the historic Rutli Meadow, where the nation was born out of resistance to Austria in 1291, were to be cancelled because the local authorities refused to pay the $170,000 cost of security protection against disruption by skinheads and neo-Nazis. Hayek, the 'outsider' who had always had an ambivalent relationship with his adopted country, together with a Swiss fellow businessman, modestly dipped into his estimated $3 billion fortune to put up the money. Thus it was that a Lebanese-American, who had become the world's 273rd richest person, helped save Switzerland's national day.

EUROTUNNEL 46

1987 | France / UK

> "I believe the commercial advantages of this tunnel would be enormous."
> WILLIAM EWART GLADSTONE, 1888

Infrastructure

The Channel Tunnel linking Great Britain and France opened in 1994, overcoming centuries of mistrust and enmity between the two nations, separated by only 22 miles of sea. When on 1 December 1990 the two halves of the undersea service tunnel met 130 feet beneath the seabed of the English Channel (*la Manche* to the French), it became possible to walk on dry land from Great Britain to continental Europe for the first time since the end of the last ice age some 10,000 years ago. The story of the Channel Tunnel is long, arduous and packed with incident – and continues to this day.

European union – workmen holding the flags of Britain and France rolled back 1000 years of hostility when the two countries' excavation crews met in the middle of the Channel Tunnel, 30 October 1990.

The idea for a tunnel beneath the English Channel was first proposed in 1802 by a French engineer, Albert Mathieu-Favier. Passengers would travel in horse-drawn coaches along a road lit by oil lamps, and an island in mid-channel would provide fresh air and rest for the horses. The estimated cost was £1 million in the currency of the time. With the resumption of hostilities between Britain and Napoleon's France the following year, Mathieu-Favier's proposal was quickly forgotten.

> **'I BELIEVE THE COMMERCIAL ADVANTAGES** of this tunnel would be enormous … there is now some chance for common sense and the exercise of that spirit of enterprise that has been at all times among the noblest characteristics of our country.**'**
>
> William Ewart Gladstone MP, Leader of the Liberal Party, House of Commons, London, 27 June 1888

HANDS ACROSS *LA MANCHE*

From 1865 onwards, with Britain and France having been at peace for an unprecedented 50 years, successive British governments in correspondence with the French considered, supported and rejected the idea of a tunnel on technical, commercial or military grounds. In 1875 the underground-railway engineer Peter William Barlow suggested a floating steel tube across the Channel. The idea was rejected, but both French and British governments passed bills enabling a concession to build a tunnel; this expired with insufficient funds having been raised. Trial borings continued to take place on both sides, and rival companies sprang up, such as the South Eastern Railway and Submarine Continental Railway Company.

When in 1882 the Channel Tunnel Company looked set to raise sufficient funds, a wide-spread panic orchestrated by figures such as the poets Robert Browning and Alfred Lord Tennyson prompted the British Board of Trade to veto the project on the grounds that invaders would too easily be able to attack from the Continent. Prime Minister William Gladstone rejected the proposal in 1884; his U-turn in favour in 1888 came too late, and there was no further attempt until 1922, when a tunnel was bored 400 feet out from the chalk cliffs between Folkestone and Dover, before political objections again put paid to the project.

A DREAM (EVENTUALLY) COMES TRUE

The Second World War, Britain's postwar bankruptcy and the Cold War all conspired against further tunnel proposals. In 1955, however, with the Marshall Plan reconstructing Europe, Britain abandoned its opposition to a tunnel wide enough to accommodate Soviet tanks. The Tunnel sous la Manche (Tunnel under the Channel) study group reported in 1960 and recommended two main railway tunnels and a smaller service tunnel. Work began in 1973, but the test tunnel bored from the British side had only extended 820 feet when the first OPEC oil shock of 1974 and subsequent worldwide recession again caused the project to be abandoned on grounds of cost.

When in 1984 the British and French governments put out requests for tenders to build a privately funded link across the Channel, the 1973 plan resurfaced in essence as the preferred of four options – a road tunnel, a bridge, and two different proposals for rail tunnels. On 12 February 1986 the two governments signed the Franco-British Channel Fixed Link Treaty in Canterbury, Kent. Ninety-eight years after Gladstone's speech to Parliament, the dream of a Channel Tunnel was finally coming true.

THE END OF INSULARITY

For the British in particular this marked the beginning of the end of isolation from 'the Continent', which could only be reached either by expensive and time-consuming air travel or by the (then) monopolistic and insanitary cross-Channel ferries. The cosmopolitan strata of British society already cooked and ate French cuisine, sent their children to France on exchanges and as au pairs, drove French cars, and in some cases educated their children at the French Lycée in London. The turning over of the first gigantic Tunnel Boring Machines (TBMs) at Sangatte near Calais and Shakespeare Cliff near Folkestone sounded the death knell for Anglophobia and Francophobia.

> ## Tunnel troubles
>
> A fire aboard a shuttle train carrying trucks and trailers in 1996 caused £200 million of damage, but without loss of life. Over a dozen asylum seekers attempting to enter Britain died attempting to ride or jump onto moving trains until in 2002 the French closed the refugee centre at Sangatte, the two countries having agreed to take their own share of would-be migrants.

Over the next three years, 13,000 workers tunnelled simultaneously from both sides of the Channel through the chalk stratum beneath the seabed under the management of the Anglo-French Trans-Manche Link, a consortium of ten construction companies and five banks from the two countries. Eleven TBMs were used to drill, excavate, shore up and remove material from the three tunnels.

On 1 December 1990, guided by laser, the two halves of the service tunnel met, and tunnellers Phillipe Cozette and Graham Fagg cut the opening under the eyes of the world's press. The French laid on a champagne buffet, and the British tea and sandwiches. The difference between the centrelines where the two halves met was measured vertically at just 2.3 inches and horizontally at 14.1 inches. The two main rail tunnels met on 22 May and 28 June 1991 respectively; when each pair of TBMs met, the French machine was dismantled and transported back down the tunnel, while the British TBM was diverted into the rock and concreted in place for ever.

By the time the Queen and President Mitterand officially opened the tunnel on 6 May 1994 in a ceremony held at Calais, the project was already a year behind schedule and 80 per cent over budget, at an estimated cost of £10 billion. The burden of debt and flawed forecasting over volumes of passenger and freight traffic would haunt Eurotunnel plc in the UK and Eurotunnel SA in France for many years. In 2007, after a four-year battle against bankruptcy, Eurotunnel plc/SA was restructured in an unprecedented deal driven by French shareholders. The deal proposed writing off over £2 billion in debt and eventually handing 87 per cent of the company to its creditors.

THE 'CHUNNEL' IN OPERATION

Eurotunnel offers three principal services: a shuttle for vehicles, the Eurostar passenger service linking London, Paris and Brussels, and freight trains. By 2005, 8.2 million passengers a year were travelling on the Eurostar trains, while the shuttle trains were carrying over 2 million cars, 1.3 million trucks and over 77,000 coaches. The numbers of passengers on Eurostar were expected to rise substantially with the opening of the high-speed Channel Tunnel Rail Link between the entry point to the tunnel at Ashford in Kent and St Pancras in London in 2007. The Channel ferries, which once tyrannized generations of travellers, were forced into greater competitiveness and levels of service for those who preferred a sea crossing to a 20-minute journey cocooned in their cars in a shuttle train beneath the seabed at speeds of up to 100 mph.

Above all, the tunnel engendered a new Euromindedness on both sides of the Channel. Day trips on business and shopping between Paris, London and Brussels became the norm, while French migration increased to southeast England, as did British home ownership in France. As an engineering feat, the Channel Tunnel merits comparison with the first transcontinental railroad in North America, Tapline in Saudi Arabia and North Sea oil production. The American Society of Civil Engineers has declared it to be one of the Seven Wonders of the Modern World.

1802
Albert Mathieu-Favier proposes a tunnel beneath the English Channel.

1875
Peter William Barlow suggests a floating steel tube.

1882
The British government **vetoes** a tunnel proposal on security grounds.

1922
An attempt to construct a tunnel is **abandoned after 400 feet**.

1973
Work on **another tunnel** begins, but **is abandoned** the following year.

1986
The British and French governments sign a **treaty** to build a tunnel.

1990
The two halves of the **service tunnel** meet.

1991
The **two rail tunnels** are completed.

1994
The Channel Tunnel is **opened**.

2007
The opening of the Channel Tunnel Rail Link at last provides **high-speed access for rail passengers** on the English side.

ENDEMOL

1994 | Netherlands

47

> 'Television is actually closer to reality than anything in books.' CAMILLE PAGLIA

**Broadcasting
Reality TV**

Endemol – the company name is an amalgam of the names of the founders – is a television production company based in the Netherlands. It is worth over $5 billion, and its core product is programming that suspends traditional conventions of privacy, turns humiliation into entertainment and nobodies into celebrities, and combines the values of the Roman amphitheatre with the world of *The Truman Show*.

The origins of 'reality' television date back nearly four decades. In 1969 the documentary *A Married Couple* followed a Canadian family over ten weeks, recording the worsening relations between the man and woman. In 1972 some 10 million viewers tuned in over a year as the parents of a Californian family become estranged to the point of divorce. The 1974 UK series *The Family* shrewdly observed the dysfunctionality of another 'normal' couple. The traditional boundary between documentary and drama remained intact in these programmes.

But in 1992 the series *Sylvania Waters*, chronicling the lives of a brash, racist and foul-mouthed Australian family, turned its matriarch, Noeline Baker, into a celebrity. The 'docu-soap' was born. In the same year MTV's *The Real World* assembled seven young New Yorkers in a loft apartment and shot them for six months, attracting 700,000 viewers a week. In 1996 *Jennicam* self-chronicled the life, sex included, of Jennifer Ringley, a 20-year-old student in Carlisle, Pennsylvania, this time connecting the video footage to the internet. At the height of its popularity the expanded, subscription-driven site was receiving between 3 and 4 million hits a day, and its 'heroine' hundreds of emails from unknown fans. In 1997 Sweden's *Expedition Robinson* caused the

> 'IN THE FUTURE, everyone will be famous for 15 minutes.'
> Andy Warhol, 1968

new 'reality' format to become the subject of a debate in the country's parliament after one of the participants, a Bosnian emigrant to Sweden, committed suicide.

190　COMPANIES THAT CHANGED THE WORLD

ENDE VERSUS MOL

Endemol's founders, Joop van den Ende and John de Mol, came from very different backgrounds – one in theatre production and the other in television entertainment. Van den Ende was older and more successful; de Mol, the grandson of a bandleader, had been a teenage disc jockey and a compulsive risk-taker from a young age.

When he was 28 his company, John de Mol Productions, was only saved from bankruptcy by investment from another former disc jockey and successful music entrepreneur, Willem van Kooten. Van Kooten backed de Mol's idea of creating and exploiting new television formats, and de Mol soon repaid his confidence, launching shows for Rupert Murdoch's Sky in the

> '*BIG BROTHER* WILL BE FOR **ENDEMOL** what Mickey Mouse is for Disney.'
>
> John de Mol, 1999

Netherlands in parallel with his own new daily music shows such as the *DJ Cat Show*. De Mol also acquired the Dutch rights to *Family Feud* and sold Merv Griffin's *The Wheel of Fortune* to Belgian and Dutch channels.

De Mol was determined to outdo his rival Joop van den Ende – with whom he was on good terms – and coming up with a new format to push the envelope. *The Shirt from Your Body*, broadcast in 1984, was a chat show without a host, in which the audience asked questions of a celebrity guest. *Medical Centre West*, a melodramatic hospital drama, confronted issues such as euthanasia head-on. In *All You Need Is Love* straight and gay people were encouraged to act out

***Big Brother's* 15 minutes of fame** – British reality TV celebrity Jade Goody and Indian film actress Shilpa Shetty fought it out on camera in the modern-day equivalent of public humiliation in the Roman amphitheatre.

their romantic feelings for each other live in the studio, while in *Love Letters* the prizes included a live wedding. De Mol called his new format 'emotainment'. In 1994 he and van den Ende merged their foreign operations while keeping their Dutch companies separate and competing. They called the new company Endemol, and with 2500 hours of programmes and a turnover of £150 million a year the merger made them the largest independent producers in Europe.

PROJECT X

In 1996, as the dotcom boom got going, one-third of Endemol was floated on the Amsterdam Stock Exchange. The issue was 18 times oversubscribed, but the backlash from the company's participation in a failed secret bid to snatch the rights to broadcast the Dutch Football League from public broadcasters damaged the share price. De Mol and his colleagues personally paid off Endemol's losses. Investors were impressed but de Mol was less so with the 'teenage scribblers' – financial analysts often just out of university who influenced the fortunes of public companies. It was in this climate that the Dutch public broadcaster KRO asked for a new programme idea to fill a gap in the schedules. De Mol and three colleagues sat down one evening and talked late into the night. They came up with the idea of locking people in a house for one hundred days and filming them day and night as viewers voted to evict them one by one until only a single person was left to win a fortune. The idea variously excited, shocked, appalled, disgusted and gripped them and their colleagues. They called it 'Project X'.

Two years would pass, during which time the movie *The Truman Show* satirized the commercialism of 'reality' programming, while young people across America showed an increasing willingness to prostitute themselves, sometimes literally, on camera and interactively through the web. Shows such as *Who Wants to be a Millionaire* attracted vast audiences in the UK and sold to Disney in the USA. Throughout this time de Mol tried and failed to find a Dutch broadcaster for 'Project X' – by this time known as *Big Brother*. By 1999 Endemol's share price had fallen, and de Mol's persistence and risk-taking over *Big Brother* was bringing the company close to the edge. The first deal, with HMG, the owner of the small Dutch Veronica channel, saved Endemol and would remake its fortunes hundreds of times over. *Big Brother* was alive, and while the Dutch media speculated that the experience might provoke suicide among participants, de Mol was considering a multi-billion dollar merger with the British Pearson media conglomerate and telling his team that '*Big Brother* will be for Endemol what Mickey Mouse is for Disney.' A week later *Big Brother* was a smash hit in Holland and de Mol had turned down Pearson's offer. Bart and Sabine, two housemates in the first series, had been shown apparently having sex on camera and Sabine had been evicted from the house. *Big Brother* captured half the 13-to-34-year-olds watching television in the Netherlands, and decimated the ratings both for the nightly news on the public channel and a rival soap produced by Joop van den Ende – an Endemol show.

> **'THESE PEOPLE ARE PROSTITUTING THEMSELVES** to media conglomerates. It's very troubling.'
>
> President Bill Clinton on *Big Brother* contestants

BIG BROTHER GOES GLOBAL

Big Brother was sold by Endemol (UK) to Channel 4 in the United Kingdom and CBS in the United States. In these and other national versions the production and cast of housemates would be 'homegrown'. In 2000 the German version, broadcast by RTL2, provoked outrage from the prime minister of the Rhineland-Pfalz region and the Catholic Countrywomen's Association. What had upset them was the apparent sexual contact between two of the house-mates on camera – which helped to generate 30,000 press articles during the run and catapulted the programme and the channel to the top of the ratings. In the same year, shortly before the dotcom bubble burst, de Mol, van den Ende and Endemol accepted a €5.5 billion cash and share offer from the Spanish telecom and media corporation Telefonica. After the sale van den Ende retired, worth a billion euros, and de Mol was worth even more.

In each roll-out of the *Big Brother* format the same pattern recurred to a greater or lesser degree, according to variations in local mores. The programme was an even bigger hit in Spain than in Germany or Holland, the flashpoint again being romance between a couple. In Italy the head of Endemol's production company in Rome consulted with the pope's confessor, and incurred the wrath of the pontiff himself, and of the intellectual left. But as elsewhere, *Grande Fratello* cruised up the ratings. In the United States, President Clinton told ABC News: 'How can these people, particularly the parents, abandon their families and children for a chance at money and dis-grace.' When the interviewer suggested that certain events in the pres-ident's life had been played out in public, Clinton replied: 'That's the problem. Privacy should be protected. My lack of privacy is the direct result of my position as President of the United States ... These people are prostituting themselves to media conglomerates. It's very trou-bling.' Clinton's statements again guaranteed the attention of younger viewers and pushed *Big Brother* up the ratings.

TIMELINE

1992
The Australian series *Sylvania Waters* marks the birth of the 'docu-soap' and 'reality' TV.

1994
Joop van den Ende and John de Mol found **Endemol**.

1996
One third of the company is **floated** on the Amsterdam Stock Exchange.

1999
Endemol launches **Big Brother** in the Netherlands.

2000
Big Brother launches in the **USA, UK, Germany, Spain and Italy**. Many other countries follow.

2000
Endemol accepts an acquisition offer from **Telefonica**.

2005
Endemol is **partly floated** again.

2007
Telefonica decides to sell its 75 per cent share.

The first United Kingdom flashpoint was class rather than sex, when 'Nasty Nick' Bateman, with a privileged background and a broking job in the City, was revealed to have manipulated his housemates until exposed and confronted by diminutive, dyslexic builder Craig Phillips. Thirty million web hits later, Bateman was evicted for breaking the rules and sold his story to a tabloid newspaper. In Germany, Zlatko, the tone-deaf Macedon-ian car mechanic who had never heard of Shakespeare and tried to remove his chest hair with nail scissors, became a 'trash hero' who issued his own bestselling music CD, unsuccessfully entered the heats for the Eurovision Song Contest, and in the end drove back home to his mother in a Porsche. Similar tales of notoriety and fleeting celebrity have flickered around the show in countries as diverse as Australia, India, Portugal, Bahrain, France, Mexico, Denmark, Colombia and Nigeria.

'CIVILIZATION AS WE KNOW IT'

Endemol's best-known creation coincided with the world-changing convergence of television, telephony and the web, and proved that governments and public-interest groups can no longer control or manipulate public opinion through television – particularly among the young. By

2005 viewers had switched on *Big Brother* more than 18 billion times and cast more than 1 billion votes. In 2005 Endemol was partly floated again and listed on the Euronext exchange. In 2007 Telefonica announced its intention to sell its 75 per cent share; one of the interested parties, who had exited in 2004 as one of the richest men in Europe, was John de Mol.

As the Australian-born British-based writer Germaine Greer has observed: 'Reality television is not the end of civilization as we know it, it *is* civilization as we know it.' Another way of looking at the phenomenon is to identify the difference between participating in a quasi-life, and getting a life. The choice, like the vote, is up to the viewer.

EBAY

1995 | *USA*

48

'People are basically good. ' PIERRE OMIDYAR

Online auction hosting

eBay began life in California's Silicon Valley as an impromptu auction board on the website of a ponytailed Paris-born Iranian-American software programmer called Pierre Omidyar. The first item sold was Omidyar's own broken laser pointer, which went for $14.83. When he emailed the winning bidder to remind them that it was broken, the buyer replied: 'I'm a collector of broken laser pointers.'

Omidyar assembled a list of friends with items for sale: a toy powerboat, an Amiga games console, a 1989 Toyota Tercel, a pair of autographed Marky Mark underpants. This was the genesis of AuctionWeb, an online 'community of users' with a quirky sense of individual uniqueness, very different to the sort of customers who are processed through a shopping mall. Omidyar believed 'people are basically good', and initially charged users no fee; but as more and more business flooded in he added a charge on completed transactions to cover his internet costs. The first staff were recruited from the user community: they included a former actor who assumed the online persona of 'Uncle Griff', a 50-something cross-dressing dairy farmer who kept his dead mother in a closet with her mouth duct-taped shut. Another, known only to users as 'Skippy', was a systems expert who claimed to live in a cave with a pet vole.

> **'EVEN WHEN TRANSACTIONS** reached $300,000 a month the banks wouldn't lend us any money.'
>
> Pamela Omidyar, wife of the founder, on the early days of eBay

FROM COMMUNITY TO CORPORATE

Early funding for the business was non-existent, except through the modest commission taken on sales. As these mounted the company could not keep up: with no receptionist, let alone book-keeper, sacks of uncashed cheques lay around the makeshift offices. As Pamela Omidyar recalled: 'Even when transactions reached $300,000 a month the banks wouldn't lend us any money.' This hippy-ish ambience belied the fact that Pierre Omidyar already had a track record in Silicon Valley, where he had sold a software company to Microsoft and made himself a millionaire in the process.

In 1996 Omidyar hired Jeff Skoll as the first president of the company, and the community of users took the next step towards becoming a corporate. Critically, Omidyar also wrote to the 'community' with the cornerstone statement of his 'grand experiment': buyers and sellers would be encouraged to give a rating to everyone they dealt with, posting this with an additional comment online for the benefit of all. This was the 'feedback forum' that would become one of AuctionWeb's unique selling points. In the same year, AuctionWeb entered into a licensing deal with Electronic Travel Auction to sell air tickets and other travel products.

A WORLDWIDE BAZAAR

In 1997 Omidyar secured $5 million in venture capital, and in the same year an eBay public relations manager fabricated the myth that the company was founded to enable Pamela Omidyar to trade a collection of Pez candy dispensers. In 1998 eBay hired Meg Whitman – Harvard MBA, ex-Procter & Gamble, Hasbro and Disney – as CEO and president, with the aim of bringing eBay to market on Nasdaq. This made Omidyar and Skoll billionaires, and 75 employees became millionaires. Whitman took eBay and its 'netizens' from an online yard sale to one of the world's leading brands; she has maintained this position with very few mistakes ever since. Butterfield & Butterfield, a bricks-and-mortar auction house acquired in 1999, did not pay back and was sold on to Bonhams at a modest loss. In the same year, eBay's computers crashed for 22 hours, costing $4 million in lost revenues

What's in a name?

Omidyar officially changed the name AuctionWeb to eBay in 1997, although AuctionWeb was already trading under the name. eBay was Omidyar's second choice. His preferred name was EchoBay.com, to match his consulting firm, Echo Bay Technology Group, but he discovered that EchoBay.com was already taken by Echo Bay Mines, a gold-mining company. His second choice turned out to be the gold mine.

and wiping $5 billion off its market value. Whitman's handling of the crisis was widely praised, and squashed critics on Wall Street.

eBay itself has shopped widely, acquiring ownership or control of Alando, which became eBay Germany in 1999, Mercado Libre and Lokau in South America in 2001, iBazar in France in 2001, EachNet in China in 2003, Baazee.com in India in 2004, Internet Auction Co. in South Korea in 2004, Marktplaats in the Netherlands in 2004, Gumtree in the UK in 2005, Loquo in Spain in 2005, Opus Forum in Germany in 2005, and Tradera.com in Sweden in 2006. eBay also owns PayPal, the online money-transaction facility – for which eBay users had demonstrated a preference over eBay's own Billpoint system. Another acquisition was Skype, the internet telephony service, bought in 2005 for $4.1 billion.

IT'S COMMERCE, BUT NOT AS WE KNEW IT

Every day, millions of collectibles, appliances, computers, pieces of furniture and other items are bought and sold on eBay. Approximately 1.3 million sellers and traders around the world use eBay as their primary or secondary source of income. In 2003 bids for a human kidney and the virginity of a Florida student reached into the millions before the items were withdrawn. Likewise the nation of Iraq – conveniently situated on the Uzbekistan–Syria superhighway, with historical sites, presidential palaces and 'oil, oil, oil' – opened at 99 cents and reached $99 million before eBay deleted the item. In 2004 a cough sweet sucked by Arnold Schwarzenegger was offered for sale but withdrawn by eBay on the grounds that its owner was still alive.

> **'BEYOND FULFILLING A FINANCIAL FUNCTION,** trade also satisfies another human need – social contact.'
>
> Jeff Skoll, president of eBay 1996–8, writing in 1999

In 2005 the wife of a British disc jockey auctioned off his Lotus Esprit sports car with a Buy It Now price of 50 pence after she heard him flirting with a model on air. The car was sold within five minutes and collected the same day. In the same year a Volkswagen Golf previously registered to Cardinal Joseph Ratzinger (who had been elected Pope Benedict XVI) was auctioned on eBay's German site for €188,938.88. The winning bid was made by the GoldenPalace.com online casino. Also in 2005, Sinn Fein attempted to auction a surveillance device planted by MI5 in its Belfast headquarters. When eBay removed it from the website saying that Sinn Fein had violated two sections of the eBay user's agreement, Sinn Fein accused eBay of censorship. The most expensive item sold on eBay to date is a Gulfstream jet for $4.9 million.

FULFILLING A HUMAN NEED

eBay's spectacular growth has seen its founding ideal of a 'community of users' survive intact, and has unleashed a capacity to create 'social capital' among individuals in an increasingly isolating post-industrial world. Jeff Skoll, writing in *Forbes* magazine in 1999, noted: 'Beyond fulfilling a financial function, trade also satisfies another human need – social contact. In the course of a transaction, a buyer and seller may find common interests, exchange gossip and even develop a relationship.' eBay is also a barometer of the darker side of human nature, and is vulnerable to exploitation and abuse. Forbidden items include narcotics, Nazi paraphernalia, firearms, used underwear and human body parts. 'Shill bidding' (in which the price is artificially

1967
Birth of **Pierre Omidyar**.

1995
Omidyar founds **AuctionWeb**.

1996
Omidyar hires **Jeff Skoll** as the first president of the company.

1997
AuctionWeb is officially renamed **eBay**.

1998
Meg Whitman takes over as CEO and president, and floats the company.

2006
eBay's revenues reach **$5.9 billion**.

2007
eBay bids for UK-based **QXL**, which hosts auction sites in Switzerland and Eastern Europe.

Where real and virtual worlds meet – the eBay 'juggernaut' spawned a host of enterprises within its worldwide membership of some 222 million, changing the buying and selling habits of a generation in the process.

driven up by collusion) and fraud (in increasingly ingenious forms) are difficult to detect and combat in a consumer service based on trust. Cases of eBay 'addiction' – resulting in obsessive spending, ill-health and debt – are not uncommon, notably in the UK, where 10 per cent of all internet time is spent on eBay. Britons are also the world's highest per capita eBay spenders.

If eBay's 222 million members were a country, they would constitute the world's fifth largest population. The world's biggest online marketplace – with revenues in 2006 of $5.9 billion and 11,600 employees – has changed the buying and selling habits of a generation. The popular saying within eBay that 'A monkey could drive this train' belies the skill and consistency with which the company sticks to its focus: the customer. This in the opinion of one analyst makes the company 'the best business model within the internet sector' and a juggernaut that looks set to run and run. By 2007 eBay had expanded to almost two dozen countries, including India and China. Pierre and Pamela Omidyar, who by this time lived back in Paris, announced they were to donate much of their wealth to Pierre's *alma mater*, Tufts University.

AL JAZEERA

1996 | Qatar

‘I think with my eyes.’

ARAB PROVERB

Broadcasting

Al Jazeera is an Arabic- and English-speaking television network headquartered in Doha, the capital of the emirate of Qatar on the Persian Gulf. Its freedom of speech is welcome to citizens of the Middle East and unwelcome to presidents of the United States. As the information hub linking the Islamic world and the West, it is probably the most influential and misrepresented broadcasting organization in the world.

Concepts of public and private life in the Middle East differ radically from those in the West. In the former, the importance of 'face' and dignity is fundamental in both tribal and urban societies. Intrusiveness and discourtesy are as taboo in broadcast journalism as they are in society. At the same time, politics is the consuming topic of conversation in tea houses and private homes across the region. The media in the Middle East, in the form of press, radio and terrestrial TV, have traditionally been under the tight control of autocratic rulers, from President Nasser of Egypt to Saddam Hussein of Iraq, from Colonel Gaddafi of Libya to the ayatollahs of Iran. In opposition to the version of events promulgated by the official media are the unofficial versions disseminated in the *souk* – the bazaar – as potent and rapid a conduit of information as many a Western TV channel.

The Western concept of the 'freedom of the press' is as alien in many areas of the Middle East as the 'democracy' that America and the United Kingdom tried to export to Iraq following the invasion of 2003. Within its own terms of reference, however, the media in the Middle East mirrors the societies of the region in the sophistication and complexity of its language and terms of reference. Key issues include the relationship of Islam to the state; the identity of individual nations versus the *umma* or 'nation' of Muslims; liberalism versus

'VICIOUS, INACCURATE AND INEXCUSABLE.'

US Secretary of Defense Donald Rumsfeld gives his opinion of Al Jazeera's coverage during the 2003 Iraq War.

conservatism; the repression of women versus their emancipation; republicanism versus monarchy; modernization versus loss of heritage and identity; and public and private attitudes towards the state of Israel. The history of the media in many parts of the Middle East and North Africa, from Algeria to Iran, is one of suppression, censorship, shutdowns, exile, persecution and murder.

THE INFORMATION REVOLUTION

All these uses, abuses and taboos began to be disrupted in the mid-1990s with the coming of satellite TV and the internet, both media that could not easily be manipulated or suppressed. The king of Morocco was no longer immune to criticism from modernizers on websites and blogs. Islamic 'jihadist' fundamentalism exemplified by Osama bin Laden and Al-Qaeda played its obscurantist terror agenda back against modernity through the same channels. This liberating and sometimes subversive freeing up of information media has had profound effects and implications around the world.

Qatar is a conservative emirate bordering Saudi Arabia, whose oil and natural-gas revenues have made it the 11th-richest per capita country in the world. In 1995 the present emir seized power from his father in a bloodless coup while the latter was in Switzerland. Evolutionary rather than revolutionary change followed. Women were given the vote and a new constitution was enshrined. Most unusually, the new emir granted $150 million to start a television station. When the BBC World Service Arabic station, trusted for its impartiality in the Middle East, was shut down by the Saudi authorities after it refused to bow to their censorship, many staff joined the new station over the border in Qatar. It was called Al Jazeera – 'The Island'.

TIMELINE

——— 1996 ———
Formation of **Al Jazeera**.

——— 1999 ———
The Algerian government tries to disrupt an Al Jazeera broadcast airing the **views of dissidents**.

——— 2001 ———
Al Jazeera broadcasts video tapes in which **Osama bin Laden** seeks to justify the 9/11 terror attacks.

——— 2001 ———
Al Jazeera's **office in Kabul** is destroyed by a US missile.

——— 2002 ———
Bahrain accuses Al Jazeera of being **pro-Israel** and bans it from reporting within its borders.

——— 2003 ———
Al Jazeera's **office in Baghdad** is destroyed by a US missile.

——— 2006 ———
Al Jazeera launches its **English-language channel**.

——— 2007 ———
Al Jazeera strikes internet distribution deal with **YouTube**.

Osama bin Laden appears on Al Jazeera Television on 17 October 2007, praising the terror attacks of 11 September, and defying the United States in its threats to attack Afghanistan's Taliban regime.

Al Jazeera was modelled on CNN and BBC World, and introduced a freedom of speech previously unknown to Middle Eastern viewers. Its agenda – to report news and air the debates of the *souk* on an informed and critical basis – was a significant event in the history of the region. Governments used to controlling the flow of information and debate were outflanked and forced into repressive measures that only underlined the station's importance. In 1999 the Algerian government went so far as to cut off the electricity supply to parts of the capital and several cities during a live debate in which dissidents implicated the Algerian military in a series of atrocities. The station also won widespread praise throughout 2000 and 2001 for its coverage of the conflict in Lebanon.

9/11 AND AFTER

This impact went largely unnoticed outside the Middle East until the terror attacks of 11 September 2001. The United States government had previously praised the station for its independence: this changed when Al Jazeera broadcast (without comment) video tapes in which Osama bin Laden and Sulaiman Abu Ghaith sought to justify the Al-Qaeda terror attacks. The station was accused by the United States government of acting as a 'propaganda' tool on behalf of the terrorists. The station replied that it was making available information relating to the most significant political event of the 21st century. Western television networks subsequently also broadcast sections of the tapes. Nonetheless, Al Jazeera apparently became a target for the Bush administration and the United States military. In late 2001, shortly after the station disclosed the whereabouts of its Kabul office, the latter was destroyed by an American missile strike during the invasion of Afghanistan.

Paradoxically, in 2002 the government of Qatar's neighbouring Gulf state of Bahrain banned Al Jazeera from reporting inside the country on the grounds that it was 'biased' in favour of Israel. This, if nothing else, suggested an even-handedness on the part of the station at odds with American accusations, and probably informed the decision in 2003 by the BBC to enter into an agreement with Al Jazeera to share resources, including news footage.

THE IRAQ WAR

After the 2003 US invasion of Iraq, Al Jazeera's reporting and transmission of pictures of captured US soldiers provoked Defense Secretary Donald Rumsfeld to describe the network's coverage as 'vicious, inaccurate and inexcusable'. (Rumsfeld himself had seen his own views accurately and fairly reported in a 2001 interview with the network.) Al Jazeera's new English-language website was shortly afterwards attacked by American computer hackers, one of whom was subsequently prosecuted. The network's reporters were banned 'on security grounds' from the floor of the New York Stock Exchange and Nasdaq. In April 2003, after Al Jazeera had disclosed the whereabouts of its Baghdad office to the US military in order to protect its staff, a US missile struck the building, killing reporter Tareq Ayyoub.

The following year, when the station broadcast anonymously-sent videos showing Al-Qaeda kidnap victims pleading for their lives and reading out propaganda messages under coercion, Al Jazeera's Iraq office was closed by the Iraqi government and US forces. Contrary to popular myth, Al Jazeera, unlike other websites, has never shown the beheading of a hostage.

STRIKING A BALANCE

When Al Jazeera opened its English-language channel in 2006, the Murdoch-owned Fox News channel in the United States repeated the 'beheading' allegations, even though these were erroneous. In 2007 the channel struck a deal with YouTube, the videoclip site, and received millions of hits, on one occasion being placed ahead of the likes of socialite Paris Hilton.

Al Jazeera's contribution goes beyond press freedom in the Middle East. The channel carries news from around the world by satellite and cable to 50 million Arabic-speaking and 80 million English-speaking viewers. Its multiracial, multicultural staff include former members of ABC, CNN, the BBC and the US Marines. Its coverage and reporting of the West is every bit as balanced and professional – and essential – to the Middle East as its coverage of the Middle East is to the West.

GOOGLE

1998 | USA

'You can make money without doing evil.'
GOOGLE CORPORATE PHILOSOPHY

**Internet searching
Online advertising**

50

Google is an internet search engine developed by two post-graduate students at Stanford University. A decade later Google Inc. was generating advertising revenues in excess of $10 billion per year. The name Google derives from a play on the word denoting the number 1 followed by 100 zeroes. The founders are among the youngest billionaires in the world; neither has got round to finishing his doctorate.

Larry Page's father was a professor of computer science and artificial intelligence, while his mother taught computer programming, both at Michigan State University. Sergey Brin was born in Moscow to Jewish parents who emigrated to the United States in 1979; his father was a mathematician and his mother an economist. Page and Brin were 24 and 23 when they met as graduate students in computer science at Stanford University in 1995. The differences between them were evident from the beginning in virtually every area, except one: a common interest in how to retrieve relevant information from massive online data sets. They realized that whoever found the fastest and most reliable way would take home the biggest prize yet in the short, world-changing history of the internet.

A BRIEF HISTORY OF SEARCH ENGINES

The origins of 'hypertext' search engines lay before the internet with Gerard Dalton's SMART information retrieval systems developed at Cornell and Harvard. In 1990 a McGill undergraduate had developed the 'Archie' (archive) system for knowledge-sharing, and word of mouth produced 'Veronica', 'Jughead' and 'Gopher'. The invention of the World Wide Web in 1991 by the Briton Tim Berners-Lee was soon followed by the 'Excite' web-based search engine, developed by undergraduates at Stanford. In 1994 'Yahoo! Directory' expanded the number of documents held online, and in the same year Lycos did the same again. The greater the volume of data held online, the more difficult it was to find what you wanted. The problem was one of the biggest challenges in computing.

Larry Page had already developed a theory to match the complexity of the task. Page's PageRank algorithm assigned a numerical weighting to each element of a hyperlinked set of documents, with the purpose of quantifying its relative importance within a data set. Page and Brin joined forces and developed a prototype search engine based on PageRank called 'BackRub' that analysed the relationships between websites and measured their relative importance. Their paper, 'The Anatomy of a Large-Scale Hypertextual Web Search Engine', caused a buzz on campus and would go on to become the tenth most-accessed research scientific paper at Stanford University. Page, who had already achieved celebrity on campus by building a working printer out of Lego, assembled the prototype hardware that would carry the search technology in his dorm room, scrounging the parts on campus and, according to Google lore, 'maxing out' their credit cards to buy a terabyte of disks at bargain prices.

> "**WORK SHOULD BE CHALLENGING** and the challenge should be fun." Google corporate philosophy

Their first search engine went online through the Stanford University website as google.Stanford.edu: the name was a play on the word 'googol', which denotes the number represented by the numeral 1 followed by 100 zeroes. On 14 September 1997 they registered the domain google.com.

SEARCHING FOR INVESTORS

Brin meanwhile set about finding potential licensees for their technology. In spite of the fact that 'dotcom fever' was virulent in Silicon Valley, there were no takers. 'As long as we're 80 per cent as good as our competitors,' one portal CEO told him, 'that's good enough. Our users don't really care about search.' David Filo, one of the founders of Yahoo, encouraged

Google founders Larry Page (left) and Sergey Brin were the youngest billionaires in the internet gold rush. Their mission to organize the world's information was enabled by a brilliant advance in applied statistics.

them to set up a search-engine company of their own; he would later back up his support with his chequebook.

Meanwhile, a near-penniless Page and Brin were rescued out of the blue by the remarkable figure of Andreas von Bechtolsheim. 'Andy' Bechtolsheim had himself dropped out of the PhD programme at Stanford to co-found Sun Microsystems – named after Stanford University Network – and made a fortune. Bechtolsheim immediately saw the potential of Google, but, as Brin recalled, he was pressed for time: 'So he said, "Instead of discussing all the details, why don't I just write you a check?"' The cheque, for $100,000, was made out to 'Google Inc.' and sat in Page's desk drawer for a couple of weeks while he and Brin set up the company so that they could open a bank account. Others, including family and friends, followed on the strength of this. The investment would make them millionaires and net Bechtolsheim and his associate David Cheriton nearly $1.5 billion.

> '**TO ORGANIZE THE WORLD'S INFORMATION** and make it universally accessible and useful.' Google's mission

EXPONENTIAL GROWTH

In 1998, without having completed their doctorates, Page and Brin 'took leave' from Stanford and set up Google in Menlo Park, California. The office was part of a friend's garage and included a parking space for the new company's first employee, Craig Silverstein. The relaxed corporate style and philosophy – 'You can make money without doing evil' and 'Work should be challenging and the challenge should be fun' – soon became mantras. Google's ease of access and the speed and accuracy of the PageRank search technology soon generated a loyal and growing following among the online community in California, the most advanced state of the world's most advanced economy. Already the servers run by the small team in the Menlo Park garage were answering 10,000 search enquiries a day. Within four months, coverage of Google had appeared in *USA Today*, *Le Monde* and *PC Magazine*, the latter naming Google one of its Top 100 websites and search engines.

> **'I'VE GOT MY KIDS BRAINWASHED – You don't use Google, and you don't use an iPod.'**
> Steve Ballmer, CEO of Microsoft

By the time of the move in 1999 to University Avenue, Palo Alto, and the coming on board of $25 million in investment from two traditional Silicon Valley rivals, Sequoia Capital and Kleiner Perkins Caufield & Byers, Google was handling 500,000 searches a day, and the 25 or so employees were again running out of space. The solution was the Googleplex in Mountain View, California, where what were by this time 3 million searches a day and rising could be handled amid an open-plan environment that featured lava lamps, large pet dogs, rubber exercise balls that doubled as mobile office chairs, weekly roller hockey games and a free canteen run by the former chef to the Grateful Dead. Google developed its first ten foreign-language versions, began selling advertisements associated with search keywords, and introduced the Google toolbar. By the end of 2000, after barely more than two years in existence, Google was handling more than 100 million search enquiries a day.

DIVERSIFICATION AND DEBATE

Eric Schmidt, who was appointed as CEO in 2001, was an experienced Silicon Valley hand, older than the founders, towards whom he defined his role initially as 'adult supervision'. Under Schmidt, Google pushed to find partners worldwide and expanded both from within and by acquisition like a 'normal' company. The 1.6 billion web documents in the index rose to 3 billion by the end of 2001 and 4.28 billion by 2004. Google's initial public offering that year brought a market capitalization of $23 billion, making many employees paper millionaires, an achievement in which Schmidt played a key role in the aftermath of the dotcom crash and in the face of scepticism on Wall Street. Since then, Google has bought Keyhole Corporation, opened a European office in Dublin, grown to 8 billion web pages, launched Google Earth, bought YouTube for $1.6 billion and the DoubleClick web-page advertising company for $3.1 billion, outbidding Microsoft and others by more than $1 billion, and ensuring an eightfold return for DoubleClick's private equity owners. Google has also explored partnerships with Simon Fuller, creator of *Pop Idol*, in internet television, and with Apple's iPhone over mobile access to the internet.

Google's mission 'to organize the world's information and make it universally accessible and useful' is masterminded from the Googleplex and carried out through 10,674 'Googlers' employed around the world. Their relatively low salaries are balanced by generous shares in the equity growth of the company. Eric Schmidt's 80/20 rule dividing time into existing and new work has generated a number of new Google products. The challenge will be to keep the relevant bits of this vision in the face of Google's seemingly inexorable growth into email, video sharing, online mapping, book publishing, and radio and television. Other popular search engines – MSN, AOL, Yahoo – lag behind by comparison. The claim 'If you succeed on Google you succeed on the web' is impossible to refute. Controversies have of course arisen, as is only appropriate to a truly disruptive technology, but these also reflect a creeping distrust of Google's growing scale. These controversies include issues relating to book copyright, personal privacy (specifically regarding user addresses and search habits), and cooperation with regimes, notably in China, at odds with Google's opposition to self-censorship.

A CLASSIC AMERICAN SUCCESS STORY

Page and Brin are true children of the semiconductor age. Theirs is a classic American success story, and one that testifies to the faster pace of growth and change in information technology than in any other industry. Their brilliant and original invention has gone from a dorm room to 450,000 servers on low-cost 'farms' around the world and 80 million users a month. They are among the world's 30 richest people, and two of the youngest billionaires. Page and Brin have bought a Boeing 767 for their personal use; they are investors in the pioneering electric automobile manufacturer, Tesla Motors; they are still 'on leave' from their Ph.D. programme. The PageRank patent is credited to Larry Page and assigned to Stanford University, which is itself named after another US business phenomenon, Leland Stanford, one of the men behind the first transcontinental railroad that joined up America.

Microsoft's volcanic CEO Steve Ballmer has been quoted in *Fortune* magazine: 'I've got my kids brainwashed – You don't use Google, and you don't use an iPod.' Most of the world disagrees. 'To google' has entered dictionaries in its own right. In the time it has taken to read this, several hundred thousand more visitors have searched and found what they were looking for.

TIMELINE

1973
Birth of **Sergey Brin and Larry Page**.

1995
Page and Brin meet at **Stanford University**.

1997
They register the domain **google.com**.

1998
Foundation of **Google Inc**.

1999
Google sets up its headquarters in the '**Googleplex**'.

2001
Appointment of **Eric Schmidt** as CEO.

2004
Google goes **public**.

2005
Launch of **Google Earth**.

2006
Google acquires **YouTube**.

2007
Acquisition of **DoubleClick**. Google **shares pass $700**.

BIBLIOGRAPHY

1   Smith, Vincent and Spear, Percival *The Oxford History of India*, Oxford 1958; Morris, James *Heaven's Command* and *Pax Britannica*, London 1979

2   Quinn, Stephen and Roberts, William *An Economic Exploration of the Early Bank of Amsterdam, Debasement, Bills of Exchange and the Emergence of the First Central Bank*, Federal Reserve Bank of Atlanta Working Paper, 2006

3   Trinder, Barrie *The Industrial Revolution in Shropshire*, 1973

4   www2.dupont.com

5   Brendon, Piers *Thomas Cook: 150 Years of Popular Tourism*, London 1991; Hamilton, Jill *Thomas Cook: The Holiday Maker*, London 2005

7   www.rwuea.com

8   Read, Donald *The Power of News*, Oxford and New York 1992

11   Yergin, Daniel *The Prize*, London 1991; Sampson, Anthony *The Seven Sisters*, London 1975

16   Hofman, Philip B *General Johnson Said*, New York 1971; Mantle, Jonathan *A Family of Companies: Johnson & Johnson in the United Kingdom*, London 1999

17   www.ibm.com; Levinson, Charles *Vodka-Cola*, 1980; Klein, Naomi *No Logo*, London 2000; Black, Edwin *IBM and the Holocaust*, New York 2001

18   Nevins and Hill *Ford: Decline and Rebirth*, New York 1962; Wilkins and Hill *American Business Abroad: Ford on Six Continents*, New York; correspondence between Ford-Werke, Cologne and Dearborn, Henry Ford Museum Archives, Dearborn; Mantle, Jonathan *Car Wars*, London and New York 1995

19   www.freewebs.com/vintagehoover; www.about.com

20   Yergin, Daniel *The Prize*, London and New York 1991; Sampson, Anthony *The Seven Sisters*, London 1975; Monroe, Elizabeth *Britain's Moment in the Middle East*, London 1963; Bakan, Joel *The Corporation*, London and New York 2004

21   www.boeing.com

22   *Time* magazine, 5 August 1929; www2.goldmansachs.com

24   www.unilever.com

25   www.kingkullen.com; www.fundinguniverse.com/company-histories

26   www.emigroup.com; www.alanturing.net

28   Schaller, M *The American Occupation of Japan: The Origins of the Cold War in Asia*, New York 1985; Kennedy, Paul *The Rise and Fall of the Great Powers*, London 1988; Mantle, Jonathan *Car Wars*, London and New York 1995

29   Margolius, Ivan and Henry, John *Tatra: The Legacy of Hans Ledwinka*, London 1990; Mantle, Jonathan *Car Wars*, London and New York 1995

31   Kamprad, Ingvar and Torekull, Bertil *Leading by Design: The IKEA Story*, London and New York 1999

33   Yergin, Daniel *The Prize*, London 1991; Sampson, Anthony *The Seven Sisters*, London 1975; Field, Michael *The Merchants*, London 1984; *Trans-Arabian Oil Pipe Line Company Brochure*, New York 1961; *Handbook for American Employees*, Arabian American Oil Company 1952

36   Howell, Georgina *In Vogue*, London 1975; Rawsthorn, Alice *Yves Saint Laurent*, London 1996

37   www.nokia.com

38   www.nike.com; Nike, Inc 2007 Annual Report; Klein, Naomi *No Logo*, London 2000

39   www.intel.com

40   Robinson, Jeffrey *The Risk Takers: Portraits of Money, Ego and Power*, London 1985 and 1990; Jackson, Tim *Virgin King*, London 1995; Branson, Richard *Losing My Virginity*, London 2005

41   www.microsoft.com; Albuquerque Tribune Online; www.abqtrib.com

42   www.woz.com; www.apple.com

43   Bakan, Joel *The Corporation*, London and New York 2004

47   Bazalgette, Peter *Billion Dollar Game*, London 2005

49   Al Jazeera websites; Arab Press Freedom Watch www.apfw.org; Jones, Jeremy *Negotiating Change: The New Politics of the Middle East*, London and New York 2007

INDEX